# Newtown Alive:

## Courage
## Dignity
## Determination

**Rosalyn Howard, Ph.D.**

**and**

**Vickie Oldham, M.F.A.**

# DEDICATION

**Co-author Vickie Oldham, M.F.A.**

My heartfelt gratitude to my grandparents Shelley and Viola Sanders who became parents to me (at age 2) and my sister, an infant, after our mother's untimely death. Unconditional tough love, constant encouragement, support and protection from racism were the hallmarks of my childhood. I appreciate all of my teachers at Amaryllis Park and Booker Elementary Schools who gave me their best in the nurturing Newtown incubator. I'm especially thankful to our neighbors, church friends, community organizers, civil rights pioneers, leaders of social clubs and countless ordinary people like Isaac Cooper, a cab driver, grocers Herbert and Catherine Jenkins and their brother Lawrence, the butcher. They made Newtown a special place for a child like me and fearlessly fought on my behalf when I didn't understand the nature of the battle and couldn't fight for myself.

**Co-author Rosalyn Howard, Ph.D.**

With sincere gratitude, I wish to dedicate this book to the people of Newtown and other areas of Sarasota who opened their homes, their hearts, and their memories, allowing us to portray a more complete history of the first African American communities of Sarasota, Florida. While reading and listening to their interviews, I was swept into the lives of current residents and their ancestors who summoned, on so many occasions, the courage to defy being relegated to second-class citizens. They triumphed in large and small ways that truly inspired me. It has been my honor to work on this project and I hope that this book, in celebration of its centennial, will awaken a revitalized spirit in Newtown.

# CONTENTS

# ACKNOWLEDGEMENTS

*"No matter what accomplishments you make,
somebody helped you."*
*- Althea Gibson*

The massive task of completing an initiative such as the Newtown Conservation Historic District project Phases I and II can only be accomplished through collaboration. The NCHD team, task force, volunteers, city and county government leaders, Newtown and Overtown families and supporters, higher education partners and business owners understood our mission and worked with us to bring untold stories to life.

**NCHD Team**
Vickie Oldham
Consultant and Community Scholar

Dr. Rosalyn Howard
Cultural Anthropologist

Christopher Wenzel
Architectural Preservationist

Dave Baber
Historical Preservation Consultant

Mark Jackson
Finance

Kacey Troupe
Photographer

Jim Flynn
Videographer

Beatrice Sims
Spaghetti Ninja Graphic Design

*"Maybe we are not here to see each other*
*but to see each other through."*
*Anonymous*

## Newtown Citizen Historic Task Force

Fredd Atkins
James Brown
Jetson Grimes
Trevor D. Harvey
Wade Harvin
John McCarthy
Robert L. Taylor

## NCHD Volunteer Researchers

Hope Black
Dawn Cannavo
Phyllis Gipson
Lillian Granderson
Ellen Heath
Dr. Delores Penn
Les Porter
Dr. Keith Parker
Dr. Cheryl Smith
Alysia Crawford

## Reviewers

Debbie Trice
James and Yvonne Brown, Retired administrators
Dr. Edward E. James II, *Black Almanac* Director/Producer/Host
Dr. Louis Robison
Robert C. Hayden
Erin Dean, Ph.D. Associate Professor of Anthropology, New College
of Florida
John McCarthy

*"Lots of people want to ride with you in the limo, but what you want is someone who will take the bus with you when the limo breaks down."*
*- Oprah Winfrey*

## Partners
Newtown and Overtown Residents
Willie Charles Shaw, Mayor of Sarasota
Dr. Clifford Smith, City of Sarasota Office of Neighborhoods
Newtown Community Redevelopment Agency Advisory Board
Lorna Alston, Newtown Redevelopment Office
Dru Jones, Newtown Redevelopment Office
Rowena Elliott, Newtown Redevelopment Office
Manasota Association for the Study of African American Life and History
Hon. Charles E. Williams, Chief Judge-12th Judicial Circuit State of Florida
Charlie Ann Syprett, Chair of the Sarasota County Bar Association Diversity Committee
Melanie Thomas, Ringling College of Art and Design
Larry Kelleher, Sarasota County Historical Resources
Dr. Tashia Bradley, Wilberforce University
Cultural Resource Center, North Sarasota Public Library
Jenny Acheson, Photographer
D. Shenell Reed, social media strategist
Dr. Roy L. Baptiste
Daryl Waters
Sonya Waterhouse
Rosa Lee Thomas
Tempo News
Eileen West
Henry Richardson
Michael Suarez
Jack and Mary Emma Jones Family
Fredd and Shelia Atkins Family
Horras and Willie Mae Sheffield Family
John Mays Family
Che Barnett
Helen Dixon
Wendell Fletcher
Michael Dixon
Charlie Rivers
Donald Haygood

Dorothye Smith
Jackie Woods
Jeraline Baker Graham
John Rivers Family
Wright and Sarah Bush Family
Tarelton Cherry

Thelma Upshaw
The Coffee Loft
Mary Tinson
Kathy Byrd Pobee
Glenda Williams
Patrick Carter

We gratefully acknowledge the contributions of the late Annie M. McElroy, author of *But Your World and My World: The Struggle for Survival, A Partial History of Blacks in Sarasota County, 1884-1986*. Published in 1986, this was the first history book that focused on the African American experience in Sarasota County. It provided an invaluable foundation for our research by filling in many gaps in the existing records and revealed information about historic events, places and people that may not have been accessible today.

# CHAPTER 1: NEWTOWN ALIVE:
## INTRODUCTION

The story of the historical and present-day African American communities of Sarasota, Florida — Overtown and Newtown — is one that has been little known and not well documented. Yet, it is an important story that shares parallel experiences with other African American communities across the US. The personal accounts from community residents and other information that you will read within the book may make you laugh, may make you angry, and may make you question what you thought you really knew about the history of the City of Sarasota. Certainly, you will find many details that were left out of mainstream historical accounts of the city.

The first free African Americans began to settle in Sarasota in 1884. They and their descendants have been important partners in the development of Sarasota's institutions, infrastructure, culture and social history. They helped carve Sarasota out of the wilderness by clearing snake infested land for real estate developers; laying railroad ties; building houses, roads and bridges; planting and harvesting citrus and celery fields; and helping to plat golf courses. They were an integral part of Sarasota's early days as a thriving community, working for the Ringling Circus; tapping pine trees to collect the resin for turpentine; mining dolomite; laboring as domestics and drivers for the city's affluent white residents; and establishing businesses of their own. They also helped move the city into the modern era by graduating from colleges and universities with degrees in various professions; becoming school teachers and administrators; challenging Jim Crow laws in the pursuit of their civil rights; and serving as elected public officials.

African American residents made their homes first in Overtown and, later, Newtown. They especially valued religion, family and education; accordingly, churches and the Booker School triplex were cornerstones of both communities. Jim Crow laws that mandated their segregation from the broader Sarasota community necessitated forging a path to survival through self-reliance. Thriving business districts developed to provide vital goods and services when downtown shops in Sarasota were off limits just because of the color of their skin. Self-help organizations were formed to meet various needs. African American and a few white physicians administered medical care to residents, although many people never utilized these doctors; they depended, instead, on midwives, home remedies and folk medicine.

Formal education for African Americans was forbidden during slavery and difficult to access for decades after abolition. This is why the majority of the early residents could not read or write. Their education was not a priority for state and US government officials. African Americans in Sarasota took the initiative and made education one of their most important objectives, starting schools in homes and churches by 1910. They viewed becoming literate as the most promising path toward improving their lives and the lives of their children. After the US Supreme Court's 1954 Brown v. Board of Education decision struck down the legality of "separate but equal," unequal educational opportunities persisted in the Sarasota school system, which resisted school desegregation for eight years after the Supreme Court ruling.

As you read some of the oral history interviews, you will notice that not all of the persons interviewed speak in what is called "Standard English;" many of them, especially the elders, did not have the luxury of having a lengthy or formal education. They recall having to quit school, sometimes in the elementary grades, to care for younger brothers and sisters while their parents went to work. Or they had to go to work themselves as children or teenagers in hot celery fields, snake-ridden turpentine camps, restaurants, or as domestics. Others traveled with their families as migrant farm workers for months at a time, missing many school days. For many years, education for African Americans went only to eighth grade; there was no high school available to them.

Speaking in "Standard English" has less do with a person's level of intelligence than the opportunity they have had to learn it. As a cultural anthropology professor, NCHD team member Dr. Rosalyn Howard taught a sociolinguistics course called Language and Culture, which is the study of how social factors, such as gender, occupation, region, social class, ethnic dialects, education, formal/informal situations and bilingualism affect a person's speech. How you speak reflects many factors, including the level of familiarity with the person to whom you are speaking and the situation in which you are speaking. You speak differently with your friends, for example, rather than your boss, or in front of an audience. That ability to change the way you speak is called "code-switching." Vickie Oldham, who grew up in Newtown, has a great degree of familiarity with the majority of people interviewed for the project. At times, the interviewer and interviewee are "gonna" code-switch, and "kinda" speak the way they would in a casual conversation with a friend. Enjoy reading the rich details of the history and culture of the people of Overtown and Newtown, as well as the rich textures of their language.

Newtown residents and leaders appealed to their government representatives for more than a decade to fund a comprehensive study to document the people, culture and history of their community. Their request was finally approved in 2015 when funding from the City of Sarasota was provided to begin the research on this project.

The timing of the Newtown Conservation Historic District project to coincide with its centennial was ideal. Societal circumstances have changed dramatically over this 100-year period and, therefore, so must the ideas and strategies designed to keep this community intact and prevent losing it to the new "development" that some aptly describe as "gentrification." Newtown has a rich legacy that can only be preserved if its people are informed about it, value it and are willing to fight to sustain it. Their decades-long determination to pursue the funding to complete this community study demonstrates that they have the same strong resilience as their ancestors who built a thriving community out of what once was empty land and through which they carved roads and built houses with their own hands.

The significant contributions of the Newtown community residents to the broader community of Sarasota, Florida deserve to be recorded for posterity. While there have been a few well-written accounts of various aspects of this community, notably Annie M. McElroy's book *But Your World and My World*, and the newspaper series "Newtown 100" that was published by the *Herald-Tribune* during Newtown's centennial year of 2014, there was much more information that its residents wanted to add to the story. Rich details about the lives of Newtown's residents over the course of a century had not been available in one place and some had not been publically accessible at all. They were widely dispersed, located in public collections such as the Sarasota History Center, in private collections of photographs, letters and old newspaper articles stored away in homes, and locked in the unrecorded oral tradition of the residents. The NCHD report and this book bring these details together and shed new light on the community.

One challenge that the research team faced was that many gaps existed in the historical information available to us. The lack of written records, particularly in regard to the earliest histories of African Americans in Overtown and Newtown, is related to the fact that African Americans were not writing them, and their stories were not important to the writers of that history. The African proverb about this phenomenon is quite appropriate:

*"Until the lion tells his side of the story, the tale of the hunt will always glorify the hunter."*

While additional information has been added, the majority of this book is a condensed version of the 364-page Newtown Conservation Historic District (NCHD) project report *Newtown Alive!* that was submitted to the City of Sarasota in 2016 by the research team of: Vickie Oldham (lead consultant); Dr. Rosalyn Howard (cultural anthropologist); Dave Baber (Historical Preservation Consultant); and Christopher Wenzel (Architectural Preservationist). The original report and this book (which includes additional photographs not in the report) are intended to honor and celebrate the centennial — 1914 to 2014 — of the Newtown community. Complete copies of the original report that includes references to all of the information collected is available at branches of the Sarasota County Public Libraries and also may be accessed online (http://goo.gl/CF6Xuc).

The goal of the NCHD project is to inspire Newtown's residents: those who never left Newtown and want to help it improve; the exceptional young people who left and returned to Newtown after graduating from college, universities, vocational schools or at the conclusion of athletic careers; the seasoned leaders who have accomplished so much and shown remarkable strength of character in fighting the battles of racism and discrimination; and the generations who, unfortunately, know little about the historical challenges as well as achievements of their ancestors and living relatives.

Redevelopment and revitalization efforts are being pursued to raise the consciousness of this community, to tear down substandard housing in order to provide decent living conditions, and to rebuild "social bridges" that were destroyed between the African American and the greater Sarasota communities. An important example of this need for bridge building is the relationship between the Booker Schools and the Newtown community that was negatively impacted by school desegregation policies. The heart of the community — the Booker schools and its dedicated teachers — was ripped out during the school desegregation process. Rather than improve education, the Sarasota School Board's actions served to disrupt the cohesive fabric of the Newtown community and made the lives of many African American students and teachers miserable. These actions can be viewed as retaliation for being forced, under threat of losing funding, to adhere to the Supreme Court's mandate to desegregate the Sarasota schools.

Newtown is a resilient community, however. We are hopeful that redevelopment projects will be beneficial to its residents and not only to outsiders whose interests, some believe, lie closer to gentrification rather than revitalizing and maintaining Newtown as a community. The community needs all of its residents to actively participate in this process to keep Newtown Alive!

Addressing the importance of the NCHD project, Newtown resident Fredd Atkins, who has served several terms as Mayor of the City of Sarasota and City Commissioner, made this statement to a *Herald-Tribune* reporter:

> *The community will not only learn more about their history and their forefathers' history, they'll also learn to respect the struggle and respect the opportunities they have now... A lot of the things going on today go contrary to this struggle. I think the project will help young people, and new people coming here, celebrate our history and our community.*

# CHAPTER 2:
# OVERTOWN AND NEWTOWN:
# THE EARLY SETTLERS

Although Lewis Colson is widely considered to be the first free African American to settle in Sarasota, there was, in fact, a community of free African Americans who lived in the Sarasota Bay area long before his 1884 arrival. When Florida was a sovereign territory of Spain, it became the southern route of the Underground Railroad for people of African descent enslaved on the plantations of the Carolinas, Georgia, and Alabama. In 1693, the Spanish King promised them that if they escaped and crossed into Florida, they could live as free people. The only two conditions required freedom were that they 1) adopt Catholicism and 2) join forces with the Spaniards to fight against the Americans who were trying to take over their sovereign territory. A community called <u>Sarrazota</u> was formed in the Tampa-Sarasota Bay area, believed to have been located near the point where the Bradenton and the Manatee Rivers meet. Sarrazota had also been called Angola, according to a land claim document filed by two Cuban fishermen in 1824.[1] Its residents included a variety of people. There were free people of color, formerly enslaved Africans (some referred to as Black Seminoles) and Seminole Indians. All had been driven out of their villages and towns in various parts of Florida by earlier American incursions into Florida.[2]

From the late 17th century, Florida was a place where freedom-seeking Africans who escaped from southern plantations found a haven of safety among the Seminole Indians or the Spaniards. The Adams–Onis Treaty, signed in 1819, eliminated that sanctuary. The treaty changed Florida from a territory of Spain to a territory of the US and Provisional Governor Andrew Jackson was determined to banish all of the Seminole Indians and re-enslave African Americans, even free persons of color. Jackson wanted to conduct a raid on Angola but was denied permission to do so by the US Secretary of Defense. Determined to achieve his ends at any cost, Jackson persuaded a band of Coweta Creek Indians, his allies, to destroy Angola in 1821.

Historian Canter Brown Jr. describes this community in his journal article, "The Sarrazota or Runaway Negro Plantations: Tampa Bay's First Black Community."[3] Brown explains that John Lee Williams, one of Florida's early historians, drew a map of the location and published it in his book *The Territory of Florida*.[4] Williams personally observed the remains of Angola in 1828, seven years after its destruction. He described it as a 'Negro plantation' located at the point between a stream entering the bay and the Oyster River — a place called Negro Point; he was referring to the point where the Braden and Manatee Rivers meet.[5] Williams states that the plantation at one time had been cultivated "by 200 negroes. ... The ruins of their cabins, and domestic utensils are still seen on the old fields."[6] According to Brown, "Once established [in 1812], the negro plantation at or near Sarasota Bay proved a magnet over the next several years for other black refugees. When the Negro Fort on the Apalachicola River was destroyed by American forces in 1816, the displaced blacks built villages all the way to Tampa Bay."[7]

Most historical accounts of Sarasota Bay's earliest residents omit reference to these African and Native American populations. Before there was an Overtown, before there was a Newtown, an African and Native American community called Sarrazota or Angola existed in the Sarasota Bay area.[8]

Vickie Oldham, lead consultant of the Newtown Conservation Historic District (NCHD) Project, became aware of Brown's research while working on a documentary short film about the history of Sarasota in 1992. Twelve years later, Oldham revisited the story again while producing another documentary for the county government access television station. The project was called "Reflections: A History of Sarasota County." The effort led her to launch the interdisciplinary research project "Looking for Angola" in 2004, which started the scholarly research investigation designed to physically locate the community. The destruction of Angola in 1821 effectively eliminated the presence of free African American people in the area for more than 20 years after the end of the Civil War, according to currently available documentation.

## SARASOTA'S LATER SETTLERS

Sarasota, Florida was a small fishing village in a swampy environment when the earliest white settlers arrived around 1842. "On maps dating back to the time that the area was controlled by the Spaniards it was known by its Spanish name, *Zara Zote*, which became [Anglicized to] Sara Sota."[9] Robert E. Paulson surveyed and platted the original town of Sara Sota for the Florida Mortgage and Investment Company in 1885. An 1897 Sarasota Real Estate Agency advertisement designed to attract new residents described the town as follows:

A charming location, containing some 200 inhabitants on Sara Sota Bay, about midway of its length and 50 miles from Tampa. The town is exceptionally well favored by nature, standing as it does on a crescent shaped, land locked bay, affording the best anchorage for small vessels on the coast, with an unrivaled view of the Gulf and its islands. The streets and avenues are from 60 to 80 feet wide and the town is skillfully planted. Sarasota is justifiably celebrated for its fish, oysters, clams and the game, while the well-known fishing grounds of the Tarpon, or Silver King, are about two miles from the wharves.[10]

## OVERTOWN

After the Civil War, the type of advertisement above attracted not only whites to the area, but also African Americans seeking employment opportunities and ways to better their lives in the growing town. Rather than migrate to the northern states, as many African Americans did, Overtown's residents came primarily from other cities and towns in Florida and surrounding southern states, beginning in the 1880s.

> Agents traveled throughout the rural South to recruit laborers and skilled workmen to come to and build new cities in Florida. As a result, African Americans were instrumental in the construction of buildings, bridges, and the Seaboard Air Line Railway in Sarasota.[11]

Overtown became the first African American community in Sarasota. Settlers were ready and willing to work hard to build their lives and the community. Racism, segregation, menial jobs and poverty were stiff challenges against their efforts, however. Based on oral history and some written accounts, a determined spirit developed out of that struggle.

Establishing a variety of businesses was done out of necessity since Jim Crow laws were in full effect in this southern city and African Americans could not be served in white-owned restaurants, and could not shop in white-owned stores. As stated by Glossie Atkins:

> We couldn't get into any of the places downtown. There was a dress store on Main Street. We weren't allowed to go in there. And if we did try to go in there, they would 'ig' us. They would pay us no attention.[12]

Eventually, African Americans were permitted limited shopping privileges in some of the downtown stores, particularly the larger chain stores, such as J.C. Penney and Sears Roebuck. Most often, however, they were served at the rear door and could not try on clothing like white customers could. Out of these discriminatory circumstances, a strong entrepreneurial spirit was born.

According to J. Whitcomb Rylee, by the 1910s and 1920s a thriving black business and residential community existed:

> Along today's 6th Street and Central Avenue. The 1920s Florida land boom led to substantial development in the Overtown area, new churches, business blocks, hotels, an outside movie theater, many of them black owned and made possible by the Boom Time prosperity which trickled down to the laborers in Overtown.[13]

The successful application filed on behalf of Overtown's nomination to the National Register of Historic Places stated that:

> One of the most successful enterprises in Overtown was the Hudson-Essex Automobile Dealership. In one month during the peak of the Florida real estate boom, the Hudson-Essex dealership in Overtown sold more automobiles from that dealership than from any other dealership in the country. Local businesses including the White Star Pressing Club, Willis Mays grocery, Royal Palm Pressing Club, Elite Pressing Club, Hurrikleen Pressing Club, the outside movie theater called the Airdome Theater on 5th Street, Superior Printing Company, the Sarasota Ice Cream Company, lunch counters such as one owned by Samuel Albright, Community Service Filling Station, Kluver & Cladin Billiards, Rolfe's Dry Goods, and the Leader Department Store, provided work for local residents during the 1920s.[14]

Of paramount importance to the culture of Overtown were church, school, and family. Community members' faith in God, to whom they looked for strength, hope and a way to cope with life's challenges, led them to congregate for interdenominational services in individual homes and in churches in Manatee County until they could afford to construct their own churches.

In those early days, churches were the foundation of the community. Not only were they places of worship, they provided a space for children to learn school lessons as well as Bible lessons. Importantly, churches were also places where African Americans could exercise some independence, occupy positions of authority and build their self-esteem, essential elements of humanity that were denied them in their daily lives in segregated Sarasota. African Americans settlers were segregated from the white population, except while working. Early Overtown settlers did not simply complain about their unfortunate and unfair circumstances. They established self-help, benevolent organizations and businesses to provide for their needs, creating a nurturing environment where everybody was "family."

The first free African American to settle in Sarasota was Lewis Colson, a formerly enslaved man who arrived in 1884. He worked as an assistant to surveyor Robert E. Paulson.[15] Colson was also a fisherman and landowner. He married Irene, who served as a midwife providing critical medical assistance to the African American community that, due to Jim Crow laws, had very limited access to most medical services.

The Colsons are celebrated for their numerous contributions to the African American community and the city. They are credited with the establishment of the Bethlehem Baptist Church, the first church built by and for African Americans. Lewis and Irene Colson sold the land to the church's trustees for the nominal sum of $1. Essentially, it was a gift. The original church building was located on the corner of present day 7th Street and Central Avenue in Overtown. John Mays, a church trustee and founding member of Bethlehem Baptist Church, was also a carpenter. He, along with the help of others, built the church. The church remained on that site until 1973 when a new building was constructed in Newtown at 1680 18th Street.[16] Rev. Lewis Colson was ordained in 1896 and became the church's first pastor in 1899. He served in that capacity until 1915. Colson Street, located between US 301 and Tuttle Avenue, was named in his honor.

Jim Crow laws prohibited African Americans from lodging in white hotels. Therefore, African American entertainers visiting Sarasota who performed with multiracial troupes were not permitted to stay at the same hotels as their white counterparts. The Colson Hotel, named for but not owned by Rev. Colson, accommodated these and other African Americans travelers. The hotel was built in 1925 and opened in late 1926 at 1425 8th Street and Central Avenue. It was described in a *Sarasota Herald* article dated Dec 15, 1926 as "a 28-room hotel for black tourists and residents, constructed of fine yellow stucco on hollow tile, with a comfortable lobby with fireplace by E.O. Burns named after Lewis Colson." The hotel was later renamed The Palms Hotel.

Rev. Colson and his wife are thought to be the only African Americans buried in the Rosemary Cemetery, located in the 1800 block of Central Avenue.[17]

Rev. Lewis Colson's headstone
at Rosemary Cemetery.
Courtesy: Christopher Wenzel

The Florida Mortgage and Investment Company, for which Rev. Colson had worked, owned that cemetery and he had helped to survey it and other land holdings for the company.[18]

Overtown was bounded on the north and south sides by today's 10th and 5th Streets, and on the west and east sides by US 41 and Orange Avenue. A small area of Overtown was known as Black Bottom, where living conditions were the poorest. Overtown's location near downtown made it easy for African American workers to get to their jobs, since most had no transportation. Eddie Rainey lived in Overtown and described it as follows:

> When I was a young man, [living in] what is now known as the 'black areas,' there were two separate communities. ... One was cited as being Overtown. ... And the reason was, that area was so close to downtown. Main Street is where the jobs were. So a lot of blacks located right there on about 4th or 5th Street and you had a lot of little houses in there. Then they could walk to Main Street to get their jobs. ... This area was called "over town" [eventually the name became 'Overtown'].[19]

As described on the Sarasota History Alive website:

> The hub of the community was at the corner of Central Avenue and today's Sixth Street. It grew as businessmen, fishermen, physicians, contractors, carpenters, laborers, drivers, masons, blacksmiths, laundry workers and railroad workers made the area their home. Along today's Central Avenue were pressing clubs and lunch rooms, a movie theater, meat and fish markets, grocery and general merchandise stores, and a variety of other businesses that provided goods and services to the African American community. Residential architecture varied in size, but most houses were modest, one-story wood-frame structures incorporating front porches. From the time of the community's founding, the Black residents living and working there played a vital role in the development of both the City and the County of Sarasota.[20]

Another prominent African American early settler in the City of Sarasota was Leonard Reid. He and Rev. Colson both played large roles in the development of Overtown. An educated man, Reid arrived in Sarasota in 1900 at nineteen years old, after graduating from the Savannah [Georgia] Normal School as valedictorian of his class. Despite his level of education, however, Reid worked for a local fish merchant for several months until he was introduced to Col. John Hamilton Gillespie.[21]

Leonard Reid driving Gillespie family in a coach.
Courtesy: Sarasota County Historical Resources.

Col. Gillespie hired Reid as coachman, butler, and caretaker for his home. In 1901, Reid married Eddye Coleman who also worked for the Gillespies as a maid and cook. The Reids rented a small house in Overtown and the couple continued to work for Gillespie after their marriage. On the advice of Gillespie, Reid invested in land, purchasing four lots in Overtown from Gillespie. Reid played a vital role as a community leader by being active in local fraternal organizations and using his collection of books in his home as a neighborhood library.[22]

Sarasota was incorporated in 1902 and Gillespie was elected as its first mayor. He held this office for six terms. Gillespie, a Scottish-American, built one of the first golf courses in the state and is credited with introducing the game to Florida. Reid assisted Gillespie in laying out the design for Sarasota's first golf course and served as the first greenskeeper.[23]

Reid and his wife Eddye were founding members of the Payne Chapel African Methodist Episcopal (A.M.E.) Church of Sarasota, along with community leaders Campbell Mitchell, F.H. Haynes, and C.H. Murphy. Payne Chapel A.M.E. Church was the second church built for African Americans in Sarasota. In 1903, the congregation constructed a small wood frame building on a lot donated by the Florida Mortgage and Investment Company at Central Avenue and present-day 5th Street. That original building was replaced with a new wood frame structure in 1914 to accommodate the growing congregation.[24]

Overtown also had active fraternal organizations and Reid was a member of several: International Order of Odd Fellows Gulf City Lodge #6403; Free and Accepted Masons, Sarasota Lodge #314; and Household of Ruth #3538.[25] In her book, *But Your World and My World*, Annie M. McElroy stated that, "In recognition of Leonard Reid as one of Sarasota's early settlers and for his contributions to his community, Leonard Reid Avenue, about one block east of US 301 north of 27th Street, was named in his honor."[26]

Other early families residing in Overtown included the Mays, Washington, Bush, Carmichael, Roberts, Joyner, Wilcox, Albright, Herring, Jackson, O'Neil, Wilson, McKenzie, and Conley families. Frank Williams was the town's first blacksmith.

Willie McKenzie arrived in Newtown in 1926 with a Savannah construction firm. He worked on Charles Ringling's ten-story Terrace Hotel as well as the John Ringling Causeway. As families like the McKenzies followed the work to Sarasota, the city became home for generations of African Americans. In addition to working at skilled labor jobs, Newtown residents became landowners, preachers, real estate developers, and teachers.[27]

The 1918 Sarasota Florida City Directory listed the names of all residents and business establishments. Written next to the residents' names (wives names shown in parentheses) were their occupations and addresses. An asterisk (*) preceded the names of African Americans, or Negroes as they were called at that time, as well as the names of any businesses they owned. A sample of entries for African Americans follows, exactly as shown in the Directory. If the information was originally written as an abbreviation, the word is spelled out next to it in brackets.

**Alley Jeremiah** (Alma), fisherman, h [home] 322 14th
**Atkins Linda**, dom [domestic], h 333 12th
**Bethlehem Baptist Church**, 417 Mango Av, Rev P R James pastor
**Booker Emma E.**, prin [principal] Sarasota Col [Colored] Schl [School]
**Carmichael Edwd J** (Rosa), propr [proprietor] Royal Palm Pressing Club, h 208 12th
**Colson, Lewis Rev** (Irene), h 305 Coconut av
**Keitt Elzona**. Tchr [teacher] Sarasota Col [Colored] Schl [School]
**Mack Jno** [short for John] (Lottie), [barber] 201 12th, h same
Twelfth Street Pool Room, 319 12th, Jno Joyner mngr [manager]

**Williams, Frank T** (Madeline), blksmith, [blacksmith] 331 7th, h 313 Coconut av [Williams was the first African American blacksmith in Sarasota]

This Directory indicates that the majority of African Americans were employed as laborers, or domestics. Others were self-employed businesspersons.

In 2002, Overtown was placed on the National Register of Historic Places. This excerpt from the application described it as follows:

> The Overtown Historic District lies several blocks north of downtown and east of the Tamiami Trail. ... The Overtown community once featured a notable mixture of single-family dwellings, commercial buildings, churches, schools, and clubhouses. A great many of these have been demolished, but several notable buildings remain. One of these, the former Payne Chapel A.M.E. Church, constructed c.1927, has been rehabilitated for use as commercial offices, but it still remains a visual symbol of the focus of spiritual life in the African American neighborhood.[28]

Although the African American residents provided much needed workers for building Sarasota, their proximity to downtown prompted anxiety among some of the white population of Sarasota. In 1911, an article in the Sarasota Times suggested that Rosemary Cemetery in Overtown be moved, stating that, "The location [of the cemetery], having to pass through the colored quarters to reach the cemetery, is not desirable." As the black population increased ... [they] were encouraged to move farther north.

Charles N. Thompson, a well-known circus manager reportedly was not interested solely in making money; he wanted make the quality of life better for Sarasota's African American community. In 1914, he and his son Russell purchased 40 acres north of town for use as:

> 'Colored quarters' with 240 lots that could be bought 'on easy payments' ... several of which were dedicated for a Methodist church, a Baptist church, and a school. The developers intended to donate the deeds when the buildings were constructed.[29]

After Newtown's opening, Overtown continued to operate as the center of African American life in Sarasota. Local resident, Thomas "Mott" Washington, acquired major holdings of land in Overtown and

Newtown and built rental houses in which many African Americans lived.[30]

## MIGRATION FROM OVERTOWN TO NEWTOWN

The continued development of Newtown led to the eventual abandonment of Overtown as an African American residential area. There is disagreement about what led to the out-migration of the African American community from Overtown to Newtown: Was there a 'push' factor from white residents who wanted to develop the land near downtown Sarasota, which was closer to the beaches? Was it a matter of African Americans seizing the opportunity to move into better housing than they had in Overtown? Several differing opinions were expressed on this issue.

An article on a Sarasota-Manatee business website called *941CEO* confirms the final dissolution of Overtown as an African American enclave and cites a reason for this: "The Rosemary District ... served as the then segregated city's first African-American community. In the 1930s and '40s, the city encouraged black residents to move north into the newer community of Newtown, and then demolished many homes and buildings in Rosemary."[31]

The City of Sarasota went beyond simply encouraging them to move further north, according to J. Whitcomb Rylee:

> The 1920s Florida Land Boom also saw Overtown encircled with 'Caucasian race only' developments, with smaller subdivisions in today's Gillespie Park area along Orange Avenue to the east and Hillcrest and Valencia Terrace to the north. This effectively prevented the natural growth of the Overtown area, forcing the growth of the black population to head to the Newtown area ... The 1930s and 1940s saw the city encouraging the development of the more isolated Newtown area with the establishment of a housing project along north Orange Avenue and increased housing standards for the Overtown area. ... In the 1950s under the auspices of its "Slum Clearance Program" the City actively began to remove the housing stock of the Overtown area ... By August of [1957] the Slum Clearance Program was responsible for the removal of about 200 buildings in the Overtown and Newtown areas ... The City estimated that "Blackbottom," as Overtown was being referred to by the local White population, had 70 of the houses in need for repair and that 100 more should be demolished. There were people living in all of them. ... With the exception of

the Cohen Way Housing Project in the mid-1960s, the city had pushed most of the black population north to Newtown by the early 1970s.[32]

As the population of downtown Sarasota increased:

> At the turn of the century and through the booming 1920s, pressures arose that led to the relocation of most of Overtown's African American residents. First, development pressure downtown created a demand for growth farther north and the African-American community was edged northward. Newtown replaced the original municipal residential area that once included Black Bottom ... Overtown had constituted a complete community with small shops, social facilities, and religious centers such as the first church, the Bethlehem Baptist Church.[33]

A second pressure on the Overtown community was the discontent expressed by white Sarasotans who were forced to encounter residents when they traveled through the African American community to visit Rosemary cemetery. Dr. Uzi Baram, Professor of Anthropology at New College in Sarasota, taught a Historical Archaeology course in 2009 that brought his students to the cemetery, established in the 1880s. In his article "Learning and Civic Engagement," Baram discussed this cemetery visit:

> Beyond the town founders buried in the Rosemary Cemetery, the surrounding area is the Overtown Historic District, the first documented African American settlement in Sarasota. Starting in the 1990s, but developing a more steady flow since the beginning of the new century, the Rosemary District (formerly called Overtown) has been gentrifying as downtown Sarasota has grown over the last few years.
>
> While the Rosemary District became a traditionally poor and African American section of Sarasota, students were challenged to look at the surrounding gentrification and how it is displacing a community. The African American community had become marginalized and silenced in the memory of a place. The politics of gentrification became a powerful and eye-opening experience for many of the students.
>
> Race haunts Sarasota. Segregation is a concern from the past and for the present, with community groups whose names indicate their anxieties about the present [2009] social situation: Sarasota Openly Addressing Racism, Coalition for Inclusion and Diversity, Embracing Our Differences, and Sarasota County

Openly Plans for Excellence. One of the locations for civic attention is the Rosemary District, whose gentrification is part of a transformation of an African American neighborhood into a trendy, wealthy, diverse area.[34]

Newtown resident James Brown disagrees and offers an alternative point of view about whether African Americans were 'pushed' out of Overtown. Brown believes that there were reasons for moving from Overtown to Newtown other than, what he terms, the myth that African Americans were forced out. Brown stated:

> I think it was a matter of opportunity, upgrade. It also had something to do with land mass topography. The area from 4th Street, south to 10th Street, north between Coconut and Lemon Avenue (where the Railroad track used to be), it was sand. [There were] very few lawns. In Newtown, there was a larger area, different topography -- lawns, palm trees, and more houses were painted than in Overtown. It was a self-contained neighborhood; there was no need to leave the area. There was much more space between houses. A lot of Overtown homes were rentals. In Newtown, people could own their homes, and there is a pride in home ownership. [35]

During the 1990s, Overtown was renamed Rosemary District as the city began to attract private investors to redevelop the area by renovating older structures. What were once homes, churches and commercial structures became revitalized as offices and other types of businesses. The author of the article "Rosemary Rising" states that:

> Community leaders have repeatedly described the former Overtown neighborhood as ripe for gentrification, but progress has been uneven … When the recession hit, last decade's ambitious crop of Rosemary developers walked away from their investments or just put their projects on hold. But today, partly due to the city's recent decision to allow developers to build denser projects, developers are coming forward again.
> Vanguard Lofts, CitySide and Valencia are three of at least eight new residential and commercial developments being considered or built in Rosemary.

Ranging from dense apartment complexes to upscale townhomes, from performing arts rehearsal spaces to retail shops, the projects are giving business owners and residents hope that Rosemary's potential as a lively, downtown-adjacent, mixed-use urban community will at last be used.[36]

At this writing, Sarasota's downtown, including the Rosemary District, is experiencing a building boom that shows no sign of lessening. There are 1,000 condominium units under construction in the Rosemary District and the demand for luxury high-rise condominiums that range from $800,000 to $4 million is increasing.

## NEWTOWN

Newtown is the second historic core of Sarasota's African-American community. Many interviewees for this project described it as "a village" where everyone knew and cared for one another. Circumstances in the Newtown "village" deteriorated over time, however, due to various factors, which included: outside societal influences; the loss of influential leaders and devoted school teachers; negative impacts of desegregation and integration; and the devastating influx of drugs. All of these circumstances substantially transformed Newtown's culture over its 100-year history.

Although many families were uprooted from their homes in Overtown, the Newtown community provided improved living conditions, especially much better quality housing. Concrete-block houses were a great upgrade over the dilapidated wooden structures of Overtown. Wealthy, white Sarasotan owners of that substandard housing were no better than slumlords.

From its beginning, Newtown was advertised as a desirable settlement for Sarasota's African American community. And it was for some people. However, there were trade-offs. While the houses were nicer and there was plentiful open space for children to play, Newtown's infrastructure – electricity, running water, indoor plumbing, roads – was severely lacking in comparison to Overtown. Eventually, that would be remedied. The Wright Bush House at Maple Avenue and Dr. Martin Luther King Jr. Way was a popular meeting place for Newtown residents and visitors. It was the first home to have electricity. Bush, a business owner, personally paid the power company to provide service from a substation on Orange Avenue near 11th Street to his home. Other Newtown residents were able to connect their homes to electricity through the power lines installed for Bush's house. James Brown still has the original 1928 receipt from when the electric lights were turned on in his home! His family was among the first in his neighborhood to get electricity.

In the documentary short film "Triumphant Struggle," written, produced and directed by Vickie Oldham,[37] NCHD project interviewee Fannie Bacon remembered, "A rich, white man named Mr. Warren developed this part [Newtown]. He had a big picnic there selling lots. And I came out there with my daddy. And that's when he bought his land." Harmie Baker recalled that Mrs. C.N. Thompson had also some land in Newtown, "And she let me sell lots for her. When I sold a lot for her, she gave me ten dollars. That ten dollars went to my home to help pay for my lot." According to Mary Mack, the rate for a new house at that time was $69 down and $69 per month.[38]

From Newtown's early years through the 1940s, the street now known as Dr. Martin Luther King Jr. Way was the thriving heart of the segregated community. However, decades of disinvestment and capital flight, along with a concentration of government subsidized housing and social services, have resulted in some blighted conditions located next single family homes. Much of the neighborhood's multifamily housing has not received regular maintenance and is substantially deteriorated.

Transportation improvements to US 301 and US 41 to the east and west of the area have enabled those roadways to evolve into major auto-oriented corridors, making travel easier around, rather than through, the neighborhood. This diverted traffic from the Dr. Martin Luther King Jr. Way business corridor. Some businesses that were located there have moved to where the traffic is flowing. Over time, a substantial concentration of industrial and social services have been located between the neighborhood and downtown to the south. Half of the northern boundary of Newtown is bounded by industrial businesses, further isolating it from the larger Sarasota community.[39]

## "AN AIRPLANE COMES TO SARASOTA"

In 1946, Karl Grismer wrote the book titled *The Story of Sarasota: The History of the City and County of Sarasota, Florida.* In it, he recounted the following story describing a flight over very different areas of Sarasota:

> No old time resident of Sarasota ever will forget Thursday, April 9, 1914. Because on that day, many Sarasotans saw their first airplane. …. It was a marvelous ship. … Several of the passengers requested that Jannus [the pilot] take them over Bird Key so they could get a good look at the glistening white home just being built by Thomas W. Worcester, of Cincinnati. This was

the first expensive home built on any island in the Sarasota Bay region. ... It is now the home of Mrs. Ida Ringling North.

Flying inland, the passengers were given the opportunity to observe another type of habitation. Out on 33rd St. they could see tiny homes being erected by Negroes in the colored community of Newtown, then being opened by Charles N. Thompson. ... Previously their principal living quarters have been at black bottom, in the vicinity of 12th and Lemon. The dilapidated buildings, owned by prominent Sarasotans, were a disgrace to Sarasota. Most of the shacks had only unsanitary, open privies and not until Dr. John R. Scully became health officer, years later, was any move made to provide better sanitation facilities.[40]

In Newtown's early days, there was a lot of open space, few houses, and most roads were unpaved, as we learn from Dorothye Smith in her interview with Vickie Oldham:[41]

*(V. Oldham): What did Sarasota look like when you came [in 1948]? Would you describe what you remember?*
*(D. Smith):* Well, Newtown had just a minimum of paved streets, mainly the north portion of Orange Avenue leading up to present Martin Luther King, and a part of Osprey bus route. That was it.

Newtown Dirt Road.
Courtesy: Wendell Patrick Carter Collection.

*(V. Oldham): How many houses do you remember?*
*(D. Smith):* Well, mainly all of the people out in this area own their own homes. And they were scattered because the lower part of Orange Avenue was all bushes, ditches, and children coming from over in this area sometimes walked across the ditch on a board to get to school. And teachers walked too because there were a minimum of cars in the community. Everybody knew everybody who had a car in Newtown.

Eddie Rainey, who began a postal service career as a clerk at the Suarez gas station in 1963, questions the rosy image of the "good old days" in Newtown, as some of the other interviewees described them. "I was here," Rainey said. "I was here when it was dirt roads, and broken down buildings that they used as schools. When I think back, I didn't realize I was deep in poverty."[42]

By 1960, Newtown was home to about six percent of Sarasota County's population, or about 7,000 people. In the 1960s, Newtown flourished with several restaurants, grocery stores, service stations, a drug store, repair shops, beauty parlors, barbershops, and a doctor's and a dentist's office.[43] The 2010 census recorded a population of 8,442 persons.[44]

Gentrification is a persistent threat to Newtown, according to some residents, and is causing great concern. One of the reasons that the NCHD project has such critical importance to the residents is that, despite their best efforts to prevent it, development in the City of Sarasota has already swallowed Overtown, renaming it the 'Rosemary District.' They fear that development may one day swallow Newtown. Newtown residents do not want their proud heritage to be lost forever, should that occur. Change is an inevitable fact of life, but the history of Newtown should be recorded for posterity in the event that this historical community dissolves into greater Sarasota, as have many African American urban enclaves in other US cities.

---

**ENDNOTES**

[1] Caldez, Jose Maria and Joaquin Caldez land grant applications, Spanish Land Grants (Unconfirmed Grants, 1828), film file 2.1. (Microfilm available at John German Public Library Special Collections Department, (Tampa), Florida A & M University, Tallahassee and Tampa Public Library).

[2] Brown, Canter Jr., "The Sarrazota or Runaway Negro Plantations: Tampa Bay's First Black Community 1812-1821." Tampa Bay History Vol. 12, Issue 2. 1990. pp. 5-29. See also Howard, Rosalyn. "Looking For Angola": Public Anthropology and the Archaeological and Ethnohistorical Search for a Nineteenth Century Florida Maroon Community and its Circum-Caribbean Connections. *Florida Historical Quarterly*, 2013, 32-68; Howard, Rosalyn. "Black Towns of the Seminole Indians." In Poynor, R. ed. *Africa in Florida: Detangling Diasporas in World Culture*. Gainesville: University Press of Florida. 2012.

[3] "The Sarrazota or Runaway Negro Plantations." 5-29.

[4] Williams, John Lee. *The Territory of Florida: 1775-1856 or, Sketches of the topography, civil and natural history, of the country, the climate, and the Indian tribes, from the first discovery to the present time, with a map, views, &c.* New York, A.T. Goodrich. 1837.

[5] Williams, *The Territory of Florida*, cited in Brown, "The Sarrazota or Runaway Negro Plantations, 7, 8.

[6] Williams, *The Territory of Florida*, cited in Brown, "The Sarrazota or Runaway Negro Plantations, 8.

[7] "The Sarrazota or Runaway Negro Plantations.

[8] "The Sarrazota or Runaway Negro Plantations.

[9] Sarasota, Florida: Paradise on the Gulf Coast. *The Western & Central Florida Cooperator*. April 2014.

[10] Sarasota County Historical Resources.

[11] National Register of Historic Places Registration Form.

[12] "Triumphant Struggle," a 20-minute documentary short comprised of edited sound bites from 13 oral history interviews, was written and produced by Vickie Oldham in 1992. It was commissioned by Community Video Archives, Incorporated and is available throughout the Sarasota County Library system.

[13] Rylee, J. Whitcomb. "History of Overtown." 1997, 2.

[14] National Register of Historic Places Registration Form. Overtown Historic District. Blackbottom; Florida Master Site File No.8S0420. 2002.

[15] LaHurd, Jeff. "Early African American Settlers." *Herald-Tribune*. April 16, 2014.

[16] McElroy, Annie M. *But Your World and My World: The Struggle for Survival, A Partial History of Blacks in Sarasota County 1884-1986. Black South Press. 1986*, 2; Grismer, Karl H. The Story of Sarasota: The History of the City and County of Sarasota. Florida. Tampa: M. E. Russell and the Florida Grower Press, 1946.

[17] "Early African American Settlers."

[18] *But Your World and My World*, 2.

[19] Interview with Vickie Oldham. September 4, 2015.

[20] "Leonard Reid Family House." http://www.sarasotahistoryalive.com/history/buildings/leonard-reid-family-house/

[21] In 1902, Gillespie was elected the first mayor of Sarasota when the town was incorporated and held this office for six terms. He also served his community as Justice of Peace four years and Notary Public ten years. He was affectionately

known as "Colonel" in this community."
https://www.scgov.net/History/Pages/JohnHamiltonGillespie.aspx

[22] National Register of Historic Places Registration Form.

[23] "John Hamilton Gillespie."
https://www.scgov.net/History/Pages/JohnHamiltonGillespie.aspx

[24] "The Colored Methodist Church of Sarasota." Sarasota Times. April 21, 1910.
Subjectfiles, Sarasota County Historical Resources.

[25] But Your World and My World, 5-6.

[26] But Your World and My World, 6.

[27] http://www.sarasotagov.com/LivingInSarasota/Contents/PublicWorks/PublicWo
rksHistoricTerrace.html

[28] National Register of Historic Places Registration Form.

[29] National Register of Historic Places Registration Form.

[30] National Register of Historic Places Registration Form.

[31] Levey-Baker, Cooper. "Rosemary Rising." 941CEO, Real Estate. September 4,
2015.

[32] History of the Newtown Community.
http://www.sarasotagov.com/Newtown/history.html

[33] "Newtown History." http://www.sarasotagov.com/Newtown/history.html

[34] Baram, Uzi. "Learning Service and Civic Engagement." In Michael S. Nassaney
and Mary Ann Levine. Archaeology and Community Service Learning.
Gainesville: University Press of Florida. 2009.
117.

[35] Interview with Dr. Rosalyn Howard. January 31, 2016.

[36] "Rosemary Rising."

[37] "Triumphant Struggle."

[38] Comments made by Mary Mack at the Historical Preservation Board Meeting,
April 12, 2016.

[39] History of the Newtown Community.
http://www.sarasotagov.com/Newtown/history.html

[40] Grismer, Karl. "The story of Sarasota: The History of the City and County of
Sarasota, Florida. M.E. Russell. 1st edition. 1946.

[41] Interview with Vickie Oldham. August 2015.

[42] "Looking Back and Ahead." http://newtown100.heraldtribune.com/looking-
back-ahead/

[43] http://www.sarasotagov.com/Newtown/history.html

[44] Newtown-North Sarasota Redevelopment Office. Demographic Summary. April
2014.

# CHAPTER 3: SYNOPSIS OF THE ORAL HISTORY INTERVIEWS

## Eddie L. Rainey Jr.

The smelly city dump was located on the north side near the African American community off North Washington Blvd. Eddie L. Rainey Jr. remembers the long-legged, long-necked cranes hovering. He rummaged through trash to find other people's treasures. His enterprising dad, an expert carpenter, plumber and electrician owned land and constructed homes for Black residents off Highway 301 near the dump and along Pershing Avenue when no other builders would. His uncle, Lloyd Haisley, a Booker High School principal made him read afterschool, then explain passages. The Florida A&M University graduate enlisted in the army in 1952. Looking for work, he saw a flyer about the postal exam, took the test and passed. Rainey retired from the U. S. postal service. His house was located in the 1600 block of then 33rd Street. *"I was raised in this community. I can't say that I ever felt unsafe. Sarasota is a great little town. I will live here forever."*

## Jesse Johnson

*"This is a millionaire town. People come from all over the world here. My little area is heaven to me."* Cement finisher Jesse Johnson came to Sarasota in 1963 to escape lynchings in Greenwood, Mississippi. Outspoken about the issues of the day there, he feared for his life. After living in Miami for a year, he came to Sarasota because *"the people showed outsiders love."*

Behind Town Hall, the Brass Rail and on the side of Can Major's store, he gambled and shot dice daily, sometimes earning $3,000 to $4,000. While standing on the corner after hustling for three years, a man came by in a truck asking for laborers who knew construction. Johnson was convinced he could quickly learn the trade and did. His new job was heading to work sites at 3 a.m. to pour cement, frame up buildings and tie steel in condominiums on the barrier islands of Siesta Key, Longboat and Bradenton Beach. *"I used to hate coming down from being 10 floors up."* By 3 p.m. Johnson was back on the corner socializing.

He helped to construct the Siesta Key Bridge, Sarasota commercial properties and public housing facilities. *"I found jobs just standing on the corner. Everybody ain't doing wrong that you see standing on the corner. I stood up on that corner and worked every day."*

### Patrick Carter

Most summers as a kid, retired NFL player Patrick Carter played outside all day with neighbors' kids. *"We'd make up our own games playing dodge ball, stick ball, and football in the streets, sometimes with a pine cone."* Carter was a wide receiver but became one of the best tail ends in the league. He played football at Florida State University and Riverview High School. The FSU Hall of Famer said his greatest moment happened in the freshman year at college. *"I had a great game. My grandma called the next day to say she saw me on TV and all of her friends saw me and called her. It was meaningful to me that she was so proud."* He credits Riverview High's coach James Ward for having a hand in his choice to play for the FSU Seminoles. *"I only made him look at all of his options,"* said Ward. *"He did all the right things and it was my job to make sure that he saw everything that was out there for him."*

### Sheila Sanders

Sheila Sanders has a sweet smile but don't mistake it for weakness. She organized a boycott of Sarasota Federal Bank as a third grader at Booker Elementary School. At that time, her class learned money management by filling out savings deposit slips for their pennies, dimes and nickels, but the students could not take tours of the bank like children from other schools. Sanders persuaded her classmates to send deposits to Palmer Bank, which they could tour. Her actions foreshadowed future activism. The teenager proactively participated in the NAACP accompanying leaders John Rivers and Maxine Mays to local and state meetings. Sanders learned about the political process by reviewing the agendas of school board meetings and attending the meetings, taking the city bus. *"Some things won't be said just because you're sitting there. I learned I didn't have to concern myself with 'being as good as,' by sitting and listening. I was already better."*

Rivers rode through town with a bullhorn, registering voters. William "Flick" Jackson was publisher of the African American newspaper, *The Weekly Bulletin*. *"Some people were leaders, but they weren't obvious leaders. They were quiet leaders, people who were independent and didn't have to depend on somebody for their income."* Jackson and Rivers joined Sanders and Edward James II as plaintiffs in a lawsuit against the City of Sarasota. They successfully pushed for single member district voting that opened the way for African American representation on the Sarasota City Commission.

### Jetson Grimes

At some point, most little boys in Newtown sit in Jetson Grimes' chair for a haircut. Grimes is an entrepreneur and a community organizer. He picked up activism from his mentor Robert "Bud"

Thomas, also a barber. At the urging of her sister, Grimes' mother left Georgia to find work in the homes of wealthy Sarasota families. She contracted tuberculosis and was placed in a treatment facility leaving her baby in the care of a godmother.

Grimes' guardian, Lenora Madame Brooks, a midwife of Cuban descent delivered many of Newtown's children because Sarasota Memorial Hospital was inaccessible to African Americans. Brooks was considered a neighborhood physician. Her husband, also Cuban, made cigars in a nearby space on 35th Street. Newtown residents gathered around the radio at their house to hear boxing matches. At 11, Grimes was cared for by an aunt, another entrepreneur who operated a janitorial service in the early '50s. Business ownership is in his DNA. He can't escape it; and after 37 years of entrepreneurship, he doesn't plan to.

### Rev. Jerome Dupree

Rev. Dupree slowly walked to the podium at Selby Gardens to memorialize a friend during a service. He eloquently recited "When the Earth's Last Picture is Painted" by Rudyard Kipling from memory. His presence and presentation was a healing balm just as it has been for countless Newtown audiences at churches, schools and civic gatherings. The admired speaker has a repertoire of six more inspirational poems by famous authors: "The Creation" by James Weldon Johnson, "The Psalm of Life" by Henry Wadsworth Longfellow; "Invictus" by William Ernest Henley; "If" by Kipling; "The House by the Side of the Road" by Sam Walton Foss; and Psalm 27. A fourth grade teacher, Marthenia Riley recited poetry and encouraged Dupree to appreciate the spoken word. Dupree listened. Other high school teachers, Esther Dailey and Janie Poe, were strong influences. *"[Poe] said if you're behind, you have to run twice as fast as the other person in order to catch up. And once you catch up, you have to run as fast to get ahead."*

Dupree began a teaching career at age 21. After 10 years, he left the profession and held several positions including neighborhood director of

Metropolitan Life Insurance. He returned to the school system at age 34. He was fast tracked to school principal and was elected to the Sarasota City Commission in 1995 serving as mayor from 1998 to1999.

The advice and wisdom of Koinonia Baptist Church's pastor, former Booker High School principal and a veteran educator is sought by civic and nonprofit organizations. An admirer posted this description of Rev. Dupree on Facebook: *"Newtown's prince, an awesome man of God with unwavering love and a precious human being."* Rev. Dupree's oral history interview was provided by the New College of Florida Oral History Program.

### Dr. Louis Robison

Dr. Louis Robison was age 13 when his family moved to Sarasota from Overtown, in inner city Miami. His community there was diverse. Not so much in his adopted hometown of Newtown. It was a predominantly Black and rural neighborhood with mostly unpaved streets. Robison entered 7th grade at Booker High School where Roland Rogers served as principal. *"Teachers required excellence in terms of academic expectations. It was difficult to get away with anything because the community was so small. Music was a contributor to my success in life,"* said Robison who played tuba in the BHS band, a crowd favorite at parades.

A transfer to Riverview High School from Booker during integration disrupted the lives of classmates but the mature teenager had already experienced transitions and knew how to navigate them. Robison attended college and rose through the ranks as a school administrator. He later became principal of RHS. Under his leadership, *"with the help of a great team"* the school went from a "C" school to an "A."

### Dr. Fannie McDugle

Young and fearless describes Dr. Fannie McDugle who moved to Sarasota's Overtown at age 15 from Atlanta with her family in 1947. She attended Booker High School from 7th to 8th grade, then left to attend a private boarding school in Cordele, Georgia. Profits from her mother's dress shop and her father's paycheck from Sarasota Memorial Hospital paid the tuition. McDugle went to school to become a nurse but didn't like it. Instead, she attended cosmetology school. She participated in Woolworth sit-ins and entered dress stores on Main Street to integrate them as a member of the NAACP. *"We'd all go in as a group. It felt good doing what was right."*

### Helen Dixon

At age 17, Helen Dixon's father Charlie Jones came to Sarasota from Madison, Florida, in 1921 after his father died. Her mother moved from Ocilla, Georgia. Dixon played in the yard on her family's four-acre property. She made toys out of a five-gallon syrup can, punched holes in it, filled it with dirt and attached a clothes hanger. One of her dad's employers gave him with a "play house" equipped with electricity, a refrigerator and a stove. It was moved to their property and used to feed neighbors in need. When Newtown Day Nursery opened, Dixon was among its first students. *"My sister and I were the first two students to attend. We were really excited because it meant we would get to play with other kids during the day. We loved it."* Her father worked for Davis Lumber Company and was John Ringling North's chauffeur. The outspoken Newtown leader constantly advocated at City Hall on behalf of African American residents for street lights, mail delivery and Booker High School's teachers and students.

*"The teachers would say, 'Miss Jones, please tell your daddy to come out to the school. We need more money.' He would go downtown and, next thing you know, the teachers would get a little raise."* After constructing many homes, the entrepreneur opened a plumbing and electrical business, Charlie Jones and Sons. He helped construct the historic Wright Bush house on Dr. Martin Luther King Jr. Way.

### Alberta Brown

Alberta Brown is known in the Newtown community for her sumptuous southern-style Sunday throw downs – a big roast seasoned to the bone, a large pot of collards, long pans of buttery yams, melt in your mouth mac-n-cheese and moist cornbread with crispy edges. It is as if a small army of people are dinner guests. Extended family members, church friends and drop-ins are part of the platoon stopping in for a plate. Brown's family members were sharecroppers from Alachua County.

They moved to Palmetto and found work picking tomatoes and green beans. Brown later worked as a live-in on Siesta Key for a physician's family. She took care of the couple's little girl. When help was no longer needed, she followed in her sister's footsteps, training to become a cook.

The position at her next job evolved into more. Jane Bancroft Cook, heir to the Dow Jones & Company family enterprise was looking for a cook. Through a recommendation from a previous employer, Cook met a tall, soft-spoken woman and hired her on the spot. Brown recalls the interview that day. *"She looked at me and said, 'oh, you're beautiful.'"* What followed was a friendship with Cook until her death in 2002 and a lifelong kinship with the family that remains today.

## Johnny Hunter Sr.

The publisher of *Tempo News* enjoyed playing games such as horseshoes, marbles, hopscotch, ping-pong and baseball. He lived in Overtown. Better housing caused a family move to north Sarasota. Hunter recalls the prominent educators who taught at Amaryllis Park and Booker Elementary Schools, as well as Booker High School. The teachers lived near the schools where they worked. Prominent entrepreneurs such as funeral director Jerome Stephens, electrician and plumber Charlie Jones, and Neil Humphrey, owner of Humphrey's Drugstore all lived in Newtown.

The visible presence of community leaders made a tremendous difference in the lives of children and their parents. Hunter says the dismantling of the community began with integration and the migration of African American residents once their economic levels changed. *"People started moving out, instead of improving their own neighborhoods. I always felt we needed to improve our own neighborhoods."* After high school, the newly minted graduate enlisted in the U.S. Air Force. After fulfilling the commitment, he returned home to work, but always dreamed of owning a business. He opened several operations. A brush with the law almost cost him everything, but a vow made in prison changed his life forever.

## Rev. Kelvin Lumpkin

Atlanta is a city that attracts African American professionals because of its economic opportunities; and the arts, music and cultural scene. It is the place where Rev. Kelvin Lumpkin planned to make a life after graduating from Bethune Cookman College. Stories told by his mother and father about African Americans ordering meals at the back door of the first McDonald's were distasteful.

He didn't have the same experience at the fast food chain, but was stopped by the police for "driving while Black" with two friends after football practice. The young man accepted the call to serve in ministry, similar to many in his family; then returned home to start a new church. His place of worship, among the fastest growing, most diverse in Sarasota is making a difference in the lives of parishioners.

## Prevell Barber

Prevell Barber's birth mother passed away when the little girl was only three years old. She lived with her grandmother in Georgia until her mother's sister and husband took over as surrogate parents.

In the summer, Barber came to Sarasota to work in her uncle's grocery store. She sold cookies sometimes eating more than were sold. The high school graduate entered Florida A&M University to major in elementary education and minor in history. Years later, as a second grade teacher, she reluctantly applied to the University of Chicago, was accepted and attended graduate school each summer for six years to earn a master's degree.

When local activists pushed to integrate Lido Beach, Barber was in the carload of freedom fighters with Neil Humphrey, Allease Suarez and her brother in law to take a stand in the sand amid name calling. *"Well God made the water. It wasn't made by man so it should be exposed to everybody,"* Barber said. On weekdays, the group drove to Lido to step into the water and heard the "n-word" hurled. *"I had heard it so much; it didn't bother me."* Through many civic and social organizations such as the Royal SaraMana Club, Barber and a cadre of Newtown community women organized debutante cotillion balls to mentor and introduce young African American women to society.

### Nathaniel Harvey

Born in 1924, Nathaniel Harvey is the soft-spoken, powerhouse patriarch of the Harvey family. He is the son of Lewis and Saphronia Harvey. His ancestry is Native American, specifically Seminole. His father worked on the celery farm located in east Sarasota.

Like his father, Harvey also found work, harvesting celery. Other workers washed, packed and shipped the crop. The labor force lived close to the farm in a place called Johnson Camp and worked from "can't to can't" beginning before sunrise in the early mornings and ending the day at sundown. Harvey's teachers were Annie M. McElroy, author of *But Your World and My World* and legendary educator Emma E. Booker. *"She was a great lady. She was very strict, but was good. She meant what she said and said what she meant."*

At age 16, the young man met his bride Mary Lee whose lineage was African American and Cherokee. The couple had seven children and enjoyed 73 years of marriage. Harvey says the lack of access to medical care caused the untimely death of his mother and brother. He praises the changes occurring in Newtown. Sarasota NAACP president Trevor Harvey is his grandson. Sunday meals with chicken, rice, lima beans and family time brought Mr. Harvey joy. He passed away on August 31, 2016.

### Trevor D. Harvey

Trevor Harvey and his family survived the flames and smoke of a house fire. Windows had to be shattered to open a way for escape. They lost everything and started over. *"It was horrific. It impacted*

*me, my mom and sisters because we didn't know what would happen."* He attended the Helen Payne Day Nursery. The young man came of age in the late 70s and 80s when Newtown's business district was bustling with stores such as Can's, Jenkins's and Moore's Grocers, Joe's Bicycle Shop and Humphries Drugstore.

In its heyday, there were close to 100 shops along what is now known as Dr. Martin Luther King Jr. Way. Harvey hopes the business corridor will thrive again. He put college on hold to manage a company, and then later sent a strong message to his children and mentees by becoming a college graduate. Harvey is president of the Sarasota NAACP and area director for the Florida State Conference overseeing seven NAACP branches. *"I started out with a desire to make a difference in the community."*

## Betty Jean Johnson

Betty Jean Johnson is a voracious reader who loves traveling to faraway places through books. Her teacher Prevell Barber stoked an appreciation for the written word. *"I always had to read something in her class or around her. The fact of it is when I read I could travel. We didn't have TV until later on."* Johnson thought her college education would lead to a career in social work.

Instead, a high school class in "library procedures" changed her trajectory after she graduated from Gibbs Junior College in St. Petersburg. Back then, Manatee Community College, now known as State College of Florida was off limits to African Americans. Mary Emma Jones, a well-respected entrepreneur and community leader, orchestrated the hiring of Mary Thomas at the Sarasota Public Library.

Thomas helped Johnson land a job there. The facility was not a welcoming place for African American patrons. Johnson understood what Newtown residents encountered. *"For a book report, I had to go to that library for a book because we didn't have it at the Booker library. There were stacks closed to Blacks. The lady at the desk had to go to the stacks to get the book. When I started working there, those same people were there."*

For years, a perplexing question dogged Johnson. *"What can I do to get more Blacks to use the library?"* A solution to the conundrum came while preparing to work a split shift. She would ask the boss for use of an old book mobile the library was about to replace with a new one. The idea was nixed but administrators provided an outreach van that made books accessible to African American children.

From a van to a storefront library operating on a shoestring budget, Johnson and supporters kept pushing, even though for years their efforts seemed fruitless. Finally, the North Sarasota Library opened as a result of the seed of an idea that Johnson planted.

## Wade Harvin

*"Something happened to me at the Ace Theater,"* said Wade Harvin. *"Well, my first kiss!"* Harvin's favorite memories of Sarasota occurred when the family moved in June 1945 from Mother Jones' Rooming House in what was known as "Black Bottom" to Delson Quarters at 821 Grove Street in Overtown. He grew up surrounded by charming, caring neighbors and playmates whose eyes were always set on achieving what seemed impossible. Educator Janie Poe's two sons Cupid Reece and Booker T. became doctors; their brother, Spurgeon was a principal. *"Janie Poe Goodwin prepared me not for business, not for 4-year college, she was getting me prepared for life."*

A bishop and 11 preachers are products of that loving incubator. As soon as the school year ended to jumpstart the summer, Harvin's dad packed the family car and took his sons north to pick beans, tomatoes and potatoes. For the first time, the boys, including nine-year-old Wade experienced life in the integrated town of Milton, Pennsylvania, unlike segregated Sarasota. Harvin longed to stay, but the allure of close-knit Overtown beckoned. Besides he had to return to meet the woman who would become his wife.

He married Carlene Jean. Her mother arranged a trip to Detroit for the summer to visit her father. *"When she got back to Sarasota, I said 'she'll never send my wife anywhere else. This is marrying material here.' She has never been back to Detroit like that, never for a whole summer away from me. No way. No way."* Harvin was married for 52 years until his life partner died in 2015. The first African American branch manager of Coast Federal Bank participated in '60s sit-ins to integrate Lido Beach. Today, he will not step foot on its sand as a result of a hateful act.

### Mary Alice Simmons

It's early in the morning in 1955 and Mary Alice Simmons leaves her Orange Avenue apartment in public housing, on the way to school. At the bus stop is a line of African American women dressed in white uniforms heading to work in the homes of prominent, wealthy families.

At age eight, Mary's family moved to unit #10. The differences between conditions in Overtown where they lived before and the new complex were like night and day. The place had a bathroom, electricity, a yard with grass, and sidewalks. Before that, their shotgun house had no running water. They pumped water for bathing, washing dishes and laundry. There were three tubs to wash, rinse garments, and rinse again. Before Clorox, a boil pot whitened clothes. An outhouse 15 feet from the house was used. A portable oil stove was the major kitchen appliance and kerosene lamps provided light. An imaginary boundary line kept community children from veering past 10th Street. Simmons only ventured across the line to grocery shop with her grandmother. *"We would walk down Main Street and smell peanuts in the five-and-dime store. I remember asking, 'Granny can I have an ice cream cone.' She said, 'sit here.' I sat on the curb. I never forgot the place,*

*Oleander's. Granny went in, got it, and brought it outside. I looked at her, looked at the cone, looked at the people sitting inside. But you didn't ask adults questions, the end. You just did as you were told."*

### Dorothye Smith

Retired Sarasota County principal Dorothye Smith is revered by her students and colleagues. Smith, born in Clearwater, Florida is the first African American principal hired to lead Southside Elementary School located in an affluent Sarasota neighborhood. Her first job after completing studies at Bethune Cookman College was teaching African American fourth graders, first in the USO building until Booker's two-story classroom structure from Overtown was moved to Newtown. In her class were students eager to learn such as Yvonne Brown and Edward E. James II. *"Children are inquisitive. Ed always asked 'why?'"* Back then, some young career climbers lived with families to make ends meet. The 20-year old's monthly $154 salary exceeded the public housing threshold. She lived in the home of Mary Jane Wilson.

She met Jacob Smith who managed the Ace Theatre for African American patrons. *"One of my friends talked me into going to the movies with her. She wanted me to meet this cute little man."* Smith visited on his days off and stayed until catching the 9 p.m. bus back to Overtown. That was bedtime at the Wilson house.

Smith taught at Booker for 15 years until she was assigned to a Venice school in 1957 during integration. She was promoted to county reading specialist, made friends along the way, then returned to run the school in Venice again before retirement. *"The most enjoyable time that a person can have is in the classroom with the children."*

**Julian Ross Moreland and Margaret Beverly Moreland Cherry Mitchell**

Julian Ross Moreland and Margaret Beverly Mitchell Moreland are the grandchildren of Wright and Sarah Bush and the offspring of James Edward and Margaret Moreland. The Bush family used their influence to advocate for education, entrepreneurship and civic responsibility. Wright owned a general store in Overtown. *"He didn't discriminate because hell, he looked like that man back there holding that camera. He tended to everybody,"* said Julian Ross (speaking about the camera man filming his interview). His father James Edward ran a juke joint called the "Bamboo Club" on the corner of Links and then 33rd Street (now 29th Street); also a dance hall with live entertainment. *"I went to see James Brown. He learned how to skid across the floor from watching me and another guy. I could dance,"* said Moreland who recounted how his dad was run out of town for *"smacking the sheriff on the head"* with a pistol after he was hit. Outspoken Grandma Bush had the reputation of correcting neighborhood children who acted out in public.

The historic Wright Bush house located at Maple Avenue and Dr. Martin Luther King Jr. Way was a popular meeting place because it had amenities such as electricity. Black soldiers stationed at a military base near the airport met their future spouses there.

## Robert L. Taylor

Robert L. Taylor is a graduate of Morehouse College. Admittedly, his was a charmed life free of heavy chores at home. The goal set for the seven-year-old was to become the first college graduate in the family. That meant no hanging out with friends on the corner in Overtown. The neighborhood had a few restaurants, a barbershop, a hotel and Bethlehem Baptist Church on the corner of Central Avenue. There were no doctor's offices. *"There was no medical care, no doctors. We used cobwebs, cotton balls and turpentine to treat everything. I went to the dentist as a 15-year-old, but the instruments were tarnished and disgusting. I didn't go back to the dentist until I was 25."*

Studying hard, Taylor earned the title of salutatorian at Booker High School. An academic scholarship to attend college followed. He served in the military, finished college on the GI bill and returned home to work small part-time jobs at the recreation center, a furniture store, on a construction crew, and cleaning sewers (he pauses). *"It has only been recently that I could talk about some instances without bursting out crying. People don't know what racism really is."*

The part time job at "The Rec" eventually turned into full time employment. Some days, Taylor spent 15-20 hours making sure the pool and other facilities were ready for children. He was the manager, a certified swimming instructor and pool operator who planned all programs because the center was the *"only game in town."*

## Dr. Harriet Moore and Estella Moore-Thomas

Estella Moore-Thomas owned Moore's Grocers when African American residents couldn't shop at other grocery stores. The Newtown business that still bears the family's name supplied the community with groceries and fresh produce. Before Moore's, she rented a store in the building once occupied by Eddie's Fruit Stand. Harriet D. Moore, her daughter helped run the store. *"We were one of the few stores that gave credit to people,"* Moore chimed in.

Moore grew up in Sidell, Florida, located 50 miles east of Sarasota in a turpentine camp. The home remedies used to treat illnesses consisted of turpentine, Epsom salt, castor oil and cobwebs. *"When I came here, we didn't have electricity. I opened the door of the refrigerator and the lamp fell and broke.*

*Right there, just cut it to the bone. They filled it up with cobwebs. No stitches or nothing. No doctors, but I lived through it."* The elder Moore didn't finish high school because the responsibility of helping at home as a teenager stood in the way, but she made sure her children received the best education. Harriet earned a doctorate degree and is principal of McIntosh Middle School. *"The way that it used to be, I miss that rallying around people who didn't have and making sure that nobody went hungry around here."*

## Dr. Rachel Shelley

Dr. Rachel Shelley has *"literally lived in every single public housing complex in Sarasota: Project Lane, Cohen Way, the 'Old Project.'"* But her most treasured memories are the hours spent at 2924 Maple Avenue. Her grandmother's wooden house was surrounded by a fence located less than 1 1/2 blocks from Booker High School where sounds of the BHS marching band permeated the community. Neighborhood children played games outside such as "red light, green light" kick ball, and "hide-n-seek." They were free to venture through the neighborhood and run to Jenkins Grocery, Mr. Joe's Bicycle Shop and Neil Humphrey's Drugstore for errands.

The house rule was to be home before sundown. From kindergarten to second grade, she attended Booker Elementary then transitioned to Phillippi Shores Elementary School. An experience with a third grade teacher transformed her life forever. *"I graduated from Riverview High School when I was 16, but what I don't recall is anyone explaining honors, advanced placement or dual enrollment classes for the chance to earn college credits. I am absolutely adamant that we have these conversations with the students at Booker High School."* Dr. Shelley is principal of Booker High.

### Dr. Thomas Clyburn

Dr. Thomas Clyburn can still hear the sound of his patent leather loafers on the floor of a Blue Bird bus, stepping out of his seat, walking down the aisle to the front, then down the steps on the first day of school in 11th grade in an unfamiliar setting. Earlier that day, Clyburn showed up for class at Booker High School where he was an honors student, but was asked to wait outside the main office. He didn't know why. A bus pulled up. *"Are you Thomas Clyburn?"* driver Robert Graham asked. *"Yes I am,"* the teenager replied. *"I'm here to take you to school, not here."* The driver and passenger took the route from Myrtle Avenue to North Washington Boulevard to Sarasota High School. Students were everywhere. *"Good luck. I'll come back to pick you up."* The bus driver dropped him off in front of the gothic style building. When he stepped off the bus, the world in front of him froze.

*"Everyone was looking at me. My pulse rate in my throat went to the roof."* He had walked to the administrative office. *"It was really, really, really quiet. The principal [Gene Pilot] introduced himself. He asked a few questions."* Then a teacher escorted him to homeroom. Some students were silent. Some whispered. *"That was my first day. It was a challenge. You would think those days would get better over time, but in many ways they got worse."*

Clyburn, no longer in Booker's cocoon of nurturing teachers and classmates was left to navigate a place he entered for the first time. Clyburn was chosen for a pilot program to integrate Sarasota County schools in 1963. *"I was sitting in homeroom looking out of the window. A kid with a big German shepherd walked toward the building. I heard a loud pop. Six men racing toward me said 'get in the center. Don't say anything. Follow us.' We went to the principal's office. They locked down the school to look for the student."* Willemina Thomas, a BHS classmate was also selected to participate in the SHS pilot program, but their paths never crossed. Clyburn's specialty is behavioral psychology. He was university director of learner affairs at Capella University.

### John Rivers

John Henry Rivers is the former president of the NAACP's Sarasota branch. He moved to Sarasota from Mobile, Alabama in 1951 in search of work to support his family. Instead, Rivers found himself in the midst of a struggle for racial equality.

In the 1950s and 1960s, Sarasota was a hotbed of segregation. Rivers accepted the challenge to fight for the integration of beaches, the school system and local politics as a leader of Sarasota's Civil Rights Movement. He registered voters and announced poll locations by riding through Newtown with a bullhorn. He fought battles for (but not limited to) equality in employment, salary, mail delivery, service at restaurants, and banking. Mr. Rivers' oral history interview was provided by the New College of Florida Oral History Program.

### Shelia Atkins

Shelia Cassundra Hammond Atkins was born in Manatee County in 1952, but grew up in Newtown. Her mother Delma Hammond was a cook in the Caples Mansion where the little girl scampered when allowed. Her father, John Hammond was a butler. The Hammond family lived in the carriage house on the grounds situated along Sarasota Bay and traveled back and forth to Alabama every six months when Ralph and Ellen Caples returned home for the summer. (Alabama is where they first met the couple.)

Mrs. Caples named Shelia, according to stories shared by her mom. Atkins attended high school during integration and has lived in Sarasota for over six decades. She and her husband, former Sarasota Mayor Fredd Atkins are active in the community. The paraprofessional aide is employed at Alta Vista Elementary. Mrs. Atkins' oral history interview was provided by the New College of Florida Oral History Program.

### Dr. Edward E. James II

Newtown residents know Dr. Edward E. James II as a community advocate and civil rights leader who stands in the gap insisting, resisting, refuting, and disrupting arcane systems that block equal opportunity. As producer and host of the ABC 7 television show, "Black Almanac" for 43 years, he covers issues that impact the African American community. The Sunday morning program is the oldest, locally produced, public affairs show in the southeast. He joined ABC 7 in 1972 as a weekend news anchor.

The Florida A&M University graduate served as a columnist and governmental reporter for the *Sarasota Journal* newspaper. He was a writer/associate producer of "Positively Black," a half-hour TV show on New York's WNBC-TV, and also worked as an editorial assistant for the *New York Post*.

With an extensive background in government and public relations, Dr. James served as the public information officer and deputy chief investigator for the State Attorney's office for the 12th Judicial Circuit of Florida, public relations director of the New York Urban Coalition, and Assistant Director of the first Urban Job Corps.

He is a recipient of the President's Award, a Lifetime Service Award and a Freedom Award, all from the Sarasota County NAACP, and was presented a Lifetime Achievement Award by the Sarasota African American Chamber of Commerce. Dr. James II's interview was provided by the New College of Florida Oral History Program.

### James and Yvonne Brown

James Brown still owns the home on North Osprey Avenue that was built in 1928 by his father. The lot was purchased in 1926 for $450. Brown and his wife Yvonne describe idyllic lives growing up in the African American community.

Yvonne Brown's grandparents moved to Overtown in 1925 from Quitman, Georgia. She recalls hearing stories about the family starting out in makeshift housing that resembled a tent, then transitioning into a two-story building on 14th Street, later renamed 8th Street.

*"We were happy and always had everything we needed. My friends and I enjoyed going to church, school, the movies, and there was entertainment that came once a year. It was called 'Silas Green' from New Orleans. It*

*was like a play, similar to Tyler Perry's. They crafted a big tent in a community. That was a lot of fun,"* she said.

James Brown grew up in Newtown where the police substation sits on Dr. Martin Luther King Jr. Way. Children played under the shade of two banyan trees. *"We were a happy generation. The beauty of it was that adults let us be children. As I grew older, I realized all they must have been going through,"* he said.

Teachers were motivators and had great expectations for Yvonne, James and their classmates. *"Boy, you are going to college. I don't want to hear it. You are going to college,"* educator Esther Reed Dailey told him. Brown graduated with honors in the top ten percent of his Florida A&M University class and retired as associate dean of educational services at State College of Florida. His wife retired as pre-school coordinator for Sarasota County Schools.

## Fredd Atkins

Fredd Atkins' story is a testament to the power that teenagers have to shake up institutional systems. He was reared in an Augustine Quarters "shotgun shack" located behind Horn's Grocery Store on 6th Street in Overtown.

For fun, Atkins played football and baseball on sandlots and dirt courts. A bicycle tire was easily turned into a basketball rim. "Pop up" was played with part of a rubber hose, chinaberries and a shaved palmetto limb. His aunt Ruby always kept a nice car. She participated in beach desegregation. *"I was a little boy. There was always some apprehension during the desegregation process. I have been in caravans when [the police] turned us around and sent us back to Newtown. Sometimes we'd get into the water. You stayed close to the shore.*

The family built a new 3-bedroom house in Newtown for $7,000 after his aunt hit the jackpot playing Bolita, a numbers game imported from Cuba.

He came to Newtown in 1958 when there were few new homes. *"It was a weird kind of experience because the middle class of Newtown lived in public housing. Most of the working class lived in the projects, even some teachers before they built homes."* Atkins participated in the desegregation of Sarasota schools. During the Booker School boycott, he taught at the freedom school set up at Greater Hurst Chapel A.M.E. Church. Then came integration. *"Assimilation was tough. My mother used to make me go [to school]. She'd say, 'Boy, I'm not gonna feed you if you don't make some decent grades.' I'd say, "This is just so rough. She said, 'but you better go.'"* At Sarasota High School, Fredd and his 1968 classmates Johnny Smith, Walter L. Gilbert, III and others boycotted, picketed, held protests, and took their complaints about inequitable treatment to Gene Pilot, the principal. Pilot established the "Pupil Interracial Council" to routinely address students' concerns.

A Booker High School teacher Rubin Mays, reassigned to Sarasota High School during integration, was Atkins' lifesaver. *"Anytime I was on the edge, I could go to his classroom and just sit there. No one would question why I was there. I could go and cool out. I'd just sit in and listen to his math class."* Sarasota High School students from Newtown successfully changed the lunch menu, added African American cheerleaders to the squad and pushed school administrators to recognize African American history for a week.

As a member of the NAACP's youth council, Atkins registered voters in high school, and attended school board meetings. Activism continued in college. He conducted research for the Miami attorney who filed a federal lawsuit against the City of Sarasota. Atkins' trajectory was established early. He is one of Sarasota's longest serving city commissioners, having spent 18 years in public service. He was Sarasota's mayor three times.

### Carolyn Mason

School integration caused trauma and fear for Carolyn Mason and rightly so. She lived in Overtown's "Black Bottom" located at the corner of 8th Street and Central Avenue in segregated Sarasota. There was a dividing line at 3<sup>rd</sup> Street or present day Fruitville Road. *"I call it the Mason-Dixon line. North of Fruitville was the Black community; and south was downtown for the more affluent community."* The communities did not mix. *"My senior year in high school should be my best year, but it was full of apprehension. I couldn't think past the fear of being around people I had never been around before. I didn't know what I was afraid of, but I was afraid. Somebody should have talked to the children – all of the children – about what to expect. Somebody should have said, 'You don't have anything to worry about.'"*

Mason began a career in public service after viewing a theater production in Sarasota that lacked a diverse cast. Frustrated, she became the go-between for talented African American artists and arts organizations. *"I offered myself as a bridge. I was probably on the board at one time of every arts organization in Sarasota County."* She was elected to the Sarasota City Commission and served from 1999 to 2003. She was Mayor of Sarasota from 2001 to 2003. Mason became the first African American elected to the Sarasota County Commission in 2008 and served as chair in 2013 and 2015. Social issues are the focus of her work. Carolyn Mason's oral history was provided by interviewer Hope Black.

## Willie Charles Shaw

The memory of Sarasota Mayor Willie Charles Shaw is razor sharp. He was reared in "Black Bottom," a swampy land in Newtown near Maple, Palmadelia and Goodrich Avenues. There were no street lights or curbside mail delivery. Overtown had its own neighborhood with the same name because of its rich black soil. Shaw can quickly rattle off the locations of community landmarks, dirt paths, swimming holes, citrus trees and bus routes; and the names of neighbors. Newtown's dusty roads were paved in 1968, but the first paved streets followed the route of the city transit bus. His grandmother and family members owned land along Orange Avenue and 31st Street. *"There was a time when one of Rev. Herring's cows got out and I was at my grandmother's house that lived on the corner as you come around Palmadelia Avenue. I was on my tricycle and the cow came up behind me. I remember looking over my shoulder saying, 'he got me.'"* When there was a death in the neighborhood, Mrs. Herring, Fannie McDugle, and Mrs. James formed an unofficial neighborhood association with Mrs. Viola Sanders at the helm. The women collected food and flowers for grieving families. Shaw's mother sewed a heart or a ribbon on the right sleeve of the bereaved.

The retired letter carrier attended the Booker schools with teachers Barbara Wiggins, Mrs. McGreen, Prevell Carner Barber, Aravia Bennet Johnson, Foster Paulk, Esther Dailey, Coach Dailey, Janie Poe, and Turner Covington. *"I would have to say that the entire learning experience at Booker groomed me into a leader. We were taught that you always had to be better, do better. You had to."* In high school, the teenager played the trumpet for a short time and was the "band boy" for Newtown's pride and joy, the Booker High School band under the direction of Alexander Valentine.

Shaw was among the African American students who traveled on a bus across the Skyway Bridge to attend Gibbs Junior College. He served in the

U.S. Air Force, then became a letter carrier following in the footsteps of Jerome Stephens, the first African American in Sarasota hired by the postal service.

The District 1 Sarasota City Commissioner was elected in 2011. He is serving a second term as mayor and continues the proud tradition of Black pioneers who advocate for the underserved, including veterans.

## Verna Hall

Verna Hall lives in the house where she was born in 1932. The wood structure, constructed by Rev. J.H. Floyd, is the second oldest house in Newtown. Built off the ground, the 84-year house is deteriorating; floorboards are rotting from years of rain and wind. Her father, Leo Purdy was assisting the police as a peace officer when he was killed in the line of duty while making an arrest on 8th Street in Overtown.

Sarah Ware, her mother, cooked for John Ringling North, the nephew of circus magnate John Ringling. Hall was "boarded out" and lived on Links Avenue from age four to ten because her mother was a live-in maid. Boarding the children of domestic workers was a way aging residents supplemented their incomes. *"There was nothing to do. When you were boarded out with families, it was usually older people that had grown kids that moved away from home. You played outside because the agreement was that there was a roof over my head with kind people. They kept me clean and fed. There wasn't that much interaction because they were already old and there was no way to entertain a small child."*

Hall lives near the Robert L. Taylor Community Complex. She watched as the barracks building was moved to the property from the airport army base. It once served as the USO building where African American soldiers socialized. *"I met the young man that I married at the Robert Taylor location. I danced in that building. We had community activities in that building also. It was during the time the "String of Pearls" was one of the instrumental tunes aired on the radio. They'd play those songs and we would go there and we would dance."*

**Edward E. James III**

This career climber with a University of Chicago degree and Google on his resume was a candidate for Florida House of Representatives District 72 in 2016.

Edward E. James III hears the call of public service. The fourth generation Sarasota resident worked for two years in the legal department of the world's largest tech company handling data analysis for patent litigators. Edward's epiphany to return home occurred while watching the "Dream Defenders" stage a sit-in at Gov. Rick Scott's office in 2013, during the Trayvon Martin controversy.

That his family has a storied history of Civil Rights activism, which spans over 100 years, sealed the deal to continue the legacy of leadership. *"I'm proud to be of the lineage of people who fought to get us to where we are now. My great grandmother Mary Emma Jones who was a business owner in this community for well over 40 years helped desegregate Lido Public Beach. She along with other concerned Newtown residents went out, waded in the water and dealt with physical and verbal abuse. I love Lido Beach. My great grandmother fought so that people like me could go and not be worried about anyone threatening or calling us names."*

The actions of Edward's father, Dr. Edward E. James II, triggered the desegregation of the Sarasota County Public Library. His grandmother, educator Annie McElroy, penned the book, *But Your World and My World*, which is on the shelves of many Sarasota natives. It documents the Black community's history from an insider's point of view. *"I came back to be a change agent. Newtown is beaming with entrepreneurship. It has potential. It has tradition and is one of the oldest communities in Sarasota. Things are not as they could be, but we're working to make things better."*

### Gwendolyn Atkins (top) and Henrietta Gayles Cunningham

Two retired African American public health nurses spent a lifetime healing bruises in the community. For nearly three decades, nurses Henrietta Gayles Cunningham and Gwen Atkins walked door to door in Newtown neighborhoods, public housing areas and in migrant camps teaching young mothers about child care, treating childhood diseases, monitoring the health of aging residents and making sure seasonal workers received medical services. They set up a makeshift clinic in the garage of Stephens Funeral Home. *"We'd treat infantigo and ring worms. Remember setting up a card table with a white table cloth then immunizing children for polio and small pox?"* Atkins asked her former colleague during a visit at an Ocala assisted living facility where Cunningham resides. *"That was real public health,"* said Cunningham, the first African American nurse at the Sarasota County Health Department.

The women became extended family members of their patients. The line between work and play often blurred. Nursing and being on call, accessible and always available was a way of life. It still is for Atkins. Mary Emma Jones, Allease Suarez and Viola Sanders were extremely helpful to both of the caregivers. *"If I had to do it all over again, I would choose public health nursing and I would choose serving my community. That's what I love more than anything else,"* Atkins said.

### Etienne J. Porter

Producer Etienne J. Porter considers himself a '90s child just beginning to explore life and develop an appetite for music of all genres - from Handel's "Messiah" to "Back on the Block" by Quincy Jones and releases by artists such as Michael Jackson, Guy, Salt and Pepper, Walter Hawkins and Hezekiah Walker. Born in 1979, an affinity for the arts occurred naturally. His father Bishop Henry L. Porter, pastor of the Westcoast Center writes songs, plays instruments and performs.

His mother, the late Cynthia Porter, was an actor and singer. Etienne learned how to play drums at church, then studied music and jazz percussion in college. PJ Morton of Maroon 5, Frank McComb, Melba Moore, and the Westcoast Black Theater Troupe are a few of the entertainers he has accompanied. Sarasota is his hometown and the headquarters of Drummerboy Entertainment and Recording Studio. His mission is to ensure that aspiring artists, singers, dancers and actors have a launch pad that catapults their careers to a larger platform.

*"I view the world differently than those who grew up at a time before me. I've never experienced someone telling me I couldn't go somewhere. If I was denied entrance anywhere, it was because I wasn't dressed appropriately but not based on skin tone.* Etienne sees one Sarasota, not a divided city. *"It's just as much about outreach. Sarasota must reach into Newtown and at the same time Newtown has to reach outside of itself."*

## Elder Willie Mays Jr. and Rosa Lee Thomas (his sister)

Elder Willie Mays Jr. is proud of the 78-year-old church he pastors, New Zion Primitive Baptist Church and the cement business he established 45 years ago. It is among the oldest Black owned enterprises in Sarasota.

At age 14, he stopped attending school to help his family make ends meet financially. Mays earned meager wages by working on a farm in Fruitville near where the family lived. Children in the settlement of approximately 50 residents attended school in a little church under the tutelage of Mrs. Washington and Altamese Cummings. The people walked a quarter of a mile to pump water for daily use. In 1944, the family moved to Newtown where Mango Avenue is situated between Highway 301 and the railroad tracks near the city dump. *"The smoke bothered us for years. We stayed in the house most of the time to escape that smoke. There were many white birds out there getting leftovers,"* Mays said. Thomas believes their neighbors on Mango died as a result of the fumes. She keeps a record of their names as a memorial. *"All of the people living on Mango Avenue, also Leonard Reid, most of them died,"* Thomas recalled.

Dorothye Smith was Thomas' fourth grade teacher. An unforgettable moment in her life was being chosen the 10th grade attendant of Miss Booker High School with another attendant Willie Mae (Blake) Sheffield.

### Walter L. Gilbert III

Children imitate the actions of adults. Walter Gilbert's boyhood experiences confirm that. His mother attended community meetings with her son and daughter in tow. The children had no say in the matter as she headed out of the door. At the gatherings, the young man saw neighbors and friends of the family. Something happened while watching organizers articulate their vision for Newtown and neighborhood improvement strategies. *"That was the yard man, the roofer guy or the guy you knew down the street as the garbage man. But when they came to these meetings they changed. They became super-people. They were talking about making things happen and how to do it, how we were going to go about it as a group and how we needed to form different committees. I'm sitting there looking. Wow!"*

Men such as the late Neil Humphrey Sr., a Newtown entrepreneur, and the late John Rivers, then Sarasota NAACP president, made an indelible impression on the young man who would become NAACP president himself, years later. *"[Humphrey] was probably 5'5" and might've weighed 155 pounds. If he raised his voice you could hardly hear him. I thought he was a meek little man; but in these NAACP meetings he was fire and brimstone."* Gilbert participated in a federal lawsuit against the City of Sarasota for single member district voting. The court's decision in favor of the plaintiffs opened the way for African American representation on the city commission.

### Ethel Reid Hayes

Newtown residents drive past the Helen R. Payne Day Nursery on 33rd Street to spark memories of learning how to read and count during the most critical years of their lives. Ethel Reid Hayes and her sister

Viola, the daughters of Sarasota pioneers Leonard Reid and Eddye Coleman, operated the preschool program.

Lifelong friendships formed among children who played in the sandbox and waited a turn on the seesaw, merry-go-round and swings. Both women were educated in Sarasota and went on to obtain college degrees. Hayes attended Florida A&M University for four years, acquired a teacher's certificate then began her career in education at Booker School in Sarasota.

She also excelled in music, taught summer school during World War II and eventually married Roosevelt Hayes, a Navy man. The couple briefly moved to California but returned to Florida in 1951. She obtained a master's degree from her alma mater and taught for many years. After retiring from the Sarasota County school system, Ethel became the director of Helen P. Payne Day Nursery.

Viola also attended Florida A&M and went on to work as a substitute teacher in Sarasota County, as a teacher at the Newtown Day Nursery from 1953-1970, and later, as a supervisor at Helen R. Payne Day Nursery where she was assistant director. Ethel and Viola were active in the community and lived in their childhood home built in 1926. The Leonard Reid Family House was added to the U.S. National Register of Historic Places on Oct. 29, 2002. Mrs. Hayes died in 1991. Her oral history interview was provided courtesy of Sarasota County Historical Resources.

## Anthony B. Major

Theater students at the Booker Performing Arts High School know the name Anthony B. "Tony" Major because their rehearsal hall bears the moniker. Major is the first honoree of Booker High's "Leaving a Legacy" Award. He grew up in Newtown playing baseball in the Negro League with his brother and uncles. Negro Baseball League legend John "Buck" O'Neil and Major's father were best friends. Major also played clarinet in the Booker High School band under the direction of Alexander Valentine. But switching majors from music to theater at Hofstra University changed his path.

His directing career spans decades and includes acting, teaching, producing Broadway and Off Broadway shows, and working with Academy Award winners Alan Pakula, Robert Mulligan, Robert DeNiro, Hal Ashby, Beau Bridges, Sidney Poitier, James Earl Jones, William Friedkin, Harry Belafonte, Eddie Murphy, Della Reese and Gil Lewis.

Major is program director of the Zora Neale Hurston Institute for Documentary Studies, and the Africana Studies Program in the College of Arts & Humanities; also associate professor in the Film School of Visual Art & Design at the University of Central Florida. His research at UCF led to the production of documentaries and exhibits, *Jesse L. Brown, the 1st African American Navy Fighter Pilot* (shot down during the Korean War), and *Goldsboro: An American Story*. He has produced and directed several theatre and film productions at UCF, in collaboration with the Zora Neale Hurston Festival of the Arts, in Eatonville, Florida.

### Glossie Atkins

Glossie Atkins laughs easily and sometimes uncontrollably at the thought of fun times in Overtown. The daughter of Jay and Nettie Campbell was born in Ocala on December 3, 1917. With her sister Ruby Horton as the leader, she left central Florida to work on a farm in Sarasota picking beans and tomatoes. *"We filled a bushel basket of beans for two dollars each."* The unrelenting heat and worms on the plants forced a transition from fieldwork to housework. Horton then operated a café. *"We had a good time,"* Atkins said, bursting into laughter without offering many details. She attended the oldest African American house of worship in town, Bethlehem Baptist Church. *"Oh goodness, we had good service and the choir, everything was good."* The mother of Sarasota's first African American mayor was a surrogate parent to neighbors' children. For 35 years, she worked as a domestic sewing, cooking, cleaning and rearing other parents' children. These days, she joins other mature women of Newtown to crochet scarves, quilts, and caps. *"God has been good to me. Yep. Oh my goodness. I've come a long way. He brought me and still's got me going strong."*

**Alice Faye Jones**

Mrs. Alice Faye Jones was born and reared in Sarasota. She spent much time at Lido Beach as a child. Her mother worked tirelessly as a maid on Longboat Key throughout Jones' childhood. Jones currently operates a free tutoring program called "Brothers and Sisters Doing The Right Thing" at the Robert L. Taylor Community Complex in North Sarasota. The oral history interview of Mrs. Jones was provided by the New College of Florida Oral History Program.

# CHAPTER 4: MAKING A LIVING - PART 1

## MIGRATION TO SARASOTA

After the Civil War ended, many formerly enslaved people became subsistence farmers, producing food for their own survival, and/or worked as sharecroppers. The system of sharecropping enabled landowners to take advantage of the people who farmed their land. During the year, sharecroppers often owed more money for the goods they bought at inflated prices at the 'company store' or 'commissary' than they received for the fruits of their labors. Some who worked in the cotton and celery fields and the turpentine camps of the South for weekly wages also found that they owed more than they were paid. Sharecroppers were constantly in a financial bind; it was a hopeless situation in which they would never get ahead in life. Many African Americans left these miserable conditions to seek better life opportunities in the cities of the northern, mid-western and western U.S.[1] They became part of the Great Migration in which more than six million African Americans left the South between 1910 and 1970. Often, a 'chain migration' occurred; when one family member or friend moved to and got settled in a particular city, other family members and friends would later follow to that same city. A similar migration occurred between cities in the South. Sometimes they came alone, looking for and finding jobs before sending for other family members to join them. According to Betty Johnson:

> It seems everyone was related to each other or was from the same geographical area some place other than Sarasota. When one person would relocate, if there were family members, they would all relocate there. They would invite others to come and some would help family and friends by either helping to find work or giving them a place to live until they could find their own ... Many came from the same regions such as West Florida, Georgia, Alabama, Mississippi. They relocated to this area because of the work available. Many from the village worked in turpentine fields, as farmer's hands on celery farms, tomato pickers, fruit growers and harvesters.[2]

Special agents were hired to recruit laborers for other job openings:

> Near the turn of the century, only about ten families lived in the vicinity. The African-American population swelled as laborers and skilled workmen were hired by special agents who combed rural areas of Georgia and the Carolinas recruiting workers to fill the demand in Florida's boom cities. Men and women came to be dockworkers, fishermen, chauffeurs, maids, laundresses, and cooks. They came to work the rails, the citrus farms, and the circus."[3]

The proposal to connect Sarasota to Tampa via railroad resulted in a wave of workers arriving to lay rails as the tracks were extended in subsequent years to Fruitville, Bee Ridge, Laurel and Venice.[4] Sarasota was a growing city where there were a variety of unskilled and skilled jobs available, including: seasonal laborers picking fruits and vegetables; domestic workers, both male and female; celery and turpentine camp workers; construction workers; and persons with fishing and maritime skills. Most of the people interviewed for the NCHD project agreed that the vision of a brighter future and the availability of jobs were the primary reasons that their families migrated to and settled in Sarasota.

Neil Humphrey's family was among those who migrated south to Sarasota from other Florida cities. He stated that: "My daddy and my mother lived in Plant City. And they heard about Sarasota. It seemed to have quite some prospects for a wonderful place to live, and so, they decided to move to Sarasota. They had the soda fountain, tables and chairs and some patent medicine [at their store, Humphrey's Sundries]."[5]

Although their lives were filled with hard work, in some instances it was now paying dividends to them as free people. However, for those working in the turpentine camps, on celery and citrus farms, and sharecropping, it was not. Those jobs reaped benefits primarily for the land and business owners. That was a key reason why parents who worked in these occupations were very serious about providing their children with an education that would lift them out of the endless cycle of poverty. Some of the jobs they performed were discussed by the interviewees:

**Alberta Brown,** interviewed by Vickie Oldham [6]
*(V. Oldham: Where were you born?)*
*(A. Brown): In Alachua County.*
*(V. Oldham): Tell me about your life in Alachua. The earliest memories.)*

(*A. Brown*): After my father died, we didn't have anybody to do the plowing. My mom had to get other mens to come in and work on the farm for her ... she had to pay those mens to work because my brother was too young to try to do anything like that. And so my mother, she would try to do the plowing, she would try to get people to do it. And it was very hard. We couldn't really do too much. He was only about twelve when my father died ... She called her brother, here in Sarasota, Florida, and she had a brother in Palmetto ... So she was trying to ask them what could they do to help her, and some way of getting her children to work ...

(*V. Oldham: You lived on a farm way out in Alachua County [Florida]?*)

(*A. Brown*): Yeah ... sharecropping. So after she did not have a husband to do the plowing and everything, we had to move ... and come to Palmetto where we could get work.

**Anthony "Tony" Major,** interviewed by Dr. Rosalyn Howard [7]

(*A. Major*): My grand uncle, who passed away at 100 years old, and my grandmother, who raised me, says that they all left North Florida ... just west of Quincy, between Pensacola and Tallahassee ... due to the Klan. And my great grandfather, who sent my grandmother to Sarasota, never made it. So the story is that the Klan finally got to him before he could get out.

(*Dr. Howard): And how did your family come to leave Quincy and wind up in Newtown? Did they know people there?*

(*A. Major*): Well I think that's where the work was – my understanding. And so they ended up at that time coming to Sarasota and ... I would say it was due to the type of work and stuff involved in Sarasota at the time, and other family members that were there.

(*Dr. Howard): Okay. One of the interviews that I read mentioned someone named Suit Major ... who was involved with the circus. Is he related to you?*

(*A. Major*): That's my father ... His name was Benjamin Major... my middle name is Benjamin ... and my father was known as 'Suit Major 'cause he always wore a blue suit.

**Betty Johnson,** interviewed by Vickie Oldham[8]

(*B. Johnson*): My parents were Mr. and Mrs. Saul Johnson. My mother's name is Blanche Johnson. They were born in what was known as West Florida, but Quincy, Florida is the name.

My father came to Sarasota as a young teenager … to find work. And in those days you grew up real fast, and you want to leave home. … When he first came to Sarasota, [he worked] at what was called the dolomite plant, up on 301. And then he worked in the orange groves, he picked oranges. Then he worked construction for George Higgins' construction company. And the fond memory I have of my father is that he was instrumental in the piping that brought the water into Newtown. [My mom] worked as a domestic housekeeper for a little while.

---

*African American laborers' farming and artisan skills, endurance, and dedicated work ethic played a large role in building Sarasota into the city it is today. Yet, their contributions to its economic growth have been underemphasized in the pages of Sarasota history. In Sarasota, men and women worked in a variety of positions to provide for their families and their hard work built the foundation of the Sarasota County economy.*

---

**Carolyn Mason**, interviewed by Hope Black.[9]
*(C. Mason):* My father drove a cement mixer … right over at Central and 10th Street. It was R. C. Martin Concrete, then. And my mother was a maid. … The two families that I remember lived on … 47th Street, just off of the North Trail. And they actually lived across the street from each other. And in the summer, when there was no school, I would go to work with her. … Actually I played with the kids [Laughter].

Both women and men worked on farms, as we learn from **Alberta Brown**, interviewed by Vickie Oldham. [10]

*(V. Oldham): What kind of fruits or vegetables were you helping to harvest?*
*(A. Brown):* Tomatoes, green beans, just anything that would work on a farm. … The fields had to be picked, so we would go out, work daily … even Saturdays [and], if they wanted us, for Saturdays. So it was hard. … We did all kinds of things and we met so many different peoples … a lot. On the farm, sometimes we had fifty or sixty people to pick. ... I really liked it. … And we had a good time. We start to … singing. Sometimes the mens would help us do it and, if they like you, they did most of your work anyway. [Laughter] So, we got to the place we had

relationships. Find you … a new boyfriend, you didn't have to work as hard. He would do double duty, yours and his.

*(V. Oldham: Were there more women out there than men, or more men than women?)*

*(A. Brown):* Oh much more womens than there was men, because mens could get a job. Womens, we really couldn't get a job. I mean, probably you could if you was working in a home. … About two years after I was here, my sister stopped working [in a home] and she put me to work. She wanted me to cook. So I start the cooking and so that's how I got my jobs and everything that we had.

## THE CELERY FIELDS

Courtesy: Sarasota County Historical Resources.

Agriculture was a major industry in Florida and played an important role in the development and growth of Sarasota and the region. Both citrus and celery were major crops and many African Americans in Sarasota did farm work, harvesting those crops. After the land was drained to make it available for agriculture in the late 1880s, early 1900s, and the 1920s, Fancee Farms used the fields to grow celery. According to the 1939 publication *WPA Guide to Florida*:

> Sarasota industries include the packing and shipping of celery, averaging 1,200 carloads annually, other winter vegetables, and citrus fruits, production of fertilizers, and the manufacturing of automobile trailers. An unusual industry is the mining and preparation of dolomite a carbonate of magnesium discovered in 1935 that serves as an antacid fertilizer.[11]

Dolomite Mine watercolor paintings.
Courtesy: William Hartman Collection.

Although not located in either Overtown or Newtown, the celery fields of Sarasota and Manatee counties were an important source of income for African Americans who lived in Newtown and Overtown and played an important role in the growth and development of these communities. During slavery, African Americans were responsible for the cultivation and harvesting of crops. After Emancipation, their experience was used to their own benefit and became an important source of income for them. There is a good deal of information on the history of the celery industry in Sarasota, but, not surprisingly, little or no documentation on the contributions of the African American workers in the fields. There is a brief comment in the *WPA Guide to Florida* about that community:

> The local Negro settlement, east of the railroad, has its shops, churches, recreation centers, and rows of shacks. The majority of inhabitants, 30 per cent of the city's total population, are engaged in agricultural pursuits, and a few find employment as hostlers and roustabouts with the circus, returning to Sarasota in the fall to pick up odd jobs in canning factories, packing houses and as gardeners.[12]

The information that is available has come primarily from the personal stories of the celery workers, the writings of Annie M. McElroy in her book *But Your World and My World*,[13] and the archived photos in the Sarasota History Center. The research involved in creating a Panel Exhibit (an example shown below) at the Sarasota County Historical Resources and the Cultural Resource Center at North Sarasota Library fills some of the gaps in the literature about the history of Newtown and the role[s] played and contributions made by celery field workers who lived there.

Lily Lacy. (Linda Black Turner's grandmother).[14]
Courtesy: Cultural Resource Center at North Sarasota Public Library.

Lily Lacy, was a pioneer among the African Americans who settled in Sarasota. Arriving in 1938 with her husband, Lily worked in the celery fields owned by the Palmers while her husband worked as a stiller at the Bee Ridge Turpentine Camp. She also started a laundry business. With no running water, she would have family members pump water from the community well. She would wash and iron clothes using an open fire to heat the irons and palmetto leaves to coat the iron giving clothes a starched look.[15] Linda Black Turner recalled in an interview that:

> [Granny worked at] the Palmer Farms. They had to take their food with 'em. She would always keep her head tied up and she would put a pan on top of her head and tie it. And she would walk down the railroad tracks [from her home in Bee Ridge]. She'd walk to Fruitville and Palmer Boulevard ... in that area where they had all the farms. She worked on the muletrain.[16]

The mule train was a moving packinghouse on the celery fields in Fruitville. c. 1949.
Courtesy: Sarasota County Historical Resources.

According to Turner:

> [Granny] had to wear those real tall rubber boots because that soil that gets on you. She was allergic to it. It would break you all out. She had an ulcer on her leg all this time, but she still worked out there on that farm. I think it was in the early '50s that she stopped. She got in so much pain that she just couldn't do the walking.[17] [Lacy's ulcer may have indeed resulted from allergic reaction to the "muck" or it could have been because the muck contained a lot of acid.][18]

Dr. Cheryl Smith and Betty Jean Johnson, two of the NCHD project volunteer researchers, reported that:

> There were three major celery farms in Sarasota proper: On Bee Ridge Road, on Fruitville Road and on Palmer Boulevard. There was also a major celery farm in Venice. Johnson Camp was a community built for the workers on Fruitville Road Farm because it was too far for them to walk every day from Newtown. It was

started around 1930. The workers there were paid approximately $3-$5 per day for back-breaking work.[19]

At least it was, however, paid work. A number of Newtown families lived in Johnson Camp before they relocated to Newtown proper; some of their descendants are still living in Newtown. According to James Brown, "My sixth grade teacher, Mrs. Hattie Johnson drove the school bus, brought the kids in from Johnson Camp to school. And there was Mrs. Goins who drove the bus from Laurel area, bringing kids up. And my teacher, Mrs. Johnson, owned her own home. That building is still there."[20]

Other businesses in that industry included the Thacker & Pearce celery farm, and the Chapman celery farm. According to Dr. Cheryl Smith:

Pictures speak a thousand words. The following photos tell a bit of the stories of the workers in the celery fields of Sarasota who made the growth and development of Newtown as well as the wider community possible. It is interesting to note that the Audubon Society's web page on the history of the celery fields identifies the workers as "migrant." At the time of the photo (below), given the similarity of other photos of the celery workers, they were more likely residents of Sarasota, permanent and seasonal.[21]

Celery farm on Palm Avenue, c. 1910.
Courtesy: Sarasota County Historical Resources.

Bell Celery Packing House c. 1940.
Courtesy: Sarasota County Historical Resources,
Bell Brothers Collection.

The celery fields, in which many African Americans toiled for years, are now a Sarasota County park that is popular for various recreational activities, such as biking, walking, and bird watching. No longer used for farming, the celery fields are still part of the Sarasota economy. [In 2010], "tourists and residents spent over $1.3 billion watching Florida wildlife."[22]

## AFRICAN AMERICAN CELERY CONTRACTORS AND BUSINESS OWNERS

African Americans began to establish their own businesses in the lucrative industries growing in Sarasota. As McElroy notes:

Elmo Newtown, father of Lillian Abnar, activist in her community, was the first black to contract celery in this county. He came from Sanford, Florida, bringing around 300 people from all over the state and other places. Later he leased three motels and rented rooms. The three were the Old Elk building on Osprey Avenue; Central Hotel on Central Avenue; and Colson Hotel. He was active until a few months before his death in 1936. Other farming contractors to follow were his brother Johnny Newton, Eddie Williams, Nathan Coons, Abe Jones, Mack James, Edward "Grand Pa" Gordon and Wade Thomas. All of these contractors acquired property and operated some kind of business during their lifetime.[23]

## TURPENTINE CAMPS

Another major industry in Sarasota where African Americans found jobs was in the turpentine camps. Also known as 'naval stores,' the industry started during the Colonial Era:

> The use of slave labor expanded the naval stores [turpentine] industry throughout the south. Next to cotton and rice, turpentine became one of the South's greatest exports. Slaves were organized into small camps and assigned sections of trees to work. Once trees in the section had been worked and died, the trees were cut to board. This pattern continued until the Civil War, when abolition of slavery forced changes in the turpentine industry.[24]

> Turpentine leases for land within what is now Sarasota County can be found as early as 1905, perhaps earlier. By 1910 there was a large camp in the community of Fruitville, and it was common for the camps to move as trees were exhausted or as the businesses expanded into new areas. By 1911 the turpentine industry was in the Bee Ridge area, and into areas further south such as Laurel (north of Nokomis and Venice).[25]

Cultural anthropologist and novelist Zora Neale Hurston[26] traveled to many southern towns where she visited turpentine camps while writing for the Works Progress Administration in the 1930s. She wrote about her experiences:

> Well, I put on my shoes and I started. Going up some roads and down some others to see what Negroes do for a living. Going down one road I smelt hot rosin and looked and saw a "gum patch." That's a turpentine still to the outsider, but gum path (sic) to those who work them.[27]

Following are two authors' descriptions of the industry:

> Over time, the extensive production of turpentine in the Carolinas and Georgia led to the destruction of the pine forests. Seeking new virgin timber, the industry turned south into Florida with its vast pine forests. This southward movement occurred in the 1900s. During this time the demand for labor led Florida to lease prisoners to the turpentine companies. Approximately 10 percent of the force in Florida was comprised of convict forced labor.[28]

> Laborers rented company housing and were paid in scrip, a system [of pay] that limited their purchase of the basic goods … [only to] the company commissary at inflated prices, resulting in an endless cycle of debt. African Americans were particularly susceptible to the exploitation of debt peonage, [a system of forced labor based on debts accumulated by workers], following the conclusion of the Civil War. The so-called "Black Codes" legislated by southern states during Reconstruction ensured African Americans remained under the close scrutiny and control of whites. These state laws restricted employment options for the newly-emancipated Americans, and aided [the continuation of] their exploitation.[29]

The Sarasota County Historical Commission
erected this historical marker for the Bee Ridge
Turpentine Camp in 1994.

The Bee Ridge Turpentine Camp opened in 1937. The laborers were paid by the number of trees they "boxed" by cutting a V-shaped "cat face," which bled gum into a clay or tin pot nailed to the tree. The workers' camp houses had two to four rooms. A camp commissary stocked soap, salt and basic staples for purchase (or on credit). The camp truck delivered workers to and from [Overtown and Newtown] for shopping and recreation on weekends. ... When the camp closed in 1952, it marked the end of an era. The market for turpentine was weak and the supply of pine trees small.[30]

Many of the residents moved to Pinkney Avenue[31] or Newtown, and some of the families still live in Sarasota. One of those former turpentine camp workers was Rev. Earl Vencent Samuel Black Sr. who, on September 2, 2015, turned 100 years old. He left Bee Ridge Turpentine Camp when it closed and moved to Newtown. Rev. Black related the story of his time working there to a *Herald-Tribune* reporter who wrote that:

[Rev. Black was] felling and chipping pine trees for an industry that once spread throughout the South. And the rattlesnakes. Oh the rattlesnakes. Turpentine work was notoriously hard and often dangerous. The men, almost exclusively black, spent hours in the forest surrounded by heat and wild animals. More than just work at the camps, workers lived, shopped and raised families there.[32]

Courtesy: SarasotaHistoryAlive.com. "Bee Ridge Turpentine Camp."

An article about the turpentine business mentioned that:

In the late 1930s, Berryman Thomas "B.T." Longino Sr., and Luther Franklin "Luke" Grubbs opened a turpentine camp in the Bee Ridge area. [Another] camp at Sidell was established by B.T. Longino Sr. on 12,000 acres of land on the Atlantic Coast Line Railroad about a mile south of State Road 72 (then it was called Sugar Bowl Road).

In addition to 30 houses for workers and the still, there was a cooper's [barrel maker's] shed, commissary, school and church. The Sarasota County Board of Public Instruction sent a teacher out to the school and [the woodsrider, Albert] Jones or his brother preached in the church. [33]

Albert Jones was an African American woodsrider, a supervisor of the turpentine camp workers, a position similar to the plantation overseer position during slavery. Jones "supervised the Sidell and Bee Ridge camps. T. W. Myers, another African American woodsrider, worked under Jones at the Bee Ridge camp."[34] "By the 1940s, production was in decline and by 1951 both camps were closed."[35]

Below are excerpts from another article that details the history of turpentine camps in the Manatee and Sarasota Counties' areas:

No longer forced laborers, many former slaves practiced subsistence farming and took jobs in the turpentine camps to supplement their incomes. Over time, this lead [sic] to the development of African-American communities within the turpentine camps. Large camps could have as many as 100 workers. The workers and their families would live at, or near, a main camp.

In the 1900s, the average worker in the turpentine camps relied on the company for most of his goods and services. The camp provided small shacks or shanties for the workers and their families. In addition to housing, the worker was paid monthly.

By 1910, there were five working turpentine camps in Manatee County [Sarasota separated from Manatee County in 1921]. Near Fruitville was the Hall and Cheney Camp. The R.T. Hall & Company Prison Camp was near Sandy and the Williams Camp was near Venice. The Hall and Harrison Camp was west of Cow Pen Slough, and there was an unnamed camp in the present Carlton [Reserve] area. Of these five camps, three are known to have used convict labor in addition to their paid workforce to harvest gum. In 1923, the state prohibited the practice of leasing convict labor to private companies. This had a direct impact on at least three of the camps in Sarasota County and raised the cost of production.[36]

James Brown, historian and retired State College of Florida Associate Dean, remembered that on Saturdays bus loads of workers from Johnson Camp (celery fields) and Laurel Camp (turpentine camp) would be driven into Newtown to shop for things that were not available at their camp commissaries. They would "promenade up and down Central Avenue, just walking, talking, and socializing." [37] The juke joint was a special place for socializing. A place to wind down, have a drink, and dance to some music after a long, hard week of work was definitely needed. They could find that at the juke joint!

## THE JUKE JOINT

During her research trips among African Americans in the South, made on behalf of the Works Progress Administration in the 1930s, Zora Neale Hurston, "Would go with her new acquaintances to a jook [joint] and drink, dance, and tell stories."[38] Charlie Pinkney's 'juke joint' on Pinkney Avenue transported celery camp residents to Sarasota for a Saturday afternoon to Sunday afternoon break. It was also the place for weekend recreation for some of Sarasota's turpentine camp workers. According to Gorman, Zora Neale Hurston considered the jook joint to be an integral part of black culture.[39] In her 1934 essay "Characteristics of Negro Expression," Hurston stated that:

> Jook is a word for a Negro pleasure house. It may mean a bawdy house. It may mean the house set apart on public works where the men and women dance, drink and gamble. Often, it is a combination of all these. The Negro 'jooks,' [are] primitive rural counterparts of resort night clubs, where turpentine workers take their evening relaxation deep in the pine forests. [40]

Gorman also writes that: "Similar to night clubs, jook joints acquired a particular flavor through their association with work camp culture in the South. The Federal Writers' Project's Florida State Guide linked jook joints in Florida to Negro labor in turpentine camps in the north of the state.[41]

Archaeologist Deborah Ziel, who excavated artifacts from a juke joint at the site of a former turpentine camp in Polk County, viewed the jook joint culture as an act of resistance by African Americans. As she explained:

> In the twentieth century, thousands of African Americans, especially those residing in the southern states, experienced a new frontier of enslavement and oppression — debt peonage. African Americans expressed their agency through engaging in leisure activities that asserted their resistance to this new form of slavery.[42] The term "agency" is often associated with freedom or resistance.[43]

## MISS SUSIE'S SOCIAL CLUB

> As an alternative to the jook joint, upstanding African Americans in Sarasota (such as teachers, some men of the cloth) looking for a discrete, private place could patronize a more upscale location for socializing, drinking and listening to music — Miss Susie's Social Club, located on Dr. Martin Luther King Jr. Way.

This photo shows the deteriorating remains of what used to be
Miss Susie's Social Club.
Courtesy: Kacey Troupe.

Miss Susie Linder was also a philanthropist, donating property, a bus and money to her church, New Bethel, when she died.

Miss Susie Linder was a no-nonsense club owner, according to all who spoke about her. Below are a few comments from the NCHD project Facebook page about Miss Susie's Social Club:

Jetson Grimes: recalled visiting Miss Susie's place, at age 17 or 18, only twice, dressed in suit and tie. It was a place to drink and chat for teachers (sometimes ministers). It was a private getaway to enjoy a drink. No one parked out front. Patrons parked in the back and on the street. Some entered from a side entrance. Miss Susie's Social Club was a place where residents could enjoy laughs and liquid "spirits," but teachers couldn't be seen inside or (Booker High School) Principal Rogers had strong words for them at work.

Dale W. Savage: Oh, YESSS!! I definitely have a memory from the past about this place, I pulled up in front one day back in 1976 and Ms. Susie let me know that under no circumstances could I park in front of her place ... she didn't play. It seems like she guarded that front 24 hours a day because no matter what time anybody pulled up she was there peeking out that front door window.

Yvette Williams: Miss Susie was always sweeping and telling you where to stand, and it was NOT in front of or even ON her property. I wonder if we had more owners like her now would we have had the problems on 27th Street like we have had in the past.

---

**ENDNOTES**

[1] Wilkerson, Isabel. The Warmth of Other Suns. Vintage Press. NY, 2011; Woodson, Carter G. A Century of Negro Migration. Association for the Study of Negro Life and History, 1918.
[2] Johnson, B.J. 2013. "The Village as I Knew It: 1950-." Unpublished Essay, 2.
[3] "History of the Newtown Community." http://www.sarasotagov.com/Newtown/history.html
[4] Email correspondence from John McCarthy. March 7, 2015.
[5] "Triumphant Struggle." Documentary Short Film by Vickie Oldham.
[6] Interview with Vickie Oldham, August 10, 2015.
[7] Interview with Dr. Rosalyn Howard, December 20, 2015.
[8] Interview with Vickie Oldham, August 18, 2015.
[9] Interview with Hope Black, September 22, 2015.
[10] Interview with Vickie Oldham, August 10, 2015.
[11] WPA Guide to Florida #27. Federal Writer's Project. (Sarasota section). 1939.
[12] WPA Guide to Florida #27. Federal Writer's Project.

[13] McElroy, Annie M. *But Your World and My World: The Struggle for Survival, A Partial History of Blacks in Sarasota County 1884-1986.* Black South Press. 1986.

[14] Elder, Amy A. *Sarasota: 1940-2005. Images of America.* Arcadia Publishing, 109.

[15] Courtesy of the Sarasota County History Center. Linda Turner Collection.

[16] Linda Black Turner. Interview with Ann Shank, December 26, 2003.

[17] Linda Black Turner. Interview with Ann Shank, December 26, 2003. Celery Fields History Panel: Cultural Resource Center (CRC) NSPL.

[18] http://www.sarasotaaudubon.org/capital-campaign/the-celery-fields/

[19] Personal communication. Dr. Cheryl Smith and Betty Jean Johnson, August, 2015.

[20] Interview with Vickie Oldham, August 24, 2015.

[21] Commentary by volunteer project researchers Dr. Cheryl Smith and Elaine Gambill. September 7, 2015.

[22] http://www.sarasotaaudubon.org/capital-campaign/economic-impact/

[23] *But Your World*, 69.

[24] Hughes, Dan. "The History of Florida Turpentine Camps." *Herald-Tribune.* March 15, 2004.

[25] Email correspondence from John McCarthy. March 17, 2015.

[26] Zora Neale Hurston grew up in Eatonville, Florida, a suburb of Orlando. She was a cultural anthropologist, a playwright, a novelist, and storyteller during the Harlem Renaissance period. One of her most famous novels is titled: *Their Eyes Were Watching God*.

[27] "Forgotten Chapter of History." (This website contains many photos of turpentine camp workers and related information). https://www.pinterest.com/dropdeaddiva56/forgotten-chapter-of-black-historyturpentine-camps/

[28] "The History of Florida Turpentine Camps."

[29] Ziel, Deborah L. *Which Way to the Jook Joint?: Historical Archaeology of a Polk County, Florida Turpentine Camp.* Master of Arts thesis. Department of Anthropology. University of Central Florida, Orlando. 2013, p.ii.

[30] Shank, Ann. "Bee Ridge Ridge Turpentine Camp." http://www.sarasotahistoryalive.com/history/articles/bee-ridge-turpentine-camp

[31] "The name Pinkney comes from the operator of Pinkney's Juke Joint (near where SCAT Transit headquarters are today)." Email correspondence from John McCarthy. March 17, 2015.

[32] Lopez, Yadira. "Newtown Reverend turns 100." http://newtown100.heraldtribune.com/2015/09/01/newtown-reverend-turns-100/

[33] Cleary, Joe. "Sarasota History of Turpentine and Pine Woods." Search For Sarasota Homes Blog. http://searchforsarasotahomesblog.com/blog/2013/12/12/Sarasota-history-of-turpentine

[34] "Bee Ridge Turpentine Camp."

[35] "The History of Florida Turpentine Camps."

[36] "The History of Florida Turpentine Camps."

[37] Telephone interview with Dr. Howard, January 31, 2016.

[38] Black, Hope. "Zora Neale Hurston Studies in Anthropology." Unpublished paper. March 9, 2005.

[39] Gorman, Juliet. "What is a jook joint and what is its history," 2001, 89, 114. http://www.oberlin.edu/library/papers/honorshistory/2001-Gorman/jookjoints/allaboutjooks/whatisjook.html)

[40] Hurston, Zora Neale. "Characteristics of Negro Expression." 1934. Quoted in "What is a jook joint and what is its history," 2001, 89, 114.

[41] "What is a jook joint and what is its history."

[42] *Which Way to the Jook Joint?* 6.

[43] Gardner, Andrew. "Agency, " 2008, 96. In *Handbook of Archaeological Theories*, edited by R. Alexander Bentley, Herbert DG Maschner, and Christopher Chippindale. Altamira Press, Lanham, 95-108. In Ziel, *Which Way to the Jook Joint?* 25.

# CHAPTER 5: MAKING A LIVING – PART 2

Throughout this chapter about how Newtown residents made a living, the voices of the interviewees – current or former residents of Newtown and Overtown – are prominent. Their oral histories shed light on the many ways that they and their families lived, laughed, labored and survived, often under very difficult circumstances. Providing a space for them to tell their stories of "How I Got Over," as the gospel hymn goes, is essential to demonstrating the very important roles they play in the celebration of the 100-year history of the Newtown community.

## DOMESTIC WORK

Domestic work, typically thought of as women's work — cooking, cleaning, and child care — was not only for women and had a broader definition. Employment records designated as "colored help" in the Sarasota History Center Archives provide this description of a male domestic worker:

> One example is an African American workman named Joe Gilleson: Domestic work, cutting wood, cleaning lumber for new house (several days at this), cleaning speed boat, helping on Flying Fish, hoeing in fertilizer, cleaning carpets and rugs, helping on old Cadillac, unloading Phantom, cleaning eaves, troughs on Oaks and leaves off of roof, watering, raking, spraying, wheeling sand for chimney of new house ... African American workers were given the menial tasks; they slept, ate and spent their non-working time in segregated quarters. They were referred to by the white staff as 'colored work hands' and by Mrs. [Bertha Honore] Palmer as 'my Negroes.' There is no indication that any possibility for advancement in wages or type of work existed. If, when they went into town on their nights off, there were any reports of carousing, they would be dismissed.[1]

For women, employment opportunities outside the home were very limited in the early days of Overtown and Newtown. Teaching was practically the only occupation open to women, other than domestic work or work in the celery fields, citrus and vegetable farms, and turpentine camps. Large numbers of women were domestic workers, performing jobs such as laundresses, house cleaning, child-caretakers and cooks. Their experiences varied; several interviewees indicated that they had very good relationships with employers and were treated well.

**Alberta Brown**, interview with Vickie Oldham. [2]

*(A. Brown):* My sister [Viola Sanders] stopped working and she put me to work. She wanted me to cook. So I start the cooking. ... That's how I learned to cook ... my sister taught me...On Siesta Key. ... I would take the little girl out to different places and do things with her, and it was a good job and we had a good time. When you fixed dinner it was around seven o'clock. ... After you cook and cleaned up everything and put it back just like it was, then you'd go into your room.

*(V. Oldham): So ... you would stay out there all week on Siesta Key?*

*(A. Brown):* Yes. ... Weekends, we would like to go to church ... So I stayed there for ... a long time. Maybe seven or eight years.

Alberta Brown's brother-in-law [Shelly Sanders] also worked on Siesta Key:

*(A. Brown):* He cleaned yards, cut trees down, he did all kinds of work for outside. He had so many families that he was taking care of on Siesta Key. So he did a whole lot of work out there. He did whatever they needed him to do. ... He would even plant a garden if they needed one.

*(V. Oldham): What was that like taking care of the little girl?*

*(A. Brown):* Well, I take her to the beach. We go places ... in the car, because I could drive and I could take her wherever I need to go. So it was just a nice job. Really it was. And I took care of her and she loved me, just so sweet. That whole family, though, was a beautiful family.

*(V. Oldham): Did you become a part of the family?*

*(A. Brown):* I think so, because [if not,] I don't think they would have paid me the rest of my life.

**Eddie L. Rainey**, interview with Vickie Oldham.[3]

*(E. Rainey):* Most of the adult females worked in private homes and they took care of the kids. They did the diapers, they cleaned the house. Some of our women even mowed the yards. They would wash the windows; they did everything. And I knew it was a hard life, but it was their only means of survival. In some cases, maybe the man wasn't there. The husband was not there. Well,

they were able to survive by taking the role of the husband and the wife by going to these maid jobs. They were cooks, they were a little of everything. And they raised us in the afternoons.

**Mary Alice Simmons**, interview with Vickie Oldham and Hope Black.[4]
*(H. Black): Did any women in your community back then work for white people.*
*(M.A. Simmons):* Oh absolutely, sure a lot of them were maids, yes. The women were lined [up] in white uniforms, catching that bus to go to work.
*(H. Black): Sounds like the movie "[The] Help."*
*(M.A. Simmons):* That's exactly what it was.
*(V. Oldham): Where were they going?*
*(M.A. Simmons):* All over Longboat, Siesta ... [My mom,] she would take us to work and we would play while she's vacuuming and cleaning and all. And then we got to the age where we could help her clean and we did ... We lived in the projects. Number ten, which fronts Orange Avenue. Every morning there was a city transit bus ... and the ladies would be lined up to catch that bus to go to work. All of them in white uniforms, so you knew where they were going to work ... doing domestic work. Every morning, including Sundays, the buses were there.

Sometimes dad worked three jobs, but he also had his shop. Always worked ... he was a housing inspector one time for the city. My grandpa Mays worked for the City of Sarasota. He worked on the garbage truck for the city.

**Estella Thomas**, interview with Vickie Oldham.[5]
*(E. Thomas):* Well my mother's family, they were what you would call migrant workers. They worked on farms, going different places working on farms and turpentine. So they migrated down in Myakka City. And then from there we went to this place called Sidell ... And then later my father passed away; my mother moved here to Sarasota. So that's how I got to Sarasota. I was thirteen ... I started working when I was sixteen, I didn't go through high school. Things happened - between my mom and my sister coming along ... I just got frustrated. ... I was out of school quite a bit because she [my mom] was working. ... Back in that time, there wasn't day nurseries and kindergartens ... like they have now. If some older person didn't take care of the babies, I had to stay

home to care of them, two or three days out the week and I just couldn't get no education doing that. So I just said, "Well, I guess the best thing for me to do is go to work." I went to work at Morrison's Cafeteria. I was working in the kitchen department ... veggies cleaning, getting the food ready for the cooks and then ... take it out on the line. I would go in about ten and then get off about 2:30. ... [Then] I would go home and be there. ... Pretty simple.

*(V. Oldham): What sort of other jobs did you do?*

I worked in the laundry and dry cleaner ... Bayview Laundry Cleaners. That's where I started.

## ENTREPRENEURS

Newtown's entrepreneurs opened diverse businesses, all meeting the needs of the community, such as: contractors clearing undeveloped land and building houses; grocers; restaurant owners; beauty salon operators; barbers; a Western Union substation owner; and taxicab services. (See the Appendix for a partial list of the African American-owned businesses that existed in Overtown and Newtown.)

Both women and men demonstrated creativity in finding ways to provide for their families. When they saw unfulfilled needs for services, they started businesses, inside and outside the home. Since Jim Crow laws were in full effect in this southern city, African American residents were prevented from obtaining basic services and were often treated as second-class citizens at white-owned businesses.

One interviewee told the heartbreaking story of the most embarrassing moment in his life. He was in downtown Sarasota and wet himself because there was no restroom that he was allowed to use. The only restroom designated for colored people was located at the distant railroad station.

African Americans had their own businesses in Overtown, and they also had access to a few white-owned stores downtown. According to most of the interviewees, they had little problem being served at the larger chain department stores such as J.C. Penney, McCrory's, and Sears and Roebuck, but were often not welcomed in other stores unless they were doing errands for their bosses.

Becoming an entrepreneur in Newtown was a serious matter of survival because of the distance from the African American-owned stores in Overtown. Residents created a practically self-sustained community.

They had all of the services they needed to live their lives without having to subject themselves to degrading and unsanitary 'colored-only' facilities and receiving service only at the back doors of white-owned establishments. Newtown developed a vibrant business district from the 1940s to the 1970s, which many people recalled during their interviews.

**Estella Thomas and Dr. Harriet Moore** interview with Vickie Oldham. [6]

*(V. Oldham): What made you think to start a business?*

*(E. Thomas):* Because I just realized I wasn't getting anywhere. You know, I didn't have the education that I should've had, but I just was gonna try the business. [My husband and I] talked about it and we got a bank loan ... So then we started the business ... Well the first one, we weren't there very long. Eddie's Fruit Stand. Everybody knows about Eddie's Fruit Stand. He came down one day and told me that we could rent his place because...he just wanted to go out of business. ... And we were there nine years in his place before we came, got the money, and remodeled ... Moore's Grocery ... 301 and 27th Street. ...We had all kind of fruits and vegetables, just everything. ... Fresh cheese, cracklings that you'd have to weigh, the two-for-a-penny cookies that you had, everything. ... Everyday I had people coming [to] Moore's.

*(Dr. Moore):* When they were renting Eddie's Fruit Stand, there were a number of black businesses along the 27th Street corridor, which is now MLK ... there was Cann's Groceries, Jenkins' Grocery, Bud's Barbershop, Jim's bicycle shop. There was Orange Grocery – Ms. Helen and Lee Clark on Orange Avenue, and there was Mr. McAllister, which was a dentist, right in the plaza where Cann's was. We had Carbo's. And the Suarez's – a gas station and the post office. They started the post office there. ... When we rented Eddie's Fruit Stand, one side was a store and the other side was a little area where the kids would come in, and they'd play records after school when they'd get off the bus at Pershing and 27th. And they'd have pickles and pig feet and hot sausages and hot dogs. ... So I'd sneak out and go over to that side so I could see what the teenagers were doing. That's something we had in this community because really we couldn't go to Publix and Winn-Dixie and all of that. We were not welcome in those places. So all of those businesses that were established on the corridor really, really sufficed for us. ... And then you have the businesses [in]

Overtown too. ... And so it was a flourishing community that was truly a community. That's what I grew up in.

**Rev. Jerome Dupree**, interview with Jessica Wopinski (New College student).[7]
*(Rev. Dupree):* My wife ... used to run a fishing market for her dad. And she knows all about how to clean fish, and how to cut it, and filet it, and whatnot. ... I think, she was in her early teens when she worked in the fish market. Her daddy would have her [work there], 'cause she could count ... her daddy would let her do all of the selling of the fish, because by the time the people finished picking out the fish, she already had figured it up in her mind how much it costs. She has a good mind for figures, for counting and whatnot. ... The fish market was right there on the northeast corner of Central Avenue and 6th Street. ... It's [now] called the Boulevard of the Arts.

**Carolyn Mason**, interview with Hope Black. [8]
*(C. Mason):* My grandfather was a barber, had a barbershop on Central Avenue.

**Verna Hall,** interview with Vickie Oldham. [9]
*(V. Hall):* There were two grocery stores in this area. One was Wynn's Store on the corner of Links and then 27th St. There was a Perry's Store on the end of Osprey, the east side of the street. And there was a pool hall on the right side of the street, owned by Mr. and Mrs. O'Neil, Buck O'Neil's parents.

**Jetson Grimes**, interview with Vickie Oldham. [10]
*(J. Grimes):* My aunt, I lived with her, after eleven years old. ... In fact, my aunt was one of my inspirations for what I do now. She was truly an entrepreneur ... She started a cleaning business as she cleaned eight or nine businesses downtown during that period. ... I remember the Van Sky Building, that was a famous building. ... She cleaned the Terrace Hotel. She had a couple of insurance offices that she cleaned. She had a couple of restaurants during that period that she cleaned. She had a staff of people that worked for her and I was ... working with her when I was twelve, thirteen years old. ... That was during the early '50s.

My godmother [Madam Brooks] was a midwife and my godmother raised me until I was eleven years old. ... But [she] was another entrepreneur. ... At that time midwives was the equivalent to a doctor in the African American community, because during that period, we didn't have the ability to go to ... the Memorial Hospital. ... She was a black Cuban. And she grew up in the community when she came to Sarasota. And her husband ... both of them being from Cuba. ... He made cigars and he had a business right in ... the same house where she was ... on 35th Street. ... And that's where I really [developed] a strong incentive for entrepreneurship in our community and in my rearing.

I was able to see African Americans working for themselves. And it just kinda carried over to where I'm at now. I decided to become a barber. ... I worked for Timmons' Barbershop right across the street there for three years. And then I moved down to Bud [Thomas], and I stayed there for sixteen years. And after that, I opened my own business and I've been here 37 years now.

**Dr. Ed James II**, interview with Haley Jordan (New College student).[11]
*(Dr. James II):* My grandparents had several businesses. They had a restaurant. They had a taxi service. They became entrepreneurs, after early years in their lives as domestic workers. [They] owned the first telephone in the black community and it was in their business. ... My grandparents also ran ... a regular Western Union office. And during those early years, there was a lack of paved streets and addresses. When a telegram would come for someone in the community, it would usually be addressed to "[a person's name] Newtown." And my grandparents knew almost, if not everybody, in the community. Sometimes in those early days when ... there was a death in the family or emergency and they were trying to reach somebody ... and if they knew the relative lived in Sarasota, sometime they would call the Sarasota Sheriff's Office. ... And they would send an officer out to my grandparents' restaurant and ... would say "there's a family called [XX]. They live in Colorado and they have a daughter whose name is [X] who lives in Newtown and we have this phone number. It's very important that [X] call her mother or father in Colorado. Can you help us?" And they would say, "Sure, I know [X]. I can tell you where she lives or we will get the number to her." They performed that kind of service.

**Dr. Fannie McDugle**, interview with Vickie Oldham.[12]

*(Dr. McDugle):* My mother, she was a seamstress, she had a dress shop [in] Overtown. She would make clothes and she would make curtains and the bed spreads to match. And she made church robes…

*(V. Oldham): What was the name of her shop?*

*(Dr. McDugle):* Malcolm's Seamstress Shop. She was Brenda Malcolm. My dad … worked at Sarasota Memorial. … He rolled these sick peoples in and out the operating room, to the recovering room.

After I graduated, I thought I wanted to be a RN nurse. I went back to Atlanta, Georgia, to nursing school. … And I got my RN license. … I was a nurse there for a good, good while. Then I decided I wanted to be a cosmetologist. I opened up my salon. … My shop was Goodrich Avenue, where I'm at now. Well … back in the day, the beauty shop was in the houses, and we had Dr. Margerie and Florence Fold; they had a beauty shop on they porch, [in] Overtown. Then Ms. Mary Emma Jones … she had beauty parlor, she had two operators. [She also] owned three taxi drivers and she was famous in barbequing, remember? You use to call them "Two Bone Jones." [Laughter] They wouldn't give you but two bones or three bones for a barbecue sandwich. Well, we've had businesses all over town. I can remember Can Major Grocery and … they had a drycleaners there too.

*(V. Oldham): Do you remember Catherine and Herbert Jenkins' grocery store?*

*(Dr. McDugle):* Oh yeah. That was one of the biggest, largest, nicest stores out here in Newtown. And he had a truck, and all the older peoples who didn't have cars or didn't have a way to get around to shop … they would call in and tell him what they want and he'd take orders. And then he would take the orders to them, from door to door, because the older people didn't have cars to get out to shop to buy their food.

They had what you call an ice truck. We had what you call iceboxes and you open that box and it had the big space like the freezer part up there. That's where you would put that big block of ice and keep it. … And it kept all your food cold just like we're keeping it cold now.

People did what they had to do to survive in the early days of African American settlement in Sarasota. They forged the way for their descendants to have the opportunities to follow new career paths. A prominent example is **Fredd Atkins,** three-time Mayor of Sarasota and former commissioner who said, "My Aunt Ruby was a gambler, and she owned a restaurant and a juke joint." [13]

**Dr. Louis Robison**, told Vickie Oldham that his family moved to Sarasota from Miami:

> *(Dr. Robison):* She wanted to open a restaurant here, which she did, at the corner of Pershing Avenue and 27th Street ... I think it still is called ... the Town Hall Restaurant. My mother owned that for a little while.
> *(V. Oldham): Did she come here specifically as a restaurateur or did she have to do some work before she was able to set up a restaurant?*
> *(Dr. Robison):* Some guys that used to come to Miami that were selling fish out of the back of a truck on the street ... told her about the opportunity [in Sarasota]. And we moved here in 1963 from inner city Miami. [14]

**Eddie L. Rainey**, interview with Vickie Oldham. [15]

> *(E. Rainey):* My grandfather, J.E. Rainey ... was a homebuilder ... a carpenter. He came in and purchased quite a bit of land in Sarasota and on that property he developed houses ... He made a living building houses. Back in those days, they were wood houses. Predominately the homes were built all over what we call the Newtown area. ... He built some homes and down ... Mango, I think it is. He owned property there. He built houses all around ... [But] for the most part, he was a farmer. And so that was his trade. He just knew how to do things with wood.
> *(V. Oldham): What did he do to earn money to enable him to buy that land?*
> *(E. Rainey):* My grandfather owned quite a bit of property in Georgia, Ocilla, in that area. He sold that property and got a tidy sum. So he came to Sarasota and long before there was a 301 ... he bought quite a bit of property on this side. And it was undeveloped, nothing but trees, squirrels, bears and etcetera. So he purchased quite a bit of property and from that point he began to build houses. He was just jack-of-all-trades: he could plumb, carpenter work, electrical work, everything.

**James Brown** told a *Herald-Tribune* reporter that:

Neil Humphrey's drug store [was] a community hub when [Brown] was a teenager. He ran a very neat place where you could buy your patented medicines, your sundries, your ice cream cones and what have you. Very polite, always presentable and well dressed, as all of the black merchants up and down MLK were. It was a gathering place, a central location.[16]

## OTHER WAYS OF MAKING A LIVING

The majority of Newtown and Overtown residents were not entrepreneurs; they worked for others. Some did both to make a living. The African Americans who settled in Overtown and Newtown arrived possessing many skills, which made them capable of adapting to many different types of work. Here, they tell the stories of how they and their families found numerous ways of making a living.

**Sarasota Mayor Willie Charles Shaw**, interview with Vickie Oldham. [17]
*(W.C. Shaw):* I'm Minister, Reverend, I am Commissioner, District One the City of Sarasota, and I'm presently the Mayor of the City of Sarasota. My great-grandfather and his brothers were railroad men and they came through here about 1903, bringing the Seaboard Railroad in here. They were gandy dancers ... the people who built the tracks, laid the tracks.

I'm born in Black Bottom. I'm raised in Black Bottom. I'm raised here in Newtown. ... From what is today 32nd Street, right in front of Booker, is where is where I was born and raised.
Right after Gibbs [now St. Petersburg College], I joined the Air Force, on August the 24th 1967. ... My dad was a veteran, family members had been veterans, served the country, and I, too, wanted to serve. I volunteered.

I came into the US Postal Service coming back from the military. I was at the hospital first, and then I came back into the hospital where I left while I attended J.C. [Junior College, Gibbs in St. Petersburg]. I was a [postal] carrier for eighteen years or more. ... I followed people like Jerome Stephens, who was the first black hired in the postal service here in Sarasota, Joe McKenzie, Jean Underwoods, Mr. Eddie Rainey, Glen Pinkston ... a series of very, very strong black men at that time.

**Prevell Barber**, interview with Vickie Oldham. [18]

*(P. Barber):* Well my uncle was running the grocery store and I would come during the summer [from my home in Georgia] and spend the time there.

*(V. Oldham): Did you make any money from the Carner grocery store too?*

*(P. Barber):* No, that was my uncle's store. I just worked there–I got my food from there. ... We had the meat counter and all kinds of canned goods. Oh, and cookies ... up near the front. That's what I first started selling, cookies [for] ... one cent, a penny. [Carner's] was at the corner of MLK and Persian Avenue. We had the sub-post office ... a part of the grocery store.

I didn't come here full-time until after I had finished high school. I came and worked for a while and then I went to college, ... Florida A & M. ... I majored in Elementary Education and minored in History. ... At that time, [teaching] was the only thing that the black girls could do, other than working in somebody's house. I did two years and I taught a little while, and then I went back to get the other two years. I taught in a little [city] called Archer, Florida, but I didn't stay there long. ... I was hired as a second grade teacher there, and only had two years [of college]. .... Later on, I went and got my Master's ... at the University of Chicago. ... I'd teach in the winter and go [to Chicago] in the summer. It took me about six years [to finish], just going in the summer. ... My first job was at Booker Elementary [teaching] second grade. ... Well at first it was kinda hard because everything you got to work with, you had to buy. I bought the chalk to write on the board, all the construction paper. ... The county was supposed to do that, but at that time they didn't.

**Dr. Fannie McDugle**, interview with Vickie Oldham. [19]

*(Dr. McDugle):* One uncle was a chef cook in the ... Jones Golf course. ... And the other uncle was a chef cook ... in Bradenton, Florida. ... I think it was a Marriott hotel where he was chef cook.

**Wendell Patrick Carter**, interview with Vickie Oldham. [20]

*(V. Oldham):* I remember in your family was Solomon's grocery store. I remember just going there and getting snacks and two-for-a-penny cookies and little candy and everything.

*(W.P. Carter):* Well, yes. It was actually Henry Solomon, which is actually my grandmother's uncle. But he was the proprietor of the place. And by the time I came along in the '60s though, I think he died thereabouts, right when I was born. So, I don't really remember him. But I remember "Birdie," Ms. Solomon, which is what a lot of ... people call her.

My mother taught school and she also worked for HRS ... Children's Services at that time. ... She was a high school teacher, then elementary. ... She retired [as a] sixth grade teacher. My grandfather ... that man was a jack-of-trades. He was the guy that people would call ten o'clock at night, and if they had an issue with their plumbing, he would get up out of his bed and go and help them. He was a very generous, very patient, very kind man. ... My grandmother ... worked for some of the people out on the beach, so like she was their maid or something along that line.

*(V. Oldham): Who were your greatest influences?*

*(W.P. Carter):* I would actually have to say my grandparents. Taking me in as a baby and raising [me]. Obviously my mother was in my life, but the majority of it was my grandparents. ... Their influence on me, and the stuff they instilled, as far as I could be anything I wanted to be if I put my mind to it. ... My grandmother made me promise before she died, that I graduated from college. She was like, "Well they getting that football out of you, you better get something out of them. So you promise me you gonna graduate." "Yes ma'am I will." And so ... I was actually playing professional football, but I had to go back two off-seasons to finish. And I did.

**Helen Dixon**, interview with Vickie Oldham. [21]

*(H. Dixon):* My father came to Sarasota [from Madison, Florida] in 1921 when he was seventeen years old.

*(V. Oldham): What did [he] do for work?*

*(H. Dixon):* Well that I can remember, I was a little girl, he worked at Davis Lumber Company. And then ... he was a chauffeur for John Ringling North ... one of the sons of Henry North of the Museum. Before he went there, he worked at what they called 'the Airbase,' where we have the airport now. It was for the soldiers. ... And he was a supervisor there and several of the Afro-American men worked there at the time. ... My daddy had decided to do a yard business. And he would get us up at five o'clock in the morning, especially myself because I was the

youngest, and go mow yards before I went to school. And he would allow the teachers to let us come in fifteen minutes later so that we could come home and change clothes and get dressed for school. We made money that morning doing yards and that was my money for school. And I remember us growing up, he said, "Well you need to have more than one profession. So always have two careers. So if they don't want you in one, you can do another." He said, "Always take the "*t* " off of "*can't* " and say, "I can do better." He said, "You were born free, you don't have to worry about anything else."

> *Parents who were not too distant from the era of slavery, or who perhaps had once been enslaved themselves, had a sharp sense of what it meant to be free, and often reminded their children that this was one of THE most important things about their lives ... they were born free, and they should always appreciate that fact. It meant they could do anything in the world with this freedom ..."taking the 't' off of can't." That positive attitude helped them all to weather the storms of the segregated reality they faced daily. It gave them hope for a brighter future.*

*(H. Dixon):* And then he started doing ... more mechanical stuff. And then he started working at the Ace Theater and the Ritz Theater downtown. We would clean the Ritz Theater and we used to have so much fun because all the money that I would find, I could keep that. Anything else, I could turn in. But that was our little extra change for school. So then finally, when he went to talk to the manager, he had just got a brand new 1950 Chevrolet. I'll never forget this. The owner said he was going to be fired because his car was better than his. And that was back in the day, '49 and '50s, where you didn't have a good car. And then so he decided, "Well, if I'm gonna do all this, I'm gonna go into my own business." And that's when he decided to do his electrical and plumbing business.

My mother was a maid in different homes and she used to work for William's Stationery ... downtown. I used to go with her into the house when she would cook and clean, take care of the children while they went to work. And it was like, you were happy. You weren't sad because your parents was doing that, because they took you everywhere they went. And you met the little kids, just like they were like your sister or brother. And we really had fun. We didn't have sadness at that time because they took us around. We did everything with them.

[My grandmother], she rented to people in her house, because all the property where Salvation Army is now, my daddy owned all of that. Well, it was called 921 – at their house, where they were living at that time – 921 Lemon Avenue. But he owned all the land over there and they used to call it "Charlie Jones Quarters." And it went from Lemon Avenue almost to the corner of Cohen Way.

Well see, when he came here in 1921, he lived with his great uncle. And his great uncle had the property. And my grandmother, who we call Grannie, she was the midwife. And so as time would go, they would build more houses onto that property. And he must have had about five or six houses on that property. And so, he would eventually rent to a lot of people on that property…He had several duplexes and a big house and all of that. So after my grandmother passed, then the property went to him.

When he became Charlie Jones and Sons with his plumbing, electric business he only had a third grade education, but he could talk more than you business-wise. He couldn't even write his name. My second sister taught him how to write 'Charlie Jones.'... And the people would say, "Charlie, if you had an education I don't know what I could do with you." Because he could count better in his head than you could on paper. And as I grew older, I was one of the ones that was teaching him and guiding him and driving, taking him around to do all the business. And he would say to me, "Go back and check your figures, I think you're wrong." And sure enough, I be one or two … pennies off of what he would say. But he was so sharp, what we call at time 'mother-wit.' And he knew just what to do. He could count up a figure quicker than you and add up a job and tell the people, "Well I want this and I want that." He said, "My daughter's gonna take care of this and my daughter's gonna take care of that." So he taught us how to be an entrepreneur at an early age.

He was the first licensed electrician and plumber with a dual license here in Sarasota. Because he couldn't read or write, they gave him an oral test. And they grandfathered him in with his license. … And then he trained two of his sons to do the plumbing and the electrical work. So that's how he got the name Charlie Jones and Sons.

**Nathaniel Harvey and son Leo**, interview with Vickie Oldham. [22]

*(N. Harvey):* My mother didn't work, but my father worked on the farm ... the Johnson Camp. ... That's a place they had put farmers, or people to work on a farm. There was a two-house shack: kitchen and a gearing room. ... We had to be to work about six o'clock. We leave home around 5:30, 6:00. Time to get out is right as the sun come up. We worked from "can't to can't." I'll put it that way.

*(L. Harvey):* From can't see to you can't see.
We had a school to go to. ... In Johnson Camp ...there was a little church there. We'd go to school in the church building. Later years I worked on the farm and back in them days you had to work because you made ... ten cents an hour. ... A dollar a day. ... You got paid once a week, on Friday. ... Bring it home give it momma.

*(V. Oldham): Now what was celery farming like? Describe how you did that. How did it grow?*

*(N. Harvey):* On top of the ground. And when it get ready to harvest, you had to do a thing called cutting it, put it in the packing house, wash it, pack it and ship it. It was quite a job. I just mostly done one job ... work on the farm, to grow the celery. I didn't have anything to do with the packing of it. I just helped grow it ... tend the fields, fertilize ... spray and whatever you had to do it.

Most of it was it done in the summertime, both winter and summer. ... Working on the farm is hard. Back in the [time] when I was out there, mostly everything you done, you done by hand. You didn't have no equipment. But in later years, you begin to have more of things to work with. We'd socialize in the barn at noon time. We sit down and talk about different things like ordinary people do ... on our lunch break. We only had thirty minutes to do that. You brought your own food. ... Whatever my wife put in the bucket. [Laughter]

*(V. Oldham): Did you do ever any other kind of work?*

*(N. Harvey):* Oh Lord, yeah. ... I worked for Sarasota Concrete. I worked Intra-State Terrazzo. I worked for Culligan's ... water, purified water, and all that soft stuff. My last job was a correctional officer.

*(V. Olham): Did your wife work?*

*(N. Harvey):* Yes, she worked everyday. ... She was a maid ... housework.

*(L. Harvey):* She did work for different people, in different houses. She had certain people ... Nickels and Ms. Wino. She worked for them for thirty something years.

**Johnny Hunter Sr.,** interview with Vickie Oldham. [23]
*(Hunter Sr.):* [My mother] came to Sarasota, Florida with her sister-in-law, the late Ruby Hunter. [After] they moved here, they were doing domestic work at the Terrace Hotel at the time the Boston Red Sox were spring training here in Sarasota, Florida, and they lived in the Terrace Hotel.

My senior year in high school ... I got a part-time job working after school, working at Asa's Service Station. ... The late Asa Jenkins owned a service station called 'Union 76 Station.'

I took the postal examination before I got out [of the Air Force in] ... a project called 'Project Transition.' ... We would have classes on the base and then when we got ready to take the postal exam, we would go downtown to the post office in Tampa. ... But at the time, the only thing they could guarantee was during the Christmas holidays. ... After the eight or nine days, they couldn't guarantee that they would give you anything. By this time, I was married and my wife had two kids prior to our marriage and she had twin children from me. So we facing four kids, myself and her and ... I needed a full-time regular job.

My friend and I, Pete Gillman, went to Manatee Tech to be auto mechanics. ... And then I worked for the late Willie Williams. The Williams Shell Station was where the Sunoco Station is at now. And I was his manager. So in 1973 ... I opened up "Johnny's Auto Repair." And I had a towing service. I had a very good business at the time, from '73 to '75.

*(V. Oldham): You went into the newspaper business. ... Talk about that transition.*

*( Hunter Sr.):* How I got in the newspaper business. When I was in prison I studied three things: I studied the Bible; I studied psychology; and I studied the law.

I used to write a column for the paper, "Behind Prison Walls." I wrote that monthly for the paper ... just talking about experiences. You know what the average education or grade level was at the time when I was in prison? It was sixth grade. I'm talking about from '75 'til '83 ... They thought I was a professor in prison. And everything I knew, I thought everybody knew it. You know, for me, it was just common. But it wasn't.

So when I got out, he [William Fred "Flick" Jackson] wanted me to come work for him ... Jackson started *Tempo*, I didn't. ... I contact [him], met him at Amlee Diner. ... And we talked for about four hours and I shook his hand and I said, "I'm your man." ... And then I started. ... I closed up my garage business in August of '86. ... That was 29 years ago. ... I got in the newspaper business and that's what I've been doing since I took it over in ... September '90. Just last month was my 25th year of doing this [publishing *Tempo News.*]

**Rev. Kelvin Lumpkin**, interview with Vickie Oldham. [24]
*(Rev. Lumpkin):* My mother has been a nurse for most of her life. My dad owned a cleaning business and was a custodian at Sarasota High School. ... Both were the oldest in their families, and had to drop out, support their siblings, [to] help work for the family.

**Wade Harvin**, interview with Flannery French (New College student). [25]
**(Part 1)**
*(W. Harvin):* My mother began working with ... a home laundromat, and she stayed with the home laundromat until such time as she was able to find other jobs. And from there she went to Ms. Bispham. ... My mother worked for the week. And following that, she began working at another home laundromat and worked there until she was able to find more suitable ... labor. And she continued there until, as best I can remember from that date and time.

I went to Florida Business and Vocational College. ... Started a banking career. ... Having less [while growing up] made us more ambitious. ... And when my cousins and my aunts in Crescent City heard that I was branch manager of the seventh largest branch of 35, they couldn't [believe it] — some came here just to see it. They said, "Well how'd you do that?" I said "I just tried. I just tried." And I tried to live a clean life. And that's ... what did it.

**Wade Harvin**, interview with Vickie Oldham. [26]
**(Part 2)**
*(W. Harvin):* We would go North in the summer and work in the fields ... it was exciting and it's another instance that proves that God made the world large, but he also made it small. We stopped in a place called Milton, Pennsylvania. We picked beans, we picked tomatoes, and we picked potatoes. We came away with nice clothing for school, and so forth, that we bought. As soon as

school was out, late May, we'd hop in the car and we'd head to Milton, Pennsylvania. … I was nine.

*(V. Oldham): So you'd go there for the summer at age nine and then come back to Sarasota to go to school, where you lived?*

*(W. Harvin):* Delson's Quarters. When coming from a poverty stricken background, you learn to work, parents teach you to work with your hands. And a lot of folk didn't believe the amount of bushels of beans that I could pick, bushels of tomatoes, bags of potatoes. The bags were always too heavy that we couldn't lift them so once we filled a bag, we waved to our dad and he'd come over and he'd stand them up, because you had to stand them up in a row. But it worked and there's nothing wrong with learning hard work. I have never been out of a job since I've been old enough to work. I didn't ask Coast Federal for a job, the president called me and offered the job to me. I didn't become office manager at the Rent-it-All, the owner called me and asked me would I consider it. I've worked at Sara-Bay Country Club. … I learned to do short orders. I learned how to do food decoration.

*(V. Oldham): How did you get to Coast Bank? I know that there probably were some [other] jobs.*

*(W. Harvin):* Yes, in between I was also the first black insurance salesman for Independent Life Insurance Company in this area. I didn't ask them, they asked me. What I'm saying is things have just been as if God has set steps on a ladder. All I had to do was live it. But then when Bill Overton, the president of Coast Federal, called me and offered me whatever my average sale had been for the last three years, he said, "I'll start you at that." And I was holding on to the chair just to keep from falling out of it, but I controlled myself long enough to say well, that sounds good, that sounds good. … So I left and I stood up and jumped and clicked my heels together. I walked down Main Street. I walked all the way.

*(V. Oldham): The first African American bank manager? ] Did customers come or did they stop?*

*(W. Harvin):* Some looked at me a little strange. … I went through teller training and I went through savings counselor training and finally they said, "Okay let's try it."… When they put me in the fifth largest office out of thirty-seven, I said, "Lord this is for real…" I knew all the big accounts were not the same color as I. But I had one white came to me and said, "You know, they told me you were coming. Some folks had some thoughts about you

coming over. You know what I told them Mr. Harvin? I said if they send him over to the fifth largest office of a billion-dollar corporation, he must know how to count" [Laughter]. ... They told the staff that I had inherited ..."You don't have any choice in this matter." That's what the director of Coastal Federal had said. "Wade Harvin is gonna be your next branch manager." And that was it.

**Rev. Jerome Dupree (Former Mayor of Sarasota)**, interview with Jessica Wopinski (New College student). [27]
**(Part 1)**
We used to caddy ... at the Bobby Jones Golf Course. ... When I got out of school, I worked at a place called Smacks. It was right there ... on Main Street and Osprey. It was a place where people went to eat and whatnot, and the only job I could get was from five in the evening until twelve o'clock at night. I had to wash all the big pans, and pots, and all that stuff. I did that for a couple of weeks, and when the third week came I gave him my notice ... before that week was up, my friend D. C. Bird and his uncle said they had some work available for us out in Ringling. And so we went out to Ringling and got that job with the architect. It was easy. We could go at seven in the morning and we were off by three o'clock during the day, and we didn't have to work on Saturdays and Sundays. That was a peach of a job.

**Rev. Jerome Dupree,** interview with Jessica Wopinski (New College student). [28]
**(Part 2)**
*(J. Wopinski): In our last interview, you were telling me about fishing at the old Ringling Bridge; could you tell me a little bit more about that?)*
*(Rev. Dupree):* Oh yeah. That was one of the joys of our lives. Because...fishing at the old Ringling Bridge was not only a hobby ... it was a means of making a living. ... A lot of people within our community depended on fishing for some of their meals. ... When we came here in 1939, this was very much a fishing area.

**Fredd Atkins (Three-time Mayor of Sarasota and commissioner)**, interview with Jessica Wopinski (New College student).[29]

*(F. Atkins):* I was still going to Manatee Junior College. So Fred [Bacon] told me ... this was like the summer of '79. He said, "Hey Fred! You get your degree from Manatee Junior College, we're gone have position for you." I said, "What kind of position?" He said, "Well, we putting together a grant for this counseling program, the Family Life Intervention Program." So I said, "Okay." So I went and finished my degree, and I joined the Union of Concerned Parents that January of 1980. Or January of 1979. Ronald Reagan fired all of us. ... The federal government cut all the programs, CETA, all the grants, everything. So I really just worked with them one year.

The Jacksons, Sanders, James and ... Rivers. They had filed a lawsuit in the name of the NAACP against the City of Sarasota for its method of at-large voting. While I'm at the Union for Concerned Parents, one of my jobs, other than counseling first offenders, was to do the legal research for the attorney, David Littman, out of Miami, to make sure that we got all of the information. So, I became ... decreed by the federal government ... an expert on the City of Sarasota's process. I was ... an expert witness, because I was the person that did all of the research on the microfiche and all the documents of the City of Sarasota history, from its beginning until 1979.

**Shelia Cassundra Hammond Atkins**, interview with Kaylie Stokes (New College student).[30]

My mother and father lived in Alabama, and the Caples[31] ... was traveling North. And they stopped in this restaurant my mother worked in. And my mother was a great cook, so Mrs. Caples asked my mother if she would like to come to Florida and be her cook. And so that's the reason my parents moved to Florida at some time later. ... They both were domestic workers all their lives here in Sarasota. When I was younger, I said I only would like to be a nurse or a teacher. I wanted to be a nurse at first, and I ... took some nursing classes, but I ended up teaching, because it gives me a sense of helping.

**Eddie L. Rainey,** interview with Vickie Oldham. [32]

*(E. Rainey):* We had guys working at the train station... At that time the train station was on Lemon Avenue.

*(V. Oldham): Do you remember the circus and people working for the circus?*

*(E. Rainey):* Of course I do. I remember that very, very well. Matter of fact, some of my friends worked on now what was called Ringling Circus and it was located over on what is now Circus Avenue off Beneva. You had the training camp there. That's where they kept the animals.

*(V. Oldham): What did your friends do with the circus?*

*(E. Rainey):* You take shovel and you follow the elephants [Laughter]. I mean what more can I say...You feed the elephants and you cook. Back in those days, they had a train section, I think about eight or ten cars that they would travel [in] - porters and things like that...No lion tamers.

*(V. Oldham): Did you know about anybody who worked for John Ringling?*

*(E. Rainey):* Oh yes. We called him Toto. Let me see what was his real name? I know, Haultan Banks. He took care of Gargantua. I knew quite a few. I knew Gable ... I knew Suit Major - he stayed with the circus year in and year out ... We called him "Suit" because he made the statement that as long as he worked for the circus, he was gonna try to have as many suits as he could. So he had over 50 suits and shoes. He traveled with us just like Snake Washington, back and forth. ... all of these guys, there were about twenty or twenty-five of them ... this was their permanent job. I mean they would come with a pocket full of money and go down and set the town up until it's time for them to go back on the train. And they would be gone like sometimes a year, six, seven months.

I came out [of the Army] and, after coming home ... I accepted [track] meet jobs in Sarasota for a while, not for too long. But I began it in search of a teacher's job, which I did get up in Greenville, Florida, Madison County...When I went there as coach, stayed up there a couple of years. And it was at that point that I realized, too, that the pay grade was very, very slim, very low. And later on I took the postal exam and went to the postal service ... I went to visit a friend of mine in New York. And one day we were all out looking for work, we were looking for jobs. Went down on Fifth Avenue and I saw this sign, "Take the postal exam" And I did. I took it and I had the score transferred here.

And I made a couple of calls first. They wrote me back and said I had passed the exam and that's how it all started.

In his news article "Looking Back and Ahead," Ian Cummings describes Rainey as a "pioneer in being the first black employee to be promoted up through the area's postal service, serving as a station manager and an interim postmaster at various locations. He graduated from Florida A&M University at a time when many of his peers didn't have the means."[33]

**Robert L. Taylor,** interview with Vickie Oldham.[34]
*(R. L. Taylor):* [My mother] was pastry cook at a little café on Main, lower Main. Johnny's Cafeteria. … I was groomed from the time I was six or seven, I was gonna be the first one that went to college in the family. So I didn't do anything really. Well a lot of time, while the kids out doing chores, I would be in there with my grandmother. She would be teaching me different things. And so I really lived the enchanted; I was really special to them. So all I had to do was make sure I got good grades from school. … I was a salutatorian when I graduated from Booker High. … I got an academic scholarship to Morehouse and so that's how I went to Morehouse first, in the beginning. But … I didn't finish the first semester because, once I was drafted and was '1A,' I knew it wouldn't be long before I go in the service. So I didn't go back.
*(V. Oldham): How did you make money in the early years, after you came back from the Army?)*
*(R. L. Taylor):* Well at first I didn't do any work at all because I was on the G.I. Bill and I went to college when I came back. … I went back to Morehouse.
*(V. Oldham): After graduating from Morehouse, did you come back to Sarasota?*
*(R. L. Taylor):* Yes … By that time I had a young daughter, and I came back and … had to work. So I did whatever kind of work was available. ... I didn't start at the [Rec] center.
*(V. Oldham): You mean this Robert L. Taylor Center that's now named after you?*
*(R. L. Taylor):* Yeah but it … was built for the troops who were stationed in Sarasota. See where the airport is now, it was a airbase, and they had a lot of black soldiers there. And this building was built for their entertainment, so they would have a place to come for entertainment. The USO built it for them.

*(V. Oldham): But tell me some more of those jobs that you had ...
working at the Rec center with kids in the neighborhood. That was a
part-time job. How did you make a living?*
*(R. Taylor):* Anything that came along you did it. ... Well I had
friends who worked at this Allied Furniture thing and they knew in
the morning I didn't have anything to do. So if they had a job I
could do in the morning, they would come get me and I would help
them that way. ... I didn't do much mowing lawns, but I'd done
construction, roofing. ... I had a job cleaning sewers. Anything that
you could come along to make money, you had to do it 'cause you
had to feed your family. But even before that, my senior year [at
Morehouse], I only needed one course to graduate and they didn't
offer that until the second semester. So I stayed home in the first
semester and I worked. The Florida Power Light ... built ... a
station there. And I worked there for that semester. ... And I
remember that job a lot because I laugh, looking back, how much
they paid me. By the time they took out my social security and all
that stuff, I had $34.90 left for that week's work [Laughter]. But that
$34.95 is maybe ten times as much as it is now. You could go to the
store with $10 buy a whole big bag of groceries. Well now $10 just
will get you in the door.

And then I went back to Morehouse and finished. ...
Graduated in 1950 ... [with] a degree in Business Administration
and Economics, which I never used. It was my desire, when I first
went to school, to be a CPA. ... I didn't know what I wanted to do.
And I always wanted to be either a plumber or an electrician. That's
what I wanted, but my parents had decided already what I was
gonna do. And so anyway there wasn't no where to get a internship
there anyway. Wasn't nowhere for me to learn to do it. ... But then,
when I got my senior year, and I ran into business math, I know
right then a CPA wasn't for me [Laughter]. That was the end of that.
And so I was considering going back to school when the city
manager called me, asked me would I try to start the recreation
program here.

Well, we had the little building, the USO building. We had
two employees, me and the janitor. There was nothing outside at all,
no facilities. ... The first time we had a full staff to work [was]
when they got the new building. ... I know we had two outside
janitors and one inside. And then ... we had about eight or ten
assistants within different fields — arts and crafts and different
stuff. Well, this was the only game in town. So we had a captive

audience really, because there's nowhere for them to go. Which proved good for discipline because kids don't never want to be sent home when all their friends are down here. So they always behaved. You could always use that over them. But once we got that new building ... most of the time I was programming, especially in the summer we would have three different age groups and they have to have a separate program, separate staff for each age group. So I spent the whole time planning what the programming would be. So if a parent came ... I knew what group he was with and I knew exactly where he was 'cause it was all a set program. And so once the summer was over, we go to the winter. And all during the winter I'm programming for the summer again. And all the schools would have their after-game dances here.

Robert L. Taylor Community Complex.
Courtesy: City of Sarasota and Kacey Troupe.

*(V. Oldham): When you look at this [new] building now, and you remember what it was when you first started, and you see your name on that plaque and all, what does that feel like?*
*(R. Taylor):* Well you can't really describe the feeling. ... You know it means a lot to me, but I think it means even more to my family 'cause they really pushed for it more than I did. After I retired here, I said I was tired of kids. But then I spent three years with Helen Payne Day Care. I had a group of about three and a half to five year olds for three years. Then when I rode to Bradenton, I was with the PAL Program, after-school program.

The new state-of-the-art Robert L. Taylor Community Complex replaced the old "Rec" and now provides many different types of athletic activities for Newtown youth, including: a fitness center; dance room; gymnasium; aquatic center; basketball court; volleyball court; and many others. The Robert L. Taylor Community Complex has been a community anchor for more than 60 years.[35]

**James and Yvonne Brown,** interview with Vickie Oldham. [36]
*(Y. Brown):* Both of us worked at an early age. So I worked at what was then 'Maas Brothers.' It's now Macy's. ... And earlier when we were in high school, we also worked.
*(J. Brown):* I don't have time to tell you all the jobs that I did out in the hot sun anytime, every time, to get to the college. ... Construction work for $1.25 an hour, road construction, paving, laying pipe, digging with a shovel all day. .... Then I finally got sense enough to move inside now and wait on tables at Morrison's Cafeteria, and Driftwood, and M&M Cafeteria. I always worked. I would get home from school and the next day, if it wasn't Sunday, I was up on the corner trying to catch what you call 'a hustle.' Whoever comes by wanting to hire somebody for the day, I'm gone. Working my way through college.

**Jesse Johnson**, interview with Vickie Oldham. [37]
Jesse is a cement finisher, painter, carpenter who also installs tile flooring. He has worked in the industry for 52 years. As a foreman, he supervises and trains construction crews; and is outspoken about equitable pay for construction workers.
*(J. Johnson):* The people in the city and job force thing ... they decide that they gonna fix this thing 'cause the contractor can't bring nobody in there if they ain't come through that system. Everybody got to be signed up to be able to go to work out there. And I like that ...'cause see what we did before, the two phases that I worked on out there in the garden, we made $250 a day.... And when he find out what we can do ... He started to taking his mens off. ... He say, "I talked to one of the gentlemen." I said, "What he want us to do?" He said, "Y'all over the cement." And I said, "We over the cement? You ain't paying us but a $150 a day. He got to come up with some more money if he want us to be over the cement." ... Next day ... the first truck come, we didn't pour. The second truck come, we didn't pour. The third truck out there, the operator said, "What y'all wanna do?" I said,

"We just waiting." The fourth truck come, we didn't pour. The fifth truck came, we didn't pour. The sixth truck - there was seven trucks out there. The man that we worked for come across the road running. "Why y'all ain't pouring?" They said, "Mr. Johnson want to talk to you." "What do Mr. Johnson have to say?" I said. "Yesterday, we have poured all this cement and ain't got nothing but $150, and we won't pour no more cement for no $150. ... He said, "I can't pay y'all no $250. What I can do, I'll give y'all $200. ... I said, "You didn't hear me. I told you $250." And he said, "Y'all come on and go to work."

And I wasn't angry when I told him that ... No ma'am. You have to tell people the truth. You feel good in the inside when you done told somebody the truth.

**NAACP President, Trevor D. Harvey**, interview with Vickie Oldham [38]

*(T. Harvey):* At the end of the year (in December) I finished high school. ... I was getting ready to go to...Florida A&M University in Tallahassee on an ROTC scholarship because I spent five years in ROTC in high school. ... I had all of his time on my hands six or seven months 'til graduation, so I got a job. ... A friend of mine ... was the manager of a local Rent-to-Own company called Champion TV. ... So I started working for him, just until graduation, getting ready to go off to college. ... And I got into that business, and learned that business so fast that, even before I graduated from high school, they were promoting me to an account manager. You know, here it is, I'm at the age of 17, 18 years old. I was the head Account Manager for this company. And when I graduated from high school, they wanted to promote me to a store manager. They were transferring my friend to a store up in Bradenton and they offered me the Sarasota store? And I had to make a decision. ... Go off to college? or do I go into this management position. ... I'm a young man at the age of 18, making over $30-35,000, without a college education. And ... I ... stayed and ran the company. And it was very beneficial to me. And after leaving there, I got into the insurance industry. I'm a Workers Comp. specialist. ... But I always had a passion for college, always mentoring and speaking to young people about the importance of education, and preaching that to my own children. And I had the sense that I was missing something because I had not finished college. So ... I made the decision that, if you're

going to give this message, if you're going to preach and teach this message, you need to live this message. So, I finally decided to go back to college and completed my college degree at Eckerd in St. [Petersburg] in Business Administration.

*(V. Oldham): Now where does the NAACP come into your story? How did this happen? You're president!*

*(T. Harvey):* Around the age of 20, 21 years old, me and a close friend of mine, Richard Redding, we kind of assessed the community and said, "Where are the young men our age? Where were they? What were they doing?" Because we were looking up to the Mr. John Rivers, the Dr. Ed James, the Fredd Atkins, the Mr. Rainey's. We were looking at those individuals. But that middle group was missing. ... So I decided at that point that I wanted to get involved with the community. I wanted to do something. I had no interest in the NAACP, only knew very little about the NAACP ... and the significant contributions it had made in our communities across the country. ... And then, all of a sudden, I got involved in the NAACP, got involved in the grassroots organization. I served up under Larry Lovejoy, I served up under Tony Cornish. ... As a matter of fact, I took over from Tony Cornish. Tony was in the middle of his term when him and his wife got a transfer to the Philadelphia area. And that's how I became president, because I was the immediate vice president. I'm an area director for the Florida state conference of the NAACP. I oversee seven other branches in the state of Florida for the NAACP.

**Alice Faye Jones & son Randy Jones**, interview with Nicholas Manting-Brewer (New College VISTA Volunteer Coordinator). [39]

*(A.F. Jones)*: We're located right now at ... the Robert L. Taylor Community Complex. Years ago, it used to be called the Newtown Community Center. The Rec. is what we all called it. What I do here is that I offer a free after school homework assisting program, free of charge to students from seventh grade to high school in various studies and subject areas, based upon their need. It's a program called "Brothers and Sisters Doing the Right Thing." We've been established since 2002 and it runs on volunteers. We do not have any paid staff or anything like that. Hopefully, in the near future we will.

*(N. Manting-Brewer): What did your mom do for a living?*

*(A.F. Jones)*: She was a house cleaner. She was a maid. She

worked out on Longboat Key. … That's what I thought I was going to be. … I respected and looked up to my mom, so I wanted to be like my mom. And I thought that's what I was supposed to [be], was a maid. … During my younger years, it wasn't often that we'd miss school, but when we did, it was an honor to go out there and travel on Longboat Key because it was a whole other world out there.

*(R. Jones):* Before my mom got a vehicle, we would catch the city bus to Longboat. When you'd leave one area and go into that area, everything became green. The grass, God, just evenly and everything, and the flowers. And it smelled different over there. It was just a whole different world. And so it was like, wow! Where are we? We're on a different planet! But it was just across the bridge. But you see how other people live when you enter into a whole other area, which you're not exposed to.

## Summary: Making a Living

African American settlers in Overtown and Newtown migrated to Sarasota seeking jobs. They hailed, primarily, from many small towns in Florida, and the neighboring states of Georgia, Alabama and Mississippi. Newtown, established in 1914, grew from the influx of new people who heard about the availability of jobs in Sarasota, but also from the relocation of African Americans from Overtown. Newtown became a "village" as many of the interviewees described it. Everyone pitched in to help one another, whatever the need; fixing plumbing, clearing land, constructing houses, churches and schools, and even disciplining children.

Some settlers came to Sarasota with the turpentine business. When they had taken all of the resin they could from the trees in Georgia, they had to move on to new pine forests. Florida was a prime location until 1952, when the trees' production of resin was exhausted. Turpentine extraction was hard work in the blazing Florida sun during the summer, and the snakes were a danger to workers who were constantly on guard against them. The celery fields were another place that African American migrants found work to support themselves and their families. Some people lived on the farms and in the camps where a limited number of small houses were available as living quarters for workers. Others traveled back and forth from Newtown and Overtown to work there. The camps and fields also had "company stores" that made working in these places almost equivalent to slave labor; workers would get food and other items on "credit," which they would pay back when they got paid. More often than not, their paycheck was not enough to cover the amount credited to them, and they would end up still owing money to the store. So, again, they would have to get items on credit until the next harvest. They could never get ahead in that system.

Since Sarasota was part of the segregated South, Jim Crow laws were in full effect and African Americans were very limited in the places where they could purchase goods and services. This led to innovation and creativity on the part of those who chose to start businesses - entrepreneurs – to help themselves but also help others in the African American community by providing vital goods and services. Two business districts formed and thrived in Newtown before desegregation.

People did whatever jobs they had to, no matter how unappealing in order to make sure that they had money to support their families. They suffered under the oppression of racism and threats from the Ku Klux Klan, but met those challenges with a powerful faith in themselves and in God. Social conditions and the types of jobs changed dramatically over the years and a few Newtown residents became "firsts" in various occupations including the post office, college administration, elected officials, nursing, banking, and professional sports.

**ENDNOTES**

[1] Black, Hope. 2007. Master's thesis. University of South Florida.
[2] Interview with Vickie Oldham, August 10, 2015.
[3] Interview with Vickie Oldham, September 4, 2015.
[4] Interview with Vickie Oldham, August 31, 2015.
[5] Interview with Vickie Oldham, September 4, 2015.
[6] Interview with Vickie Oldham, September 4, 2015.
[7] Interview with Jessica Wopinski, November 17, 2012.
[8] Interview with Hope Black, September 22, 2015.
[9] Interview with Vickie Oldham, November 8, 2015.
[10] Interview with Vickie Oldham, September 4, 2015.
[11] Interview with Haley Jordan (New College), October 29, 2010.
[12] Interview with Vickie Oldham, August 10, 2015.
[13] Interview with Vickie Oldham, August 24, 2015.
[14] Interview with Vickie Oldham, October 26, 2015.
[15] Interview with Vickie Oldham, September 4, 2015.
[16] "Remembering a Newtown that taught character." February 21, 2011. http://www.heraldtribune.com/article/20110221/ARTICLE/102211040/0/search?p=1&tc=pg
[17] Interview with Vickie Oldham, August 18, 2015
[18] Interview with Vickie Oldham, August 10, 2015.
[19] Interview with Vickie Oldham, August 10, 2015.

[20] Interview with Vickie Oldham, November 16, 2015.

[21] Interview with Vickie Oldham, October 19, 2015.

[22] Interview with Vickie Oldham, August 18, 2015.

[23] Interview with Vickie Oldham, October 19, 2015.

[24] Interview with Vickie Oldham, October 26, 2015.

[25] Interview with Flannery French (New College Student), November 5, 2015.

[26] Interview with Vickie Oldham, August 18, 2015.

[27] Interview with Jessica Wopinski, October 11, 2012.

[28] Interview with Jessica Wopinski, Part 2, November 17, 2012.

[29] Interview with Jessica Wopinski. Part 2, November 17, 2012.

[30] Interview with Kaylie Stokes (New College), October 20, 2015.

[31] "Ralph C. Caples and his wife, Ellen, first came to Sarasota in December 1899 by horse and buggy...Caples was convinced that Sarasota was going places and the time was ripe to invest in the area. He persuaded his friends, John and Charles Ringling, to come to Sarasota and take a look...In order to persuade John Ringling to become a permanent resident of Sarasota, he purchased the Thompson property at Shell Beach, adjacent to his estate in 1911. Ringling was convinced and purchased the Thompson property in 1911...[and] the adjoining property the next year." https://www.sarasotamagazine.com/articles/2014/11/17/caples-ringlings-sarasota

[32] Interview with Vickie Oldham, September 4, 2015.

[33] Cummings, Ian. "Looking back, and ahead." April 17, 2014. http://newtown100.heraldtribune.com/looking-back-ahead/

[34] Interview with Vickie Oldham, August 18, 2015.

[35] Newtown-North Sarasota Redevelopment Project Report. April 2014.

[36] Interview with Vickie Oldham, August 24, 2015.

[37] Interview with Vickie Oldham, September 4, 2015.

[38] Interview with Vickie Oldham, November 20, 2015.

[39] Interview at Robert L. Taylor Community Center with Nicholas Manting-Brewer, AmeriCorps VISTA Volunteer Coordinator at New College of FL, Oct 25, 2012.

# CHAPTER 6:
# EDUCATION AND SCHOOLS

## THE EVOLUTION OF EDUCATION IN OVERTOWN AND NEWTOWN

African American families in Overtown and Newtown viewed education as the paramount means by which to improve their circumstances and enrich the lives of their children. During her interview with Vickie Oldham, **Estella Thomas** confirmed that this was her goal:

*(V. Oldham):*  *Why was education important to you and making sure that your children were educated?*

*(E. Thomas):*  Because I wasn't educated. So I made sure that they were educated so they could make it in the world. Gotta have education.[1]

Besides churches, the schools were among the most deeply rooted cultural institutions in Overtown and Newtown. Like many other African Americans recently freed from enslavement, the residents were no doubt influenced by W.E.B. Du Bois and Booker T. Washington who stressed that education — from grammar school, to high school, to college, vocational or trade school — was the gateway to progress and upward mobility. Although most had been forbidden by slave owners to learn to read and write, a few had learned those skills and they taught others. No one person embodied that ideal more than **Emma Edwina Booker.**

Emma E. Booker served the Overtown and Newtown communities for many years and was a role model to many of her students and teachers alike. In recognition of her major contributions to education, three schools were named in her honor: Emma E. Booker Elementary, Booker Middle School, and Booker High School. Although she was teaching school and holding the position of

Courtesy: Sarasota County Schools.

principal at the Knights of Pythias Hall School, and later at the Sarasota Grammar School, Emma E. Booker had not yet attained her college degree. She persevered for over 20 years, attending college during the summers, to finally obtain her bachelor's degree in 1937.

The first kindergarten in Overtown was started in the home of Josie Washington in 1910. Lucinda P. Wiggins also established a kindergarten in her home. The number of students enrolled in Wiggins' kindergarten increased to the point that it had to move into the basement of the Payne Chapel A.M.E. Church.[2] In addition to their roles as places of worship, churches provided spaces for education.

The Knights of Pythias Hall School functioned as one of the first formal schools and its principal was Emma E. Booker. In 1923, the school had its first graduating class; the ceremony was held at Bethlehem Baptist Church on Central Avenue. In addition to Emma E. Booker, the teachers at the Knights of Pythias Hall School included Aravia Benton Johnson, Lucinda P. Wiggins, and Mayme Williams.[3]

Despite the lack of adequate books, supplies, facilities and salaries, Overtown and later Newtown schools had one invaluable asset – its dedicated teachers. Rather than complaining about services and materials that they were being denied by the discriminatory system, teachers placed their energies into providing the very best education possible for their students, despite those circumstances. Using their own money, teachers often purchased much-needed books and supplies for their students. Parents and teachers often collaborated on fundraising efforts to purchase school materials, sponsoring a fish fry and other events.

Teachers lived in the same community and sometimes the very same houses as their students, resulting in very close relationships. Former teacher **Dorothye Smith** stated in her interview that:

> The superintendent and the School Board members worked with the county budget and they'd give you a budget at each school, according to personnel and the needs. But most of the things you use in the classroom, you bought it, because money was kind of slim during those days. ... You had a [housing] project leading into Newtown. It's on Orange Avenue. Well, that was already in operation when I came. But we couldn't stay there because I made too much money: $154.00 a month. That was too much money to be making, living in the projects. So ... we had to live in the house with families. ... There were not any duplexes or apartments or anything where you could live. I lived in a house with a family and then when that family became enlarged and had more children, then [I] moved to somebody else.[4]

Teachers visited students' homes to discuss their progress and problems with parents directly. According to many of the persons interviewed for the NCHD project, teachers, parents, and students had a very personal connection and the teachers were very well respected. Amazingly, most of the persons interviewed could recall the names of their teachers from their elementary, middle/junior, and senior high school classes, a testament to the extraordinary role that those teachers played in their lives! Following are a few examples of these relationships:

**Dr. Louis Robison**, interview with Vickie Oldham.[5]
*(Dr. Robison):* I think there was a certain amount of fear and respect at the same time for teachers at school. ... You had the opportunity to see teachers in the grocery store, see them at the laundromat or just see them in general in the community.

When questioned by a reporter, **James Brown** had strong recollections of Principal Rogers:[6]
*(J. Brown):* What an impact. You will get a lot of mixed emotions about him, but overall I knew that for us as African-Americans to exist in a segregated world, we needed to understand the system and live within structure ... He may have been a little too structured. But on the positive side, talk about the expectations. He always said that there are no excuses, letting you know that the barriers are there but they don't have to be there for the rest of your life.

**Helen Dixon,** interview with Vickie Oldham.[7]
*(H. Dixon):* Booker High was *the* school. ... Because even though we got hand-me-downs, the teachers cared about us. They loved us. They would go and call your parents. They would get in touch with you by phone or by walking to your house.

**Anthony "Tony"Major**, interview with Dr. Rosalyn Howard.[8]

*(A. Major):* Our principal [Professor Roland Rogers] was like, very clean. He would teach us, "Cleanliness is next to Godliness." And so when you walk the campus, if there was a piece of paper on the ground, you had to pick it up, whether you put it there or not. ... So we had the cleanest school in Sarasota County, trust me. It was ... a situation at Booker where everybody cared.

**Dorothye Smith (teacher),** interview with Vickie Oldham.[9]

*(D. Smith):* At Booker I enjoyed working with the children because I was very familiar with the parents. You met the parents at church, shopping. You just knew everybody. And the principal did something that was unique. He had teachers visit the homes of each child that he or she planned to teach that year. If you had twenty-four students, you visit twenty-four homes. You knew the parents before the first day of school. You knew the children ... [when they saw me on the street they would say,] "That's my teacher."

Newtown Educators.
Courtesy: Jetson Grimes Collection.

Mrs. Quessie Hall, Mrs. Ruby Williams, Mrs. Jackson,
Mrs. Siplin. Teachers at old Booker Elementary School.
Courtesy: Remar Harvin Collection.

**Rev. Jerome Dupree,** interview with Jessica Wopinski (New College student).[10]
*(Rev. Dupree,* Former Principal of Booker High School and Amaryllis School): I always like to work through the parents. When I was a teacher in school, I would call one of my parents every evening. I would call them from the school after the kids were gone. ... And when I first started I would find out that some of those parents had had some bad experiences, because every time someone called them from the school, it was bad news. So I made sure that when I called each one of those parents of the students I had, I called them to give them good news. So when some of them asked, they'd say, "What now? What now?" I said, "What does that mean?" "What kind of problem is it now with him?" I said, "No problem. I called you to tell you that your son or daughter did a marvelous job today, and I would appreciate it if you would kind of speak to them about it, and kind of give them a pat on the back, buy them a cold drink or something like that."

**James Brown,** interview with Vickie Oldham. [11]
I tell people, I was number five in my class of 34. And you should have seen those other guys who were ahead of me. They were really, really sharp. And it goes on and on about successful people who came out of Newtown, from those same dirt streets. Some of them came from homes that did not have electricity. Some of them came from homes that did not have indoor plumbing and running water. But those were not hindrances. Those were bumps in the road. And the teachers ... accepted no excuses. You had to speak Standard English. None of the neighborhood [slang]. And she just demanded excellence and would not accept "No" for an answer.

In 1925, the first public school built specifically for African American children was constructed next to the railroad tracks at Lemon and (today's) 7th Street and was named the Sarasota Grammar School. It opened with eight grade levels. Emma E. Booker led the children in a procession from the Knights of Pythias Hall to their new school. Historian Janet Snyder Matthews described the occasion:

> As the tall woman walked, she carried a wooden-handled school bell she always rang to convene classes. Some 70 children paraded behind her as they departed their make-do classrooms at Knights of Pythias Hall and headed towards Sarasota's first school building for blacks.[12]

Some people referred to the Sarasota Grammar School as the Rosenwald School because it had been built with money supplied by the Rosenwald Fund. Julius Rosenwald, a German-Jewish businessman, formed a partnership with Booker T. Washington to build schools throughout the segregated South for African American children, and to build homes for their teachers. The Rosenwald Foundation provided what was called "seed money" and required the communities receiving funding to demonstrate their commitment to education by raising the remaining funds needed and to help construct the buildings.[13] Sarasota Grammar School was renamed in honor of its first principal, Emma E. Booker. Booker Elementary School was originally located in an abandoned WWII barracks, but in 1958 a new school was built.[14]

Booker Elementary School (Sarasota Grammar School).
Courtesy: Sarasota County Historical Resources and Dorothye Smith.

Courtesy: Sarasota County Historical Resources and Dorothye Smith.

## NEWTOWN DAY NURSERY (HELEN R. PAYNE DAY NURSERY)

Alice Turner, Luella O'Neil, Susie Reddick, Susie Newton, and Mary Emma Jones established the Newtown Day Nursery around 1930, not only in recognition of the need for early education, but also to enable women to go to work and be assured that their children would be cared for properly. It was grassroots-funded, receiving all types of donations from community members who were not wealthy monetarily, but were willing to donate their time, goods, and services to the Nursery. According to McElroy,[15] these donations that "made a difference" included: fresh milk from cows owned by Mrs. Paralee Wilson; food items and supplies from J.W. Carner and C.B. Britt Grocery and Southern Grocery and Table Supply; pastries from a bakery on Central Avenue; Winn's grocery donated food and extended the credit to the school; and food from the kitchens of concerned citizens. Other community members donated their administrative, professional and organizational expertise. Supporters of the Newtown Day Nursery also raised funds through appeals on radio programs at station WSPB, and from talent shows performed at tourist camps, trailer parks and the Municipal Auditorium (aka Exhibition Hall). In 1961, a new structure was built to house the day nursery with funds donated by benefactor Helen R. Payne and the school was renamed "Helen R. Payne Day Nursery" in her honor.[16]

There was early opposition to increasing the level of schooling for African American students beyond grammar school. The offensive argument made by whites was that there was no need for African American children to have higher education since they would find work only in menial positions. However, James Robert Dixon, fought against the odds to add a high school component. In 1935, Booker High School's first graduating class consisted of four students, three females and one male: Marthena Riley, Nacomi Williams (Carter), Annie Mae Blue (McElroy) and A.L. Williams.[17] Later, Amaryllis Park (Principal Jerome Dupree) was opened for first, second, and third-graders and Booker Junior High for seventh and eighth graders. Many graduates of the Booker schools returned to teach in the Sarasota County School system.[18] Mamie Baker Young who migrated to Sarasota from Quincy, Florida, established Sarasota's first Special Education Department in 1954. Later she created an Adult Night Program to assist people in obtaining their G.E.D. The first graduation was held in 1955.[19]

Booker's First Educators – 1949.
Courtesy: Sarasota County Historical Resources.

In 1954 Chief Justice Earl Warren wrote his landmark Supreme Court decision in the Brown v. Board of Education case, which prohibited racial segregation in US public schools. Three years after the Brown v. Board of Education decision, schools were still segregated in Sarasota. The NAACP asked the Sarasota County School Board to voluntarily desegregate. In 1961, after four more years of inactivity, the NAACP and several plaintiffs filed a successful desegregation lawsuit in federal court. In the 1962-63 school year, the first African-American students enrolled in previously all-white Sarasota Schools. The first school integrated was Bay Haven Elementary.

By 1965, the US Government had tied federal dollars to compliance with the 1964 Civil Rights Act and ordered all schools to integrate by 1967. The Sarasota County School Board came up with a plan to comply that was consistent with what many other white school districts did across the country: close the African American schools and bus those students to white schools, sometimes quite a distance from their homes.

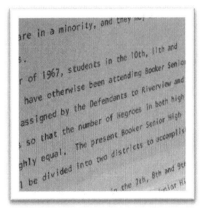

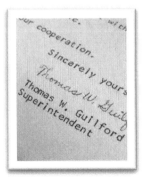

(above) Excerpts from a memo to teachers from the Superintendent of Schools, Thomas W. Guilford, about the closing of Booker Elementary School and Booker High School.
Courtesy: Jacquelyn Paulk.

In 1967 Booker High School was closed and, in 1968, Booker Junior High School followed. Originally, the community supported busing as a step forward. Eventually, however, many felt that closing the Newtown's schools had stripped away community pride and identity.

## THE PITFALLS OF SCHOOL DESEGREGATION

While segregation created challenges for African American students in Sarasota, desegregation brought serious new ones. The effects on students, teachers and families were tremendous, as described by several project interviewees. Many who were forcibly bused to all-white schools dropped out rather than continue to suffer verbal and physical abuse; some reported being spit upon by white students. White teachers were also products of a segregated culture and exhibited some of the same racist behaviors and language as students.

## STUDENTS' EXPERIENCES

**Dr. Harriet Moore**, who later became a school principal, attended Bay Haven Elementary, the first school that became integrated. She recalled her experiences there in an interview with Vickie Oldham: [20]

> I think that people were not adequately prepared for integration. I think that the law came and people said, "Okay we got to integrate so we're going to draw a line, we're going to take kids from here, we're going to take kids from here, and we're going to send them to those schools." The teachers and the students who were already in those schools were not prepared to receive African American students, nor did they know the truth about African American people. They had perceptions of African Americans as not so bright, ignorant, and what they were seeing on television. And in the '60s, what were they seeing on television that's representative of African American people? It certainly wasn't the people who were leaders in our nation. It was kind of 'Stepin Fetchit,' and prostitutes and that kind of thing. That's all they knew, what they saw on television. ... So they were afraid and they had misperceptions and misconceptions of us.
>
> So now you've got the other side: the African American children, who were now being bused out in these communities with people who did not want them there, who also had real experiences with Caucasian people. For example, you couldn't go

to the front doors for service; they had the right to refuse service to you. And they did in this community. And so that was real for us and now you want us to go to their schools? ... And so this is what we were thrust into. So was there an impact? Absolutely. Those people didn't want to teach African American children and African American children [didn't want] to be in those schools and be taught by them. Not because of hatred so much, but because, I believe, of misconceptions about who people are.

School closures caused a major rupture in the fabric of the Newtown community. In a 2013 interview by a *Herald-Tribune* reporter, former principal **Rev. Jerome Dupree** stated that, "We felt we were being hijacked. ... Of all the schools in the county, and Booker being among the oldest, why would they close our school? That was a slap in the face in our community."[21] Rev. Dupree was the valedictorian of the Booker High School class of 1953.

**John Rivers** explained some of the challenges encountered when the schools became integrated:

When they went on to integrate the schools, we had some problems right off. ... Because we talked about closing out the school here and then transporting the kids. ... So, with that, I decided at that time to call a boycott of the school system. ... The schools were receiving their funds based on attendance. And, therefore, they just decided that they didn't want that [the boycott] to work. ... So they sent the principal, assistant principal of Sarasota [High School] out here to talk to me. He said, "John, you are going to get your brain beat out, you know. You don't know what you are getting into." So, I just said, "Well, if anyone get close enough to beat my brains out, he's close enough to me to beat somebody's brains out, and that's exactly what will happen if you try to do something to me."

So, we called the boycott on a Sunday afternoon. Monday morning we had ninety-five percent of our students out of school. And we had organized the churches to open cafeterias, classrooms and everything in the churches out there. So, the kids were going to school and happy with it. A lot of New College students ... teachers and assistants. ... So everything was just working in our favor. ... And it did work. It did work, you know.[22]

## SCHOOL BOYCOTT

On May 5, 1969, a total of 2,353 African-American students (85% of the county's African-American students) boycotted the Sarasota County public schools in protest over the proposed closing of Amaryllis Elementary School and the unfair way that the schools had been integrated.[23] Even though a child might live directly across the street from the Booker campus, she or he had to be bused to an all-white school across town, a long distance from home, lifelong friends, and teachers who cared about them. **John Rivers'** and other families were concerned about their children's safety, traveling so far away from home:

> It was tough … because here's this little old six-year-old getting up four [o'clock] in the morning to get a bus and ride twenty miles away to get to school. That was tough, and disgraceful really, and rude.[24]

May 6, 1969 *Herald-Tribune* article.

## FREEDOM SCHOOLS

Not all families sent their children to the Freedom Schools that were set up during the boycott. James Brown and wife Yvonne, both educators, were concerned about the quality of education their children would receive from non-certified teachers. Their position was that, "If closure of the schools was what it took to integrate, so be it."[25] According to Rivers, and confirmed by the percentage of students who boycotted classes, however, most of the people of Newtown "were united."[26] As Susan Burns explained:

> For some of the participants, the boycott was a pivotal moment, the kind of defining event that shapes one's character and leaves a mark that lasts a lifetime. Of one fact there is no doubt: If the boycott of 1969 hadn't happened, Sarasota's Booker schools — Booker Elementary, Booker Middle and Booker High School — would not exist today.[27]

It was believed that the reestablishment of the schools within the community was a critical step in reclaiming community identity. Things did not turn out the way many expected, however. The Booker High School that reopened was unrecognizable from the one that closed.

**Fredd Atkins** attributed an ulterior motive to the way that students were assigned to specific schools during the initial school desegregation period, and still today:

> *(F. Atkins):* One of the greatest caveats of desegregation was how…to divide the Black athletes. Even right now, districting is about spreading around the wealth of athletes. It is so simple. Some of the greatest battles—when you hear about how Riverview fought to get these two blocks over here [in Newtown] or how Sarasota fought to get these two blocks over there, it wasn't about the academic concerns of African American kids. It was about the athletic prowess … their potential.
>
> Dr. [Ed] James and Al Abrams and Gene Carnegie and Fred Bacon … they got together and incorporated this not-for-profit around the Sam Shields Sr. incident. And they were able to — with us going, fighting the school board battle — to get Sam to be able to go less than one hundred yards from his house to school, when it'd been ten miles to Riverview. And so, that was part of the struggle.[28]

Atkins' opinion is borne out by the fact that two star athletes from Newtown who were forced to attend Riverview High School due to the closing of Booker High School. Tony Green and Wendell "Pat" Carter were inducted into the Riverview High School Hall of Fame in September 2015. According to many, had it not been for desegregation, they would have been inducted into Booker High School's Hall of Fame. Both men later played professional football in the NFL.[29]

**Dr. Louis Robison** attended Riverview High School during the first year of forced school desegregation. In a strange twist of fate, many years later he served as interim principal at Riverview High School for eighteen months.

*(Dr. Robison):* I can remember being the only black student in many of my classes at Riverview ... And that was difficult, particularly during the first year of desegregation, because we knew, for the most part, that they didn't really want us out there. And we didn't really want to be there. So that made it difficult in a sense. I left there and went to Florida A&M.

*(V. Oldham): I'm thinking about what it must have been like when you were named principal of that very school that you were a student at. That must have been amazing.*

*(Dr. Robison):* That was quite amazing actually ... being named the interim principal at Riverview High School. ...The superintendent of schools at the time was Wilma Hamilton ... [she] came to me and asked me if I would consider taking on the interim principal position at Riverview High School. ... I said, "Okay I'll do it. How long?" ... She said, "Oh maybe only about six months." I said, "Okay." Well, six months ended up being eighteen months ... In the eighteen months that we were there, the staff was so accommodating and so open. ... This was the beginning of school grades coming out ... meaning schools were assigned A, B, C, Ds and Fs. And Riverview High School was a "C" school at the time. ... And in the eighteen months that I served as the interim principal, we moved that school – with the help of teachers, parents and students – from a "C" school to an "A" school.

## TEACHERS' EXPERIENCES

The desegregation order proved to be a challenging experience for teachers as well as students. A study by a doctoral student found that most African American teachers did not want to be transferred into such hostile environments.[30] They had to be forced to do so, or quit, which some did. An exception to this was **Dorothye Smith**, who recalls in this interview that after teaching at Booker for fifteen years, she was transferred to the Venice schools and enjoyed it:

*(D. Smith):* It was after *Brown v. Board of Education* and you had to integrate. So they had to integrate somebody, so they integrated me. ... [I was] the first one to go to Venice [in] 1967. ... Some of the children [had never had a black teacher before and they would]

pass by me and would take the arms, pull them back. I said, "It won't come off, it's there to stay." And they would laugh. Everything was funny because I made it that way because they were inquisitive. They wanted to know and I answered questions. The children, that's what it was all about. … Somebody had to pave the way because there were other people coming along. So I didn't want to make them think it was a task they couldn't perform.[31]

According to **Dr. Louis Robison**, a Booker High School alumnus who served as a principal in the Sarasota Schools and an administrator in the Manatee County schools:

> The first year of desegregation was traumatic not only for students but for the teachers as well. … I remember [several]. In many cases these teachers saw their earlier positions from Booker minimized; they were put into assistant coaching jobs from previously head coaching positions or given music teaching positions from previously-held band leader positions. Adding insult to injury was the Teacher Strike of 1968 in Florida. … Some teachers walked out of Riverview and Sarasota High Schools. … When this happened, they lost their jobs, adding more turmoil to the already difficult transition for Black students.[32]

## THE UNION OF CONCERNED PARENTS

The Union of Concerned Parents (UCP), a community based organization (CBO),[33] was formed in 1973 by a group of parents who were outraged at the Sarasota County School Board's failure to take punitive action against a teacher who had committed a violent crime against an African American student. According to Annie McElroy:

> A white teacher had tied six black students to a motorcycle, dragging them around the football field. The Sarasota County School Board was refusing to take any action against the teacher (even though he admitted doing the act) …The Sarasota County School Board did not end the teacher's employment with them. The Union of Concerned Parents helped the parents of one of the physically abused students successfully sue the Sarasota County School Board for money damages.[34]

Frankie Davis joined the UCP staff in 1978 as the Broadcast Journalism Project Coordinator. She was among the first children to break the color barrier in 1962 at Bay Haven School, the first year that the Sarasota School Board finally complied with the 1954 Supreme Court order for all schools to desegregate.

## DESEGREGATION AND THE REINVENTION OF BOOKER HIGH SCHOOL

In 2003, Donald F. Rainone, a doctoral student in the College of Education at the University of South Florida (USF), published his dissertation entitled: *The Role of the Sarasota Visual Performing Arts (VPA) Magnet in Desegregation and Resegregation of Booker Neighborhood Schools.* The goal of his research study was to assess how Booker High School's Visual Performing Arts (VPA) magnet program affected the community.

Rainone vividly described the effects on the Newtown community during the reopening of Booker High School as a magnet school. This new status brought both welcomed changes and tough challenges to the school and to the Newtown community as well. Paved roads brought relief to Newtown students who, before white students were bused into Newtown to attend the magnet school, had to wait until it stopped raining in order to avoid having to wade through the mud to get into the school. As Fredd Atkins told Rainone, "We would have to wait until the water receded. It was like a swamp or a moat all around the school. The buses had to wait also. Or man, they'd get stuck." Rainone stated that:

> While Newtown residents were happy that the school reopened in September 1970, it came with a price. The school had few African American teachers and administrators, and a majority white student population. Fearing that to protest the situation would mean that the school would once again close, one resident said that, "We all felt like we could not let that happen. So, we sucked it up and went along to get along – right or wrong. Why is it that it is always we, the black folk, who compromise, give in? We only want a small piece. Just a taste. It's you folks who want to eat the whole darn pie."[35]

Based upon the data he collected, Rainone concluded that:

> Once the black Booker neighborhood schools were closed, the white power structure, comprised of administrators, School Board members, teachers, and influential citizens, assumed the management of a reopened Booker Campus, created an array of special programs and set racial quotas, at once integrating the

Booker Campus and alienating, by lack of meaningful black inclusion, the Newtown community. Though significant physical changes that included the removal of barbed wire fences, paving of dirt roads, and the release from Federal Court control were achieved, white control was institutionalized on the Booker Campus. Desegregation effects including busing and the magnet program produced a present-day fractious community, unable to coordinate a unified movement to demand and receive an alternative to the results of years of white rule on the Booker Campus.[36]

## RACIAL QUOTAS AT BOOKER HIGH SCHOOL

According to Rainone's research, when Jan Gibbs was appointed the Principal/Director of Booker High School, succeeding Addison Gilbert, she:

Understood the white power structure had become a mixture of influential white businesspeople or "heavy hitters." It was Gilbert's fear that, if the school was allowed to drift towards a heavy or too-black population, prospective parents and those of children already attending a "special school" and, of course, the School Board, would not be happy … [Gibbs was "charged" to prevent that from happening]. The Newtown community had never heard of the "charge" made to Gibbs [until it was mentioned in interviews conducted for this research], but suspected the Board of engaging in a tactical numbers game. [The community's] concerns and fears of what role the VPA was going to play in the makeup of Booker Campus were ignored. A School Board meeting held on May 1, 1979 established that: "Quotas in the Fine Arts Magnet Program will be maintained in the 20-50% range."[37]

This "charge" still haunts Booker High School today. When it reopened, Booker High School was no longer an all-black, community school. In fact, it was a majority-white school. Rainone confirmed this in his 2003 dissertation, stating that, "Booker High School has a white population of 62% and a black population of 25%."[38]

Principal Dr. Rachel Shelley reports that the school population statistics have changed significantly since that time. In 2015, under [her leadership], the 1,161-student population consisted of approximately 1/3 African American, 1/3 Latino, and 1/3 white students.[39]

## BRIDGES BURNED: THE NEWTOWN COMMUNITY AND BOOKER HIGH SCHOOL

According to Dr. Shelley, there were two actions by former Principal/Director Gibbs that seriously aggravated the fractured relationship between the school and the Newtown community. First, when the old Booker auditorium was demolished and rebuilt, the new structure no longer bore the name of the highly respected, first principal of the school, Roland Rogers. Second, artifacts commemorating the school's history that held great importance to the Newtown community and to alumni were tossed into the rubbish, allegedly with Gibbs' permission. Newtown residents, current students, and alumni were outraged; they were able to salvage some of the precious items from the refuse. It seemed to them that Gibbs wanted to erase all traces of the African American legacy from the Booker Campus, and this caused a huge divide. Alumni who graduated from Booker in the 1950s, 1960s and 1970s no longer wanted to be affiliated with Booker. They felt distraught because "the only thing we had was our school and they created an all-white school."[40]

## REBUILDING THE BRIDGES

Dr. Shelley recognizes that there is still a lot of work to be done toward mending the relationship between the Newtown community and Booker High School. That relationship may never be quite the same. However, she is very conscientious about building bridges between the community, current students and the alumni. That effort paid great dividends when she sponsored an event in October, 2015 that honored former students who would have graduated from Booker High School in 1968 had it not been closed down due to the desegregation order. A *Tempo News* article heralded the return of former Booker High School students. The headline read: "Emotional Welcome Home for BHS Class of 1968." The article described how:

A flood of memories and hugs turned into tears as the group listened to a surprise announcement made by BHS principal Dr. Rachel Shelley. ... Honorary high school diplomas and a proclamation were presented to class members who still hold their purple and gold [school colors] traditions close to the heart. Lifelong friendships with classmates were tested; and the close bonds between their families and teachers who lived in the same neighborhood and worshipped together were torn apart. ... Patricia Byrd-Blake recalled that, "We were split up. Some friends went to Sarasota High and I went to Riverview." Glenda Williams also became a Riverview High student. "I remember getting off the bus and there were stairs where the busses parked. From the upper floor we were spit on," she said. "We were top students in our Booker class but there, the criteria changed. There were things that happened to us that people don't understand," an emotional Williams recalled.[41]

## CHANGES IN EDUCATION IN NEWTOWN

Today, there are more non-traditional educational options for students throughout Sarasota County. These include: Sarasota Military Academy, Suncoast Polytechnic, and Westcoast School. There are also new programs being offered in the traditional school setting. As a part of the Newtown-North Sarasota Redevelopment Project, Booker High School's campus received $60 million in renovations that allowed for new academic programs and educational experiences. These include: Advanced International Certificate in Education (AICE); International Baccalaureate (IB); The Visual Performing Arts (VPA); The Law Academy magnet; The STEM Academy; Leadership Training: JROTC; Advanced Placement; Dual Enrollment; Digital Design, Career and Technical Education; and Business Supervision and Management.

The Booker High School renovation project, completed in 2013, provided employment opportunities for local residents; construction workers from Sarasota, Manatee, Desoto and Charlotte counties completed 70% of the labor.[42]

Booker High School Renovated Campus.

Courtesy: Sarasota County Schools.

In Newtown's early years, most of the graduates of the Booker Schools attended Historically Black Colleges and Universities (HBCUs): Bethune Cookman College (now University), Morehouse College, Edward Waters College and Florida A&M University (FAMU). That was largely due to the limited opportunities for African American students to gain admission to other Florida predominantly white institutions (PWIs). In later years, African American graduates of Booker had opportunities to attend a wide range of universities, both HBCUs and PWIs, including: the University of Chicago; Eckerd College; University of Florida; Bowling Green State University (Ohio); State College of Florida, Manatee-Sarasota (formerly Manatee Community College); Florida State University; University of South Florida; and others.

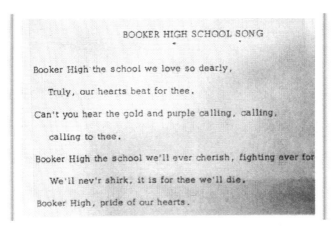

```
                    BOOKER HIGH SCHOOL SONG

Booker High the school we love so dearly,

    Truly, our hearts beat for thee.

Can't you hear the gold and purple calling, calling,

    calling to thee.

Booker High the school we'll ever cherish, fighting ever for

    We'll nev'r shirk, it is for thee we'll die.

Booker High, pride of our hearts.
```

(left) Wilberteen Thomas, mother of Vickie Oldham, was a 1953 Booker High School alumna and a Kentucky State University graduate.
She sang and played the piano at community events.
Courtesy: Vickie Oldham Collection.

## ENDNOTES

[1] Interview with Vickie Oldham. September 4, 2015.

[2] McElroy, Annie M. 1986. *But Your World and My World: The Struggle for Survival, A Partial History of Blacks in Sarasota County 1884-1986*. Black South Press, 48.

[3] *But Your World,* 37.

[4] Interview with Vickie Oldham. August 2015.

[5] Interview with Vickie Oldham, October 26, 2015.

[6] Eckhart, Robert. "Remembering a Newtown that taught character." *Herald-Tribune*. February 21, 2011.

[7] Interview with Vickie Oldham. October 19, 2015.

[8] Interview with Dr. Rosalyn Howard. November 17, 2015.

[9] Interview with Vickie Oldham. August 2015.

[10] Interview by New College student Jessica Wopinski. October 11, 2012.

[11] Eckhart. "Remembering a Newtown that taught character; and interview with Vickie Oldham, August 24, 2015.

[12] Matthews, Janet Snyder. "Booker Earned Degree While Teaching Others." *Black Educator*. Centennial Profile. 1985.

[13] "The Rosenwald Schools: An Impressive Legacy of Black-Jewish Collaboration for Negro Education." http://abhmuseum.org/2012/07/the-rosenwald-schools-an-impressive-legacy-of-black-jewish-collaboration-for-negro-education/

[14] "Booker High School." http://www.digplanet.com/wiki/Booker_High_School_(Sarasota,_Florida)

[15] *But Your World*, 40.

[16] *But Your World*, 117.

[17] *But Your World,* 39-41.

[18] "Booker High School." http://www.sarasotagov.com/LivingInSarasota/Contents/PublicWorks/PublicWorksHistoricBookSchool.html

[19] *But Your World and My World*, 50.

[20] Interview with Vickie Oldham. September 4, 2015.

[21] Russon, Gabrielle. "At Modern New Booker Campus." *Herald-Tribune*. June 29, 2013.

[22] "85% of Black Students Walk Out." *The Herald-Tribune*, May 6, 1969; and Burns, Susan. "The Boycott." *Sarasota*. June 1999.

[23] "Sarasotan students' school boycott stops neighborhood schools from closing, Florida, United States, 1969." http://nvdatabase.swarthmore.edu/content/sarasotan-students-school-boycott-stops-neighborhood-schools-closing-florida-united-states-1

[24] Interview with Kortney Lapeyrolerie. October 10, 2010. http://www.sarasota.wateratlas.usf.edu/oral-history-project/

[25] Interview with Dr. Rosalyn Howard. January 31, 2016.

[26] Interview with Kortney Lapeyrolerie. October 10, 2010.

[27] "The Boycott." Sarasota, 33-34.

[28] Interview with Vickie Oldham. August 24, 2015.

[29] "Green and Carter Inducted Into Riverview Hall of Fame." *Tempo News*. September 3-9, 2015, 1.

[30] William Allan Byrd, Jr., a doctoral student in the College of Education at the University of Miami, was encouraged by the State Department of Education and the South Florida School Desegregation Consulting Center to conduct his dissertation research on the subject of school desegregation in Florida.

[31] Interview with Vickie Oldham. August 2015.

[32] Personal correspondence. January 22, 2016.

[33] Community based organizations (CBOs) are nonprofit groups that work at a local level to improve life for residents. The focus is to build equality across society in all streams - health care, environment, quality of education, access to technology, access to spaces and information for the disabled, to name but a few. The inference is that the communities represented by the CBOs are typically at a disadvantage. CBOs are typically, and almost necessarily, staffed by local members - community members who experience first hand the needs within their neighborhoods.
http://eder671nonprofit.pbworks.com/w/page/18541471/CBOs%20-%20Introduction

[34] *But Your World*, 154-155.

[35] Rainone, Donald F. *The Role of the Sarasota Visual Performing Arts (VPA) Magnet in Desegregation and Resegregation of Booker Neighborhood Schools*, Diss. University of South Florida. Tampa, FL. 2003, 220.

[36] The Role of the Sarasota Visual Performing Arts (VPA) Magnet, iii-iv.

[37] The Role of the Sarasota Visual Performing Arts (VPA) Magnet, 222.

[38] The Role of the Sarasota Visual Performing Arts (VPA) Magnet.

[39] Telephone conversation with Dr. Howard February 4, 2016.

[40] Telephone interview with Dr. Rosalyn Howard, February 4, 2016.

[41] Oldham, Vickie. *Tempo News*. Vol. 28, No. 42 Oct 15-21, 2015.

[42] Newtown-North Sarasota Redevelopment Project Report. April 2014.

# CHAPTER 7: SEGREGATION, DESEGREGATION AND INTEGRATION

In Sarasota, as well as many other parts of the South, there were spoken and unspoken rules about African Americans' behavior in the presence of white people: no direct eye contact; what stores one could shop in; stepping off the sidewalk and into the street when a white person approached; and where the boundaries were around the African American community that should not be crossed. "Back then, in the days of segregation, black residents risked trouble almost any time they stepped outside the Newtown community. There were rules against walking downtown after dark, using certain water fountains, or trying on shoes in a Main Street shop."[1] According to Jeff LaHurd, "The Roaring '20s were among the hardest times for Sarasota's African American community. The Ku Klux Klan was often a visible presence here, with cross burnings and other forms of intimidation, both physical and psychological. Sarasota's branch of the Knights of the Ku Klux Klan, the Invisible Empire, was Klan Number 72." [2]

In her Honors Program thesis for the University of South Florida, St. Petersburg, titled, *A Bare Bones History: Lynching in Manatee County*, Hailey Erin Praught revealed details of lynching and other violence against African Americans that occurred before "The Roaring '20s" hard times that LaHurd mentioned above. In a voice at times filled with indignation that this part of her history had been hidden from her, she addressed the secrecy and silence surrounding these horrific events. Sarasota was part of Manatee County until 1921 and, therefore, was also implicated in the vicious and inhumane activities. Praught's thesis revealed that:

> Between 1890 and 1920, lynch mobs in Florida killed at least 161 black victims. According to Michael Newton, author of *The Invisible Empire: The Ku Klux Klan in Florida*, "The number of blacks lynched in Florida lagged behind the body counts for neighboring states, but Florida's smaller population made it the per capita leader in a national "lynching bee." Florida's total number of lynchings, 282 people, fell behind Alabama, Arkansas, Georgia, Louisiana, Mississippi, and Texas. But when the total number of black lynchings, 257, is compared with the black/white population for those years, Florida comes out ahead. This indicates a penchant for violence toward blacks.[3]

Praught documented the lynching of eight African American men in Manatee County. Six, murdered in 1896, were never identified. Two other men were identified as Henry Thomas and Willie English. Henry Thomas was lynched on March 8, 1903:

> For the accused assault of Ms. Porter Keen. … Rape or alleged sexual assault were the most common arguments for the need of lynching and lynch mobs — to keep uncontrolled, sexual brutes away from delicate, virginal white women. In reality, only thirty percent of blacks lynched in the South were lynched for that reason. The other sixty percent of lynching occurred for any number of reasons.[4]

Willie English, murdered on July 1, 1912, was the final lynching victim that Praught discovered evidence of in the *Manatee River Journal* article, "Mob Lynch Negro Last Monday Night."[5]

> "Willie" English, as he is affectionately called, was put in jail after being accused of assault with attempt to rape a white woman. … Sheriff Young, sleeping at the county jail to protect English, was stormed by a mob, during which "there was much reckless and dangerous shooting of pistols." [6]

Praught quoted and agreed with Sherrilyn Ifill, a law professor and President and Director-Counsel of the NAACP Legal Defense Fund, when Ifill argued that we need to talk about the past in order to make those memories public and overt so that communities can respond to them honestly.[7] According to Ifill, "The project of reconciliation and reparation for lynching is urgently needed. … The after effects of lynching continue to shape and mold the communities where these acts occurred."[8]

Rev. Earl Vencent Samuel Black Sr. was raised at the Bee Ridge Turpentine Camp. As dangerous as it was to work in the camp, he recalled, there could be even more danger lurking in everyday social settings. His mother always warned him to, "Stay in your color, stay in your place." Just looking at a white woman in 1926, when he first came to Sarasota, could be deadly. "A black man couldn't even look at a white lady. I'm telling the truth," Rev. Black said.[9]

Another example of intimidation tactics used against African Americans was an incident on the Seaboard Air Line Railway's Turpentine Track:

> Around 1924 ... one day a Negro man got on the train at Manatee and rode to a station about half way down the line. Next day, when the train stopped at that point, the Negro was awaiting the conductor and told [him] that he had been short-changed the previous day. When his language became rough and threatening, the conductor asked him to step into the coach. Inside the vehicle, the conductor quickly reached for a small revolver, cracked the Negro over the head with the instrument, and discharged a bullet into the ceiling of the coach. The Negro, terrified, blurted, "Yes Sir, you did give the right change.[10]

**Rev. Jerome Dupree** and other interviewees who discussed what life was like during segregation, stated that the rules for residents of Newtown resembled the "Pass Laws" of South Africa during the apartheid era.[11] Dupree recalled that:

> After seven o'clock, people from the Newtown community and the Overtown community were not allowed to be on the south side — go across, go past 3rd Street, which is Fruitville Road — at night. And if you did go south of Fruitville Road at night, you had to have some kind of credentials showing that you were supposed to be in that area during that time. And the police were always stationed at Five Points there ... and they could see whether or not you were going. So when we started working at the bowling alleys — we set up pins at the bowling alley before they got the automatic set-up — we had to go to the little police station. It might have been half as big as this room here, but we went to the little police station that was on State Street. It was right next to a hardware store known as Adams and Houser Hardware Store. But we had to go there and get a permit.[12]

**Carolyn Mason** agreed:

> There was definitely a dividing line. And for me, I call it the Mason-Dixon line, and it was Fruitville Road. It was 3rd Street. That was the dividing line. Because north of Fruitville or 3rd Street, was the black community, and south was downtown, the more affluent community. And there were places downtown that I could not go in because of the color of my skin.

Not until sometime in the '60s ... sometime before 1964 that we were able to go into the theatres downtown. ... I distinctly remember 'colored' and 'white' bathrooms in the train station, on Lemon Avenue, or in the Five and Dime Store, both of them on Main Street. And there were two theatres on Main Street that we couldn't go in, because of the color of our skin. We had a theatre, a black theatre, on 5th Street, just east of Central Avenue. ... I remember: riding at the back of the bus because I had to [on] the public transportation, not being able to go to Lido Beach, and having to go to Caspersen Beach, which was located in South County, just a little south of Venice.[13]

Several interviewees expressed how their parents shielded them from the worst of the discrimination and racist acts of violence. They did not feel oppressed in their childhood and were allowed to be just children, playing games and living without that constant awareness that someone would treat you unfairly because of your skin color. Of course, that feeling was made possible in part by the sheltered atmosphere that Newtown, a self-reliant African American community, provided; they had very limited contact with whites.

However, the reality of racism was quite apparent for the adults. Therefore, they established businesses that were necessary to meet the community's needs. In Newtown, residents appeared to blend Booker T. Washington's and W.E.B. Du Bois' approaches for improvement in their lives. First, education was stressed and was provided at an early age, initially in private homes. Later, education was provided in a more formal, if not traditional, school environment, an effort led by teacher and principal Emma E. Booker. Sending their children to college was a goal for many families, but attending vocational and technical schools to gain specific skills — which sometimes led to establishing their own businesses or having a profession, such as nursing — was seen as a valuable alternative to college.

The number of businesses in Newtown grew dramatically as more people moved there. That certainly followed Washington's philosophy of self-reliance and separation. But the residents of Newtown also strongly agitated for their full civil rights, including demands for better schools and for political representation. **Walter Gilbert III** states that his motivation for becoming more involved in the civil rights movement was:

Mr. Neil Humphrey, he owned the drugstore. It was a little sundry store that sold some of everything, patent medicines, not a pharmacy type drug store. He had the only business like that in our community. He was telling us how we'd go down there, what we'd say, how we were to act. He wasn't having no troubles. I'm looking at all the other people saying, "Yes sir, Mr. Humphrey." It changed my perspective. His persona changed right in my face. I wanted to be like this guy, not only business-wise, I wanted to be a leader like him.

Neil Humphrey, Sr.
Courtesy: Humphrey Family Collection.

## ACCESS TO KNOWLEDGE: THE LIBRARY

Librarian Betty Johnson.
Courtesy: *The Bulletin*.

Libraries are essential to expanding the horizons of children and adults alike. The Newtown community had no access to a public library, due to segregation, until the year 1957. That was the year that a remarkable incident involving **Dr. Ed James II** occurred. As he recalled:

If a black person wanted to get a book from the library you had to go to the Newtown Community Center to the town "Rec" center. Well, someone from the Newtown community center will call the library and say, "We have a student at the high school or just a citizen who wants a book on water conservation." So somebody from the library would take two or three books that they thought might answer what they were looking for and send it out three or four, five or six, seven, eight — whenever the next trip was — days later to the Rec. Well that changed. I'm happy to say I was part of that change. During the Christmas of 1957, during winter break from Florida A&M University, I came home ... Roosevelt Ball, A.W. Ball, Ralph Honor and myself, we went down ... to the library. And we walked in.

There was a counter just beyond the front door ... the librarian came out and said, "Can I help you?" I said, "Yes, we are going to check out some books." [I] proudly said, "We are college students. We need to do some research over the holidays." She said, "Have you tried the Newtown library? The Newtown Community Center, the library there?" I said, "That's not a library that's a joke." ... I said, "It is our plan to check out some books today and ma'am, you should call whoever you need to call so that that can happen."

She was talking to the city manager at that time, Ken Thompson. She handed the phone to me and said, "Mr. Thompson wants to talk to you," and so I said, "Hello?" He said, "Hi, I'm Ken Thompson. Who am I talking to?" I said, "I'm Ed James." He said, "Do I know you?" I say, "No, no, Mr. Thompson I don't think so and I don't know you." He said, "Well, I'm the city manager. I understand you want to check out some books from the library. I said "yes." "And I understand that you didn't go to the Newtown library," he said. I said, "There is no Newtown library. You mean those two shelves of old magazines and books with torn pages in the community center?" He said, "Do your parents know that you were there?" I said no. "What would they say if they knew you were there demanding service?" I said, "They would probably say it's about time."

He said, "Well, would you come down and talk to me? I'm at City Hall. ... I said, "OK I'll be right there." ... And that day I met Ken Thompson. I sat down and talked with him and he said ... "OK, go back to the library and get your books now." And I guess he told her it was okay if we went back. So I thought, "Now I get to legitimately check out a book." And she gave me the equivalent of a card and I told her what I was looking for. I don't even remember what it is at this point. And she went back in and helped me find it. ... And that's how the library system became integrated.[14]

Dr. Ed James II's remarkable story was history making in many respects. Thanks to his courageous actions, Newtown residents had library borrowing privileges yet still required a car, which many of them did not own, to transport them there. Librarian Betty Johnson came up with a creative solution. She started a "library in a van" to improve outreach efforts to the community. **Johnson** tells her story below:

I worked at that time what they call 'split-shift' [at the library] ... I noticed the blacks were not using the library. And that's mostly because we were not welcomed ... The library was not open to black people in those days ... It was just the attitude of the people that worked in the library. The way they treat you when you came into [it]. You knew that you were not welcome. What can I do to get more blacks to come and use the library?

So during this time, the Library Construction Act — a state project coming out of Tallahassee, the state library — had grants going for library services to what they were calling at that time 'disadvantaged' [areas]. ... The grant was to establish a library or to show the feasibility, the need for a library in the community where that grant was being used. And so the outreach program ... started; there were five stops. ... The stops were: Newtown Recreation Center, Robert Taylor; we had a stop at Orange Avenue Projects; we had a stop at Project Lane; and we had a stop at Laurel. ... That van was equipped with books on moveable carts. So the kids could come in, select their books and take them home or they could sit at the stop and read the books ... [in] a building.

So even the idea of the library, they did get to used it and ... we did outdoor movies here in this area. So this was a way of introducing this community to library services. And this is what the outreach was all about, introducing the community to library services.

The most exciting thing ... is the Cultural Center here [at the North Sarasota Library]. That is very exciting because, as I told people, I never intended it to be ... a black library, but a library with a collection of black history that everybody could use, that everybody could benefit from. ... So this is more or less what it is with that special collection here of black history and that's great.[15]

# CIVIL RIGHTS ERA: DESEGREGATING PUBLIC SPACES

The period after World War II was the beginning of the fight for the civil rights of every American, particularly those left out of the typical definition of "American citizen"– African Americans.

World War II saw an end to tolerance of racism in Newtown and the surfacing of years of quiet anger. The African-American community felt as a whole that, because African-Americans had fought and died for the country, they deserved equal treatment. Throughout the 1950s, this emerging anger became the impetus for change across the country, including Sarasota.[16]

## RESTAURANTS, CLOTHING STORES

### Dr. Fannie McDugle:

I was one of the members of [the NAACP]. ... Mr. Rivers ... was our NAACP president. ... And we had a organization ... civil rights organization. ... When we got the members together we started at Morrison Cafeteria because that's where Blacks couldn't go and we would all just get together like 25 or 30 [of us]. They get scared when we walk in there. ... And they'd just look at you. ... And we would just sit down and look at them. And the waitress was scared to come over to the table, I guess, to take our order. So, they standing there looking at us and we sitting at the table looking at them. So we did it for a whole week. ... Every day, every day. It was eleven o'clock when we went down on our lunch; that was lunchtime. And then five o'clock, that was from five to nine; that was dinnertime. ... Morrison's Cafeteria and ... Woolworth. ... We would all sit, take up all the space, all the stools. ... And then the manager would come out and look at us and be scared to say something because [of] the NAACP. They knew we were strong and you have to be careful. So they would go back.

We did it for a whole week. ... We wasn't served, but we would sit up and keep the other people from coming in. And they would cook up the food and ... nobody come in and buy it. They didn't serve us and we wouldn't let nobody come in. We integrated the restaurants and we integrated the clothing stores like J.C. Penney's, and there was a expensive store there on Main Street. During my time, we integrated [the beaches] too. They had one in between Sarasota and Bradenton Beach. ... We integrated Siesta Key too. ... It felt good to us because we were doing something that was right. ... Opened the door for YOUR generation, that's right.

## THE BEACHES

A *Herald-Tribune* article, written in celebration of Newtown's 2014 centennial reported that:

> Newtown had no beaches. Only nine miles away, others enjoyed the best beach in America, as Siesta Key has sometimes been called. The white sands of Lido were even closer. But for the kids growing up in Newtown 60 years ago, those pretty places were off-limits. Black people weren't allowed on the beach. There were no signs posted, and no such laws on the books. It was simply "understood," say people who remember those times. Rising calls for desegregation were met with resistance from white residents and hand wringing among local officials.
>
> On Oct. 3, 1955, about 100 black residents challenged the old order by piling into cars, driving to Lido and wading in the water. The simple act drew the attention of authorities and opened up an early front in the fight for civil rights here, years before the better-known victories of the 1960s.
>
> "It was a time of challenges," said **Ed James II**, a community activist who was involved in the caravans as a high school student. "They didn't want to do anything to hurt the tourist trade. But that didn't mean they weren't malicious and ironclad in what they would do, like other Southern towns." When black swimmers broke the unwritten rules at Lido Beach, they made front-page news. Some whites were outraged. Police came out to monitor the scene, sometimes interfering with the visitors and sometimes defending them. The papers of the time called it a civic crisis, and described Sarasota as a "powder keg."[17]

**John Rivers (Former president of the Sarasota branch of the NAACP)** remembered that:

> Well, everything was segregated at that time. And the beach was one of the top [places]. ... When we first started going to the beach, it was in Venice because we weren't allowed to go here in Sarasota. And going to the beaches in Venice, we had no problem at all. ... But...it's eighteen, twenty miles from here down there. And that was a long distance, unnecessary long distance. And we took issue with that. And after going there for a while, we then started to going to Lido Beach. And ... we had some problems. The reporters came, and they identified the cars, took pictures of the cars ... the tag number and all of that stuff. And from the tag

numbers, the system could pick up the names of the people. And some of the people were fired just because they went to the beach ... there. But we didn't stop at that time. We went into the water the first time.

And then the next day, they cancelled out everything, closed the beach on us. And, at that time ... I was leading the group. So, we ... left Lido ... headed back into town on the second day that we were there. Then, I decided, I said ... "Let's go back." And we turned around and went back. And, sure enough, the beach was full of people. And the policemen came back, and say, "Oh, the beach is closing again." I said, "No, no, you go on to town. If we need you, we will call you. But other than that, we don't need you."

But, by that time ... with the photos that the reporters had taken ... some of the people in the city ... identified the people that was at the beach ... their cars. And some of them was fired the next day because they was at the beach. And the remainder of us continued to go every week until it was a simple thing.[18]

In the effort to keep African Americans from going to the beaches in 1957, county officials agreed to build them a swimming pool in Newtown. Some residents were not happy with that solution, but they agreed to allow the pool to be built. Unknown to the elected officials, however, they planned to continue their beach access protests. "The day [the new pool] opened, another beach caravan set out for Lido Key."[19] As Rivers recalled:

We got that one [Lido] under control. So, we wanted to go Siesta. ... And that was a ... nicer beach. And we only had one incident. Some guy came up there with a pickup truck. ... He got out of the truck, got the bottles, and he put them under each one of the cars that we was there, that was ours. ... And I was out in the water at that time. And someone called out to me to "come, come, hurry." So, when I came out, he was still putting his bottles under the tires of the cars. And I walked right up to him and, just nearly nose-to-nose, and I said, "Look, I want you to get every bottle you had out there. ... I want them out. And I want it out now." So, he looked over and none of his people were there to support him. So, he started pulling the bottles out from under the cars. And that was a victory.

It was NAACP president Neil Humphrey [Sr.] who organized the caravans. Humphrey, a successful Newtown businessman, possessed the necessary financial independence to challenge the establishment. [20]

One of the white objectors to the African American beach-goers happened to be a man who conducted business with the residents of Newtown. According to Rivers:

> There [were] some people that didn't like what was going on [at the beach], and one was insurance [agent]. But he was collecting the insurance fees throughout the black neighborhood. So, when he disagreed with that and kind of acted up, I called his headquarters the next day and told them, "We don't want him back in our neighborhood … collecting money. …" So, sure enough, they transferred him out of here, and we didn't see him no more. [21]

## EVOLUTION OF THE SARASOTA ARTS SCENE

Artistic expression has always been a vibrant part of African American culture. In Sarasota there were limited outlets for that expression for African Americans, except in school and church plays and programs. The Heritage Players: The Black Theater Company of Florida was formed and active in Sarasota during the 1980s, with Fredd Atkins as its president.

Anthony "Tony" Major grew up in Newtown and graduated from Booker High School in 1957. He is an accomplished professional actor of stage and screen, filmmaker, producer and director. He directed the film 'Super Spook,' "the first black comedy film made during that whole '70s Blaxploitation period." According to Major, "That [film] got distributed nationally and internationally. …. And now, finally, it's on DVD and people can purchase it online." [22]

After attending college in New York City, earning a Bachelor of Arts degree in theatre arts and a Master of Fine Arts degree, he had the opportunity to meet and work professionally with many famous and award winning actors, directors and producers, including Academy Award winners Harry Belafonte, Bob Mulligan, and Alan Pakula. Major was also the Assistant Producer on "The Redd Foxx Show."

Major returned to Sarasota for two years to direct the Theater Workshop run by the Union of Concerned Parents organization from 1979-1981. The rehearsal hall at Booker Visual Performing Arts School is named "Anthony 'Tony' Major Rehearsal Hall" in his honor.

Early in his career, Tony taught at NYU Graduate Film School. He currently teaches and is the director of both the Zora Neale Hurston Institute for Documentary Studies and the Africana Studies Program at the University of Central Florida in Orlando, Florida.

The Westcoast Black Theater Troupe (WBTT) "was founded in 1999 in Sarasota, Florida, by actor, singer, director, and playwright Nate Jacobs. It is the only professional black theatre company on Florida's west coast," according to its website. [23] Etienne Porter, from Newtown, got involved with WBTT through his connections with Nate Jacobs who was his former high school Art teacher. Jacobs and gave Porter, at age 16, his first opportunity to play drums in a professional production.

The Sarasota theater scene is evolving. Jay Handelman, theater and television critic for the *Herald-Tribune*, wrote that:

> The mostly white theater scene that prompted Nate Jacobs to seek more diverse offerings in the late 1980s has changed a lot since he launched the Westcoast Black Theatre Troupe 15 years ago. ... Area theaters have diversified their offerings to attract a broader demographic and tell a wider variety of stories. [24]

## ENVIRONMENTAL RACISM IN NEWTOWN

During their interview with Vickie Oldham, Elder Willie Mays Jr. and his sister Rosa Lee Thomas discussed the hazardous conditions in which they, and many others in the Newtown area, lived while growing up. At the time that their family moved to the area, it was essentially overgrown land. **Elder Mays and Rosa Thomas** recalled that:

> *(E. Mays):* The city dump was right 'cross the railroad. The street right next to the railroad tracks. ... Very close to the African-American community. The smoke ... it bothered us for years. But we stayed in the house most of the time to escape that.
> *(R.L. Thomas):* The city dump ... it was in Newtown, between the railroad tracks. And all of the people that lived on Mango Avenue, most of them died. ... I have names of all of the people that passed away, husbands and wives.
> *(V. Oldham): Do you think it was as a result of the fumes?*
> *(R.L. Thomas):* Oh yeah. ... Because we lived quite close to the railroad track. It's called now Humphrey's subdivision. So we inhaled it. We'd walk past there as kids. We went to Booker High School. You could smell the fumes and see all the birds flying. But they did a lot of burying things underground so that ground I believe even now is very contaminated.

Rosa Lee Thomas' conclusions about the hazardous health effects for people living near the dump are confirmed by scientific data reported in the City of Sarasota Newtown Community Redevelopment Area Plan.

It states that in 2004, the City of Sarasota designated the site of the former city dump area as a 'brownfield.' The site is now called Marian Anderson Place. The Environmental Protection Agency (EPA) defines a brownfield as: "real property, the expansion, redevelopment, or reuse of which may be complicated by the presence or potential presence of a hazardous substance, pollutant, or contaminant."[25]

During attempts to develop the site, preliminary environmental testing indicated the presence of potentially harmful contaminants. To determine the extent of the contamination, the city received several assessment and pilot grants from the State of Florida and Federal Departments of Environmental Protection to collect and test soil and water samples from the site. Analysis of the samples indicated contaminants were present at the site at concentrations exceeding the Florida Administrative Code, Chapter 62-777 Contaminant Cleanup Target Levels. The determination was made that adverse environmental conditions existed within the site based on the documented level of contamination on the site and would require monitoring and remediation in accordance with Florida Department of Environmental Protection (FDEP) guidelines.[26]

A 2016 *Weekly Brief* from Sarasota City Manager Tom Barwin stated that, "the Marian Anderson site is now officially clean and no longer designated as a brownfield. We're referring to it as a 'success in the making' because there's more work to do. We're in the process of considering how the 14 acre parcel should be redeveloped."[27]

According to a January 2017 *Herald-Tribune* article, the area is still being decontaminated.

> Declared contaminated after an unauthorized landfill was set there in the 1960s, the site has long languished with little economic activity despite many efforts over the years. ... The 13-acre site along Dr. Martin Luther King Way should be redeveloped for local businesses with a private company, city administrators have suggested.
>
> The Florida Department of Environmental Protection issued a site rehabilitation completion order in 2014 for cleanup efforts on the property, and the city has until the end of this year to use the remaining $432,000 of a county grant made available for the rehabilitation.[28]

Retail stores and restaurants topped the list of most wanted [occupancies], especially a retail plaza that could offer healthy, affordable foods for low-income residents and potentially new employment opportunities, according to surveys submitted to the city. Upgraded "class act" restaurants, soul food spots and small coffee shops could also attract a younger clientele or more families to stay in the area instead of leaving the area to shop and eat, some suggested. Office space for small local businesses and the potential to build affordable housing also topped the potential priorities.[29]

## THE "DOWNSIDE" OF INTEGRATION

Despite positive changes that emerged from desegregation, there are some persons who believe that integration led to serious negative outcomes. Two of the interviewees presented their individual issues with integration. **Anthony "Tony" Major** shares his views about integration:

> There were no white folks owning anything in Newtown. Not at that time. It was all black owned. That's why I say that integration was one of the worst things that ever happened to us. Because we didn't integrate, we assimilated.[30]

Historian **James Brown** states that the Newtown community began to change when he was coming out of Booker High School [in 1957] – the community took a shift in the historical pattern. He associates that with integration:

> I understand the whole concept of integration, but when it came to our community, we lost a lot of stuff. Money went out of the community, businesses were boarded up. I understood the concept, but I don't think [the people of Newtown] were ready for integration. We are still trying to recover from it in 2015.[31]

---

## ENDNOTES

[1] Cummings, Ian. "Caravans to Lido broke beach barrier." *Herald-Tribune*. July 13, 2014.
http://newtown100.heraldtribune.com/2014/07/13/making-lido-beach/
[2] LaHurd, Jeff. *Sarasota: A History*, Chapter XI. 2006. Arcadia Publishing.
[3] Praught, Hailey Erin. *A Bare Bones History: Lynching in Manatee County*. Honors Program thesis. University of South Florida, St. Petersburg. August 5, 2009, p.14; and Newton, Michael. *The Invisible Empire: The Ku Klux Klan in Florida*. Gainesville: University Press of Florida, 2001, 33.
[4] *A Bare Bones History*, 22. (Ref. Manatee River Journal. 7 July 1912, 3.)
[5] "Mob Lynch Negro Last Monday Night." Manatee River Journal. 7 July 1912, 3.
[6] "Mob Lynch Negro Last Monday Night."

[7] *A Bare Bones History*, 45-46; Ifill, Sherrilyn. *On the Courthouse Lawn: Confronting the Legacy of Lynching in the Twenty-First Century*. Boston: Beacon Press, 2007, p.iv.

[8] *On the Courthouse Lawn*. p.xv.

[9] Lopez, Yadira. "Newtown Reverend turns 100." http://newtown100.heraldtribune.com/2015/09/01/newtown-reverend-turns-100/

[10] Sulzer, Elmer G. *Ghost railroads of Sarasota County: An account of the abandoned lines of the county and city*. The Turpentine Track: Manatee to Arcadia. Sarasota County Historical Commission, Sarasota County Historical Society. 1971, 11.

[11] "In 1866 [South Africa], a 'Pass Law' was instituted. Any Black person found outside the allowed residential area without a Pass from an employer, a magistrate, missionary, field cornet or principal chief could be arrested. Pass laws in the Transvaal, or South African Republic, were intended to force Black people to settle in specific places in order to provide White farmers with a steady source of labour." "Pass Laws in South Africa 1800-1994." http://www.sahistory.org.za/south-africa-1806-1899/pass-laws-south-africa-1800-1994

[12] Interview with Jessica Wopinski (New College). October 11, 2012.

[13] Interview with Hope Black, September 22, 2015.

[14] Interview with Haley Jordan, New College student. October 2015.

[15] Johnson, B.J. 2013. "The Village as I Knew It: 1950-." Unpublished Essay.

[16] "History of the Newtown Community." http://www.sarasotagov.com/Newtown/history.html

[17] "Caravans to Lido."

[18] Interview with Kortney Lapeyrolerie. (New College), October 29, 2010.

[19] "Caravans to Lido."

[20] Interview with Kortney Lapeyrolerie. (New College), October 29, 2010.

[21] Interview with Kortney Lapeyrolerie. (New College), October 29, 2010.

[22] Interview with Dr. Rosalyn Howard. December 20, 2015.

[23] http://westcoastblacktheatre.org

[24] Handelman, Jay. "A More Colorful Sarasota Theater Scene." http://newtown100.heraldtribune.com/2014/11/14/colorful-sarasota-theater-scene/

[25] "What is a Brownfield?" http://brownfieldaction.org/brownfieldaction/brownfield_basics

[26] Source: Florida Administrative Code (Ch 62-777), PSI, Inc. Site Assessment Report, and Florida Brownfields Redevelopment Act (Sections 376.77 – 376.84, Florida Statutes, Brownfield Designation Staff Report.

[27] "Briefs from Barwin." May 27, 2016.

[28] Murdock, Zach. "City to seek help redeveloping Marian Anderson Place." *Herald-Tribune*. January 1, 2017.

[29] "City to seek help redeveloping Marian Anderson Place."

[30] Interview with Dr. Rosalyn Howard. December 20, 2015.

[31] Interview with Dr. Rosalyn Howard. January 31, 2016.

# CHAPTER 8: POLITICS

## VOTING RIGHTS

Historically, African Americans in many communities across the US have been disenfranchised, unable to vote because of various policies and procedures put into operation by state officials with the intent to deny African Americans their rights under the 15th and 19th Amendments to the US Constitution. The 15th Amendment gave male US citizens the right to vote in 1870.[1] Not until 1920 did the 19th Amendment extend voting rights to female US citizens. Despite the fact that these amendments were intended to extend the right to vote to all citizens, many African American men and women had to meet unfair, additional qualifications in order to vote. They were subjected also to threats and outright physical violence when they tried to exercise their right to vote. This remained commonplace particularly in the South. Then, they were required to pass various kinds of "tests" before they could register to vote, such as correctly guessing the number of bubbles on a bar of soap, taking reading and writing quizzes, or paying a fee (poll tax).

Upon returning from fighting in World War II, Medgar Evers, who became a famous civil rights activist and martyr:

> Decided to vote in a Mississippi election. But when he and some other black ex-servicemen attempted to vote, a white mob stopped them. "All we wanted to be was ordinary citizens," Evers later related. "We fought during the war for America, Mississippi included. Now, after the Germans and Japanese hadn't killed us, it looked as though the white Mississippians would."[2]

It is still quite difficult to believe that in 2014, the US Supreme Court practically wiped out the progress achieved for equal voting rights over the past 50 years. In a partisan vote, the US Supreme Court ruled 5-4 to strike down Section 4 of the Voting Rights Act, a key part of the Act that monitored the actions of states with a history of denying voting rights to African American citizens.

## A TIME FOR CHANGE

Newtown has a proud history of overcoming obstacles. In the early years, most of its African American settlers were primarily concerned with basic survival. They had moved to Overtown and to Newtown seeking jobs, finding ways to support themselves and their families. It was not until some of those basic survival needs were met, and the Civil Rights Movement of the 1950s gave them powerful inspiration, that the Newtown community began to agitate for better political representation of their community in the City and County government of Sarasota.

Despite having no official titles or being elected, it is clear from the oral histories of residents that there were some highly intelligent and skilled "politicians" in Newtown. They were steadfast in advocating for just causes without fear or apology, whether it concerned equitable pay for teachers, getting a janitor in the schools,[3] or equal access to public places. Other examples include actions taken to provide the services (businesses, schools, transportation) that they needed. But in order to achieve greater progress, they needed to have a presence in the actual governing bodies of the city and county. Most of the white elected government officials felt no obligation toward them and ignored the inequitable circumstances of African Americans in Sarasota.[4]

## LEGAL CHALLENGE TO AN UNFAIR ELECTORAL PROCESS

For many years, African Americans did not have the right to vote in Sarasota. When they were extended that right, their votes had little impact because of the unfair structure of the electoral system. The system was an effective technique used by the white power structure to deny equal representation to African Americans and, therefore, access to ways to advocate for their community. Finally, Newtown citizens and the NAACP took legal action. Why was this legal action taken? **Dr. Ed James II** explained that:

> At the time of the filing of the lawsuit in 1979…five different black folk had run nine times…for City Commission and could never get elected… [In] our lawsuit, "James versus Sarasota," we were asking for five single-member districts. And we had asked the city for that so that they could do it themselves, but [they] never would. And this case rolled on for seven years. When we finally got to the point of having our day in court and the judge was setting a hearing, the city wanted to file what they called an affirmative defense. [In it] they admit that the election system is flawed, but they could correct it and we said, "No, we want our day in court.
>
> And we had our day in court. And the judge in his infinite wisdom decided we didn't need five single-member districts, but three single-member districts with one a majority-minority district, and we should be able to elect a commissioner: three single-

member districts and two at-large. ... Fredd Atkins ... won the election and became our first black elected city official. ...He was our unity candidate. ... He served several terms as Mayor and City Commissioner. ... Since that time, District One has always been represented by a black person.

Some folk will come ... here, and they'll see a black commissioner or a black mayor and think that's the way it's always been. No. There was nothing without a fight. And we had to even threaten the city's Federal Revenue Sharing Funds to get blacks in the fire department.[5]

Dr. Ed James II and other Newtown community activists demonstrated in the 1980s and 1990s the power that can be generated by forming a unified voting block within the community. This became a winning strategy. Following is a list of Sarasota's African American elected officials:

**Fredd Atkins**  Elected first African American City Commissioner and mayor, 1985. Three-time Sarasota mayor, 1987-1988,       1991-1992, and 2006-2007.

**Delores Dry**  Elected first African American female  City Commissioner, April 1995 until her death in January 1996. Rev. Jerome Dupree completed Dry's term.

**Rev. Jerome Dupree**  Elected City Commissioner; Sarasota mayor, 1998-99.

**Carolyn Mason**  Elected City Commissioner, 1999-2003; Sarasota mayor, 2001-2003; Sarasota Board of County Commissioners,       2008-2015.

**Willie Charles Shaw**  Elected City Commissioner, 2011; Sarasota mayor, 2014-2015, 2016.

**Shelli Freeland Eddie**  Elected District 3 City Commissioner, 2015; Sarasota Vice-Mayor, 2016.

**Rev. Willie Charles Shaw** is a successful politician, born and reared in Newtown. "I am Commissioner of District One, the City of Sarasota, and I'm presently the Mayor of the City of Sarasota," he said, introducing himself during his interview. Mayor Shaw indicated that the

Newtown unity, which was evident in the 1980s, is not so apparent today:

> I think that quite frequently we become distracted. … And our priorities are very difficult to set because we have not yet as a community learned how to work together. … Hopefully one of my visions is to work … across the aisle or working with others to bring about a greater understanding. Some of our arguments are very, very frivolous and I want to see the landscape change. … I want to see the benefits of a true CRA [Community Redevelopment Area] effort within this portion of the community.[6]

## THE NAACP

The National Association for the Advancement of Colored People (NAACP) had a turbulent beginning in Florida. Florida formed nine branches of the NAACP from 1939 to 1940. During the 1950s, the process of building more local branches began. The Florida State Legislature initiated actions against the NAACP and its growth in the state following the US Supreme Court desegregation ruling in 1954, Brown v Board of Education. The State Conference of the NAACP was ordered by the state of Florida to disclose the membership names.[7] However, in 1958, the US Supreme Court denied states access to the membership lists.

The NAACP has been a powerful force in the Newtown community. Its local chapter, formed in 1952, was heavily involved in the 1979 lawsuit that concluded in 1985 with a ruling requiring the creation of a redistricting plan that paved the way for the election of African American political representation in Sarasota. Before that, the NAACP led the battle to desegregate Sarasota's beaches and restaurants. During that time, the NAACP president was Neil Humphrey Sr., an independent businessman who showed no reluctance in challenging the white establishment in Sarasota. Humphrey's Sundries was a well-established business in Newtown and he had no fear of intimidation, for example, by the threat of being fired by an employer, as others did.[8] Dr. Ed James II described Humphrey as "a little man in stature, but a very, very fiery, God-fearing, kind person." Dr. James believes that, "Mrs. Prevell Barber is the only person who's alive today who was a member of the chartering branch of the NAACP in Sarasota County."[9]

John Rivers was an assistant to Neil Humphrey Sr. during the time of the beach desegregation efforts. When Rivers died in December 2014, civil rights activists in Newtown recounted his many triumphs, calling him one of the most important leaders of their generation. "He was one of the community's original freedom fighters," Dr. Ed James II said. "He helped the black community, but also he helped make the white community better." [10] The Sarasota County NAACP honored Rivers with its Humanitarian Award, shortly before his death.

When he moved to Sarasota in 1951, Rivers noted that it was far behind the times as far as desegregating its public spaces; Jim Crow still ruled and African Americans were underrepresented in positions of influence in Sarasota. During an interview, Rivers stated that:

> I came here directly from Mobile, Alabama, which is a larger city than most other cities. And I was concerned once I came here, because we were so far behind in Sarasota. We came here, and ... no minorities in any positions. No policemen ... nothing but schoolteachers ... in segregated schools. So, this was a very different thing than we were accustomed to.[11]

Rivers set out to change that, embarking on a career of activism that reshaped Sarasota from City Hall to the sands of Lido Beach. Before he was finished, he had become a revered figure in Sarasota history. Among all the Newtown leaders of the turbulent 1960s, Rivers is remembered as a kind man who also could be tough. Dr. Ed James II, another Newtown activist involved in the 1985 case, recalled how Rivers faced down threats of violence in person at times, and took his share of late-night phone calls from anonymous enemies. And, as Rivers told a historian years later, he wasn't afraid to pull aside a sheriff's deputy at the courthouse and talk about "kicking his pants off" for using racial slurs.

> NAACP president Neil Humphrey Sr. ... organized the caravans. And when it came to actively defending the caravans, Rivers was crucial, James said. "He would sometimes demonstrate what he meant, if you didn't understand it." John Rivers was a soldier on the front lines of the battle for civil rights in Sarasota.[12]

The current NAACP president, **Trevor Harvey**, is making plans for a transition from the position that he has held since January 2006. He will remain active within the state. He said in his interview that:

> I have a succession plan. It could be in two, four years. I'm laying the groundwork because I want to make sure that the work continues. I will never leave the organization, even if I'm not the president because I'm passionate about the organization and what it stands for. The mantle will be passed pretty soon. [My] greatest accomplishment? One of the things that comes to mind, I reactivated our leadership academy, our youth branch that was

dormant for a number of years. In mentoring youth, I felt that the NAACP could make a strong difference in continuing to help develop our young people and give them a sense of why it's important to be involved in the community. A lot of our young people don't understand what the NAACP is and what the NAACP does. A lot of the time we have to get them to understand that every civil liberty that we enjoy today came on the back of the NAACP. We have to teach that. It's been successful.

The NAACP and the determined residents of Newtown have conquered seemingly insurmountable obstacles on the road to political representation and power in Sarasota. Their courage to draw battle lines in the fight for justice and equality is remarkable, considering the entrenched Jim Crow laws, hate groups, lynching and other violent acts committed against African Americans throughout Florida.

Much has been achieved and yet, there is still much to be done — outwardly, in the public arena, and inwardly, within the African American community of Newtown. As NAACP President Harvey stated, "A lot of our young people don't understand what the NAACP is and what the NAACP does. They don't understand or, perhaps worse, they are not interested in the history of the organization and the importance of voting, a right often taken for granted now, but one that many people fought for and were injured or killed."

Many people — young, middle aged and elderly — do not understand how much their personal lives are impacted by politics, daily. It is time they become aware of that fact. Political involvement in Newtown and Sarasota, especially participation in local elections, is essential to making the changes that we desire to become reality. Dr. Martin Luther King Jr. had a "dream" and he understood that it took political power, gained through voting, to make that dream become reality. Whenever we see the sign "Dr. Martin Luther King Jr. Way" in Newtown, we should be reminded of the "way" he helped to lead us toward the gains in civil rights that we have today. We must also be aware that many of those gains can be reversed with every vote that we do not cast.

# ENDNOTES

[1] **Amendment 15 (1870)**

**Section 1**. The right of citizens of the United States to vote shall not be denied or abridged by the United States or by any State on account of race, color, or previous condition of servitude.
**Section 2**. The Congress shall have power to enforce this article by appropriate legislation.

This amendment was designed to protect the right of African-Americans to vote and has served as the foundation for such legislation as the Voting Rights Act of 1965.

[2] Constitutional Rights Foundation. "Race and Voting in the Segregated South." http://www.crf-usa.org/brown-v-board-50th-anniversary/race-and-voting.html
[3] Helen Dixon's father used to go to City Hall regularly to make demands for things that the schoolteachers needed (including raises) or a janitor to clean up the school restrooms after his daughter fell on a floor wet from an overflowed toilet. From an interview with Vickie Oldham, October 19, 2015.
[4] One exception was African American Sheila Sanders-Brown who was elected and served from 1980 to 1984 as the Democratic state committeewoman and as vice chairperson of the 13th Congressional District. She was also one of the plaintiffs in the 1979 lawsuit.
[5] Interview with Haley L. Jordan (New College student). October 2015.
[6] Interview with Vickie Oldham. August 18, 2015.
[7] United States Supreme Court; N. A. A. C. P. v. ALABAMA, (1958) No. 91 Argued: Decided: June 30, 1958.
[8] "60 years ago, blacks desegregated Florida beach." http://www.washingtontimes.com/news/2014/jul/19/ 60-years-ago-blacks-desegregated-fla-beach/?page=all
[9] Interview with Haley L. Jordan (New College student). October 2015.
[10] "Civil rights pioneer led era of change in Sarasota." http://www.heraldtribune.com/article/20141205/ARTICLE/141209813
[11] Interview with Kortney Lapeyrolerie (New College student). October 29, 2010. http://www.sarasota.wateratlas.usf.edu/upload/documents/TranscriptRivers.pdf
[12] "60 years ago, blacks desegregated Florida beach."

# CHAPTER 9: CHURCHES OF OVERTOWN AND NEWTOWN

Various forms of religion, spirituality, or belief in some kind of mysticism are integral to most cultures. Many religious practitioners will testify that their belief and faith in God or a higher power provides them with the strength they need to endure the challenges of everyday life. Certainly that was true for enslaved African people who were forcibly brought to the United States and other places colonized by Europeans during the 400-year slave trade. The inhumane conditions under which many managed to survive nurtured their belief that it could only have been accomplished with the intervention of a Supreme Being or God. Although their own traditional belief systems were strong, many Africans accepted the religion of their enslavers because it promised them salvation and equality in the eyes of God:

> African Americans played a major role in their own conversion, and for their own reasons. Africans brought to America initially resisted giving up the religions of their forefathers,[1] but over the years, and with the birth of new generations on American soil, accepting Christianity became part of accepting America as home. Over time, large numbers of slaves found the Biblical message of spiritual equality before God appealing and found comfort in the Biblical theme of deliverance.[2]

Historically, Baptists and Methodists were the most accepting of all Christian denominations toward people of African descent.[3] Bethlehem Baptist Church was the first church in the Sarasota area to be built by and for African Americans. It was constructed in Overtown in 1899. The second African American church built was Payne Chapel African Methodist Episcopal (A.M.E.) Church, in 1903.

The growth of a large number of African American churches in Sarasota – there are over 50 churches, ranging from services held in private homes, to large churches with local and international connections – stems from the motivation to meet the basic human needs for self-respect and strategies to cope with life circumstances. Church members believed that serving God also meant serving others, a passion expressed by several people interviewed for this project.

# BUILDING A FOUNDATION

Churches formed the solid foundation upon which the African American communities of Overtown and Newtown were built. From the 1880s, their strong Christian faith led many African Americans in Sarasota and neighboring areas to attend interdenominational worship services held inside private homes; Baptist, Methodist, Holiness and other Christian denominations all worshipped together.[4] As the number of African American settlers increased, they splintered away from the interdenominational worship services to establish separate churches for their own denominations. Between 1899 and 1928 at least ten churches were established in Overtown and Newtown. Today, there are more than 20 African American churches serving the community.

Church buildings were used not only for worship, but also for social activities, meeting places for organizations, and served as the earliest schools. Education and religion went hand in hand among the early African American settlers of Sarasota, as it still did for quite some time afterward among many of their descendants. During the school desegregation period, the Freedom Schools that emerged overnight in response to the 1969 school boycott were held at African American churches.[5]

Although students no longer have to attend classes held in churches, in order to meet the desires and needs of their community today some churches have opened private schools and/or provide supplemental tutoring and other academically oriented programs. Bethlehem Baptist Church founded the Horizons Unlimited Christian Academy preschool program in 2003, whose goal is to "prepare and motivate students to develop exemplary character and high achievement while empowering them to become God-fearing, law-abiding, productive citizens, community leaders, and entrepreneurs, within a culturally diverse global society;"[6] Horizons also has a Parents, Teachers, and Friends Organization (P.T.F.O.) that, among other things, raises funds for the school. Greater Hurst Chapel African Methodist Episcopal (A.M.E.) Church created the Seed of Academic Resources Program (S.O.A.R.), which is a K-3 program employing "teachers who can provide a caring and nurturing environment for the students and also understand the culture of poverty. The primary goal of S.O.A.R. is to improve the achievement level in reading and math of educationally disadvantaged students."[7] The Westcoast Center for Human Development (WSHD) Church established "a private, inter-/non-denominational, K-12 school. With Christianity as its foundation, WSHD serves as a training ground for leaders of the 21st century. The curriculum with college preparatory courses consistently produces students who are prepared and confident to meet the challenges of the new millennium."[8]

Over time, the number of African American churches grew rapidly. The list includes:


Bethlehem Baptist Church: 1899

Payne Chapel African Methodist Episcopal (A.M.E.) Church: 1903

Mt. Moriah Christian Church: 1913

Truevine Missionary Baptist Church: 1918

The House of God: 1922

New Bethel Missionary Baptist Church: 1924

Bethel Christian Methodist Episcopal (C.M.E.) Church: 1925

Church of God in Christ: 1925

Greater Hurst Chapel African Methodist Episcopal (A.M.E.) Church: 1928

Shiloh Primitive Baptist Church: 1930

Church of Christ: 1932

Zion Primitive Baptist Church: 1937

Koinonia Missionary Baptist Church: 1980

West Coast Center for Human Development: 1980

Trinity Christian Fellowship Center, Inc.: 2000

Light of the World International Church: 2010

Community Bible Church

Firstborn Church of the Living God

Mount Calvary Missionary Baptist Church

Newtown Gospel Chapel

Society of Our Lady Mercy

Trinity M. L. Church

Below are details about some of Newtown's churches:

## Bethlehem Baptist Church, Est. 1899

Original Church
Cornerstone

Originally the Colored Missionary Baptist Church of Sarasota, it is now known as Bethlehem Baptist Church. The Baptists were the first to leave the interdenominational worship services that they had conducted in private homes and build a church. Bethlehem Baptist Church was constructed on the northeast corner of Mango Avenue and 13th Street (present day Central Avenue and 7th Street) in Overtown.[9] It was the first African American church built in Sarasota. Lewis Colson, the first African American settler in Sarasota (1884), and his wife Irene essentially donated the land to build it; they sold the deed to the church for $1 in 1897 and the building was completed in 1899. Mr. and Mrs. Mott (Josie) Washington loaned the church money with which to purchase its first pews. "It is said that Bethlehem was the only Negro church for miles around, therefore, the group included people from Bradenton."[10] John Mays, another early Sarasota settler who was a carpenter and builder, helped to construct the church. Mays became a "noted homebuilder...[and] when the first bank opened in Sarasota, Mays was one of its largest depositors."[11] Lewis Colson became an ordained minister in 1896 and served as pastor of Bethlehem Baptist Church from 1899-1915. Bethlehem was a center of activity for religious and educational activities in the community, having the only church building at that time. Rev. Patrick Miller is the current pastor.

## Payne Chapel African Methodist Episcopal (A.M.E.) Church, Est.1903

The second church built by and for African Americans in Overtown was Payne Chapel African Methodist Episcopal (A.M.E.) Church, located near Bethlehem Baptist. Payne Chapel was named after Daniel Alexander Payne who was elected A.M.E. bishop in 1852. A group of Methodists, who had been attending Bethlehem Baptist Church or the A.M.E. Church on the Manatee River in Bradenton, got together and decided it was time to organize an A.M.E. church in Sarasota. Members of the congregation given credit for organizing the church include: The Reverend T.H. Arnold,

Leonard Reid, Jerry Allen, Richard Grice and the Reverend C. Conely. By the late 1960s, the congregation was declining and the building was deteriorating. A new Payne Chapel was built in Newtown on 19th Street and Central Avenue, and the original building was abandoned in 1975. The current pastor is Rev. Herbert Hollingsworth.

Original Payne Chapel A.M.E. Church building.
Courtesy: Sarasota County Historical Resources.

## Mount Moriah Christian Church, Est. 1913

Mt. Moriah Christian Church was located near the Bee Ridge Turpentine Camp. It served as a "school and social center as well as church" to the turpentine camp workers and their children.[12] Rev. E.W. Range was the first church leader. A prominent Newtown community member, Rev. J.H. Floyd, became pastor in 1957 (until his death in 1974) after a number of others had served in that capacity. After Rev. Floyd's death, Rev. Wesley Tunstall became the pastor.

## Truevine (Truvine) Missionary Baptist Church, Est. 1918

The church was organized in the home of Deacon P.J. Johnson and services were held at Orange Avenue and 25th Street (Robinson's Cowpen). The congregation later moved to the Van Dame Subdivision near the Booker School Complex. J.H. Floyd constructed a church building in 1952. A new church building now stands at 1947 31st Street. The current pastor is Rev. Edward Quary.

## The House of God, Which Is the Church of the Living God, the Pillar and Ground of the Truth Without Controversy, Inc., Est. 1922

Founded by Mother Magdalena Tate and her two sons who established churches from 1903-1913 in Alabama, Georgia and Illinois. The Sarasota House of God church was organized under the leadership of the late Bishop J.R. Lockley, who served as the first pastor. General Elder, M.E. Colvin was assistant pastor to Bishop Lockley; she was only the second female black pastor to serve in a Sarasota church. The first church was built in 1938, on the corner of 6th Street and Coconut, where they worshipped until a new church was constructed in 1984. The late Dr. J.W. Jenkins, a spiritual leader, educator and advocate of economic independence, was selected and ordained chief overseer.[13] Bishop James C. Elliott served as senior bishop and chief overseer of the church. He began ministry at age 12 when he was appointed pastor of a mission in Johnson Camp, a migrant camp at Palmer Boulevard and Bee Ridge Road. After receiving a bachelor's, master's and doctorate degrees, and pastoring churches in Florida, Maryland, Pennsylvania and New Jersey, Elliott was appointed in 1990 as chief overseer and senior bishop of the 100-year-old House of God Church. The current pastor is State Elder Kenneth Ellis.

## Bethel Christian Methodist Episcopal (C.M.E.) Church, Est. 1924
(originally named New Bethel Colored Methodist Episcopal C.M.E. Church.) Bethel C.M.E. Church originally shared a building with Payne Chapel until Payne Chapel was destroyed in the 1925 hurricane. Rev. Dr. John Wesley Walker Jr. is the current pastor.

## New Bethel Missionary Baptist Church, Est. 1925
(Formerly the House of God (1924), but was dedicated as New Bethel in July 1925). The church had its beginning on the undeveloped land that made up much of Newtown at that time. In 1925, under the leadership of Rev. Woodard, a lot was purchased across the street from where the Truevine (Truvine) Missionary Baptist Church parsonage is now located. Rev. C. Preston became the first official pastor and served from 1925-1927.[14] Currently, Rev. Toby T. Philpart is the pastor.

## Church of God in Christ, Pittman Church of God in Christ, Pittman Church of the Living God, Est. 1925
Initially, services were held in the home of Brother and Sister Paralee Wilson. The Newtown church was built on Church Street near 29th Street then moved to 33rd Street [MLK present day] near the corner of Osprey Avenue. The original building burned down. Elder Thomas Pittman changed the church's name to Rawson Temple Church of God in Christ. Upon his death, the name was changed again, to honor Elder Pittman.[15]

## Greater Hurst Chapel African Methodist Episcopal (A.M.E.) Church, Est. 1928
The church was originally known as Bryant Chapel, named for the first pastor. During the 1929 annual conference, the name changed. The members included Abraham Davis, Elizabeth Davis, John, Mary and Hattie Phelps, Clara Williams, and Nora and Rev. Joseph Bryant. Later members were Harmie Baker, Luella O'Neil, Johnny Pompey and Fannie O'Neil Bacon. The first cornerstone was laid in the 1940s. The church increased membership, built an annex and completed the parsonage in the '50s. During the Civil Rights Movement, it was the site of a freedom school during

the school boycott and a meeting place for community organizing for beach integration. The current pastor of Greater Hurst Chapel is Rev. Keturah Drayton Pittman.

## New Zion Primitive Baptist Church, Est. 1937

The church was founded by Elder Rice and Moderator Miller in the Fruitville community with six members who held services in a small dwelling. The church remained in Fruitville for years before moving to the Humphrey's subdivision on 27th Street where it was rebuilt. The church was relocated again to 22nd Street to a building with a seating capacity of 100 people. Since 1984, Elder Willie Mays Jr. has served as pastor. The church celebrated its 78th church anniversary in November 2015.

## Westcoast Center for Human Development, Inc., Est. 1980

Henry Porter II is lead pastor. His father, Dr. Henry L. Porter, is the founder, Bishop and Presiding Prelate of the Westcoast Center. Their global headquarters in Sarasota, Florida. Westcoast Center is among the larger African American churches in Sarasota. It operates a private K-12 school, and has an international mission.[16]

## Koinonia Missionary Baptist Church, Inc., Est. 1980

The Bethlehem Baptist Church congregation became divided due to an internal dispute that resulted in the congregation voting the pastor, Rev. Rupert Paul, out of the church in 1980. A portion of Bethlehem's congregation left with Rev. Paul and started the Koinonia Missionary Baptist Church, Inc., under Rev. Paul's leadership. Rev. Jerome Dupree retired as the pastor in 2016. Rev. Roland Gobourne is the new pastor.

## Light of the World International Church (LOTWIC), Est. 2010

Abundant Life Christian Center (ALCC), that formed in 1999, merged with Bethesda Word of Faith Church and became LOTWIC in 2010. Rev. Kelvin Lumpkin is senior pastor. He accepted the call to ministry while pursuing a bachelor's degree at Bethune Cookman University. Rev. Peter Greenidge is executive pastor.

## REFLECTIONS ABOUT CHURCH EXPERIENCES:

**Mary Alice Simmons:**
When I grew up all I knew was Bethlehem Baptist Church. There was also Payne Chapel but my aunt, my grandma, the family was Bethlehem Baptist Church.[17]

**Wade Harvin:**
We attended Bethlehem Baptist Church, which was in Overtown. And ...
our other classmates over town [later referred to as 'Overtown'] went to
the Methodist Church. It was the pastors ... [who] were great ones in
Overtown ... Dr. Hughes is probably one of the greatest ones that came to
the Overtown area. [He was pastor of] Bethlehem Baptist. Payne Chapel
had Reverend Mack. Loud — almost as loud as some Baptist preachers.
But Methodist, always kind of toned down.[18]

**Yvonne Brown:**
During the week we would have, well of course Sunday church, then we'd
go back to afternoon, BYPU [Baptist Young People's Union]. Then we'd
have evening service and during the week we would have all kinds of
activities at church ...we did a lot of plays during the holidays ... And we
also travelled back in the day to neighboring communities for church ... [I
attended] Bethlehem Baptist. [19]

**Alberta Brown** was very involved at Bethel C.M.E. church for many
years. "Oh my goodness, I was over the Director of Youths, I sang in the
choir, ran the kitchen."[20]

**Willie Charles Shaw:**
I was between New Bethel and Bethel C.M.E. Church ... Preachers were
strong. Remember, the strongest people within our community at that time
and the voices of the community were the funeral home directors, the
undertakers and the preachers.[21]

**Dorothye Smith,** a former schoolteacher and principal who attended
several churches said, "You didn't have anywhere else to go [in Newtown]
but church. So I worked in the church, teaching Sunday school ...
I attended New Bethel. I taught Sunday school at New Bethel. I attended
Hurst Chapel, which is the A.M.E. church. It didn't make any difference
... And the children [from school] expected you to come to church.
Everything they were in, they would invite you to come. So you were there
to see them in Sunday school or whatever happened at church. [22]

According to **Betty Johnson**, "Most of us attended church in Newtown.
That is, after the people started moving out from Overtown into Newtown
... I attended Greater Hurst Chapel A.M.E. Church ...We were like a
beacon church, and we were the community gathering place because of all
of the meetings that took place ... community civic meetings ... Greater
Hurst Chapel is known for school [de]segregation. When they closed
Booker, Hurst Chapel became the school [when] they were protesting."[23]

**Margaret Beverly Moreland Cherry Mitchell:**
"Greater Hurst Chapel has been a community meeting place for the NAACP and community discussions about schools, etcetera."[24]

**Nathaniel Harvey:**
Oh yeah, we went to church ... Every Sunday you had to get up, get ready for church.[25]

**Carolyn Mason:**
Churches were the center of most people's lives.[26]

The idea of the church as a place where you could find refuge, forgiveness, and support was instilled from childhood. That is what **Johnny Hunter Sr.** found in the prison ministry of **Bishop Henry Porter.**

> I told [Bishop Porter] how he could start the process. ... And so he started that in 1976 and he's been going in there [to the prisons] now since 1976. ... [After my release from prison,] I was part of Jim Russo Prison Ministry. He's dead now. ... I used to travel with him back to the prisons, sharing my testimony and did fundraisers for him. [27]

## THE CHOIRS UNION

In 1948, Mrs. Leatha Range, a long time resident of Newtown, organized the Choirs Union. This organization of nine church choirs from the African American community formed the Old Folk Aid Club in 1951, acting on a proposal made by Rev. J.H. Floyd. The Old Folk Aid Club helps to provide care for the community's aged and infirmed residents. On a motion made by Mrs. Flora Knowles, the club was established.

The choirs raised funds by selling fish and peanuts, holding beach barbecues, teas, and concerts and selling ads in souvenir booklets. Benjamin McMillan and Forrest R. Freeman produced the dedication program booklet filled with ads from banks, such as First Federal Savings and Loan Association of Sarasota, and many other businesses, such as Jenkins Grocery, Humphrey's Sundries, Suarez Service Station, Holton Seniors Funeral Home, and the 27th St. Pharmacy. Small donations also flowed in. Choirs have continued to support the Old Folks Aid Home {below), which has been renamed the J.H. Floyd Sunshine Manor. The Home's policy was liberal in treating residents who could not afford to pay for care.

Courtesy: Wade Harvin Collection.

---

**ENDNOTES**

[1] Long before Europeans conducted a slave trade on the continent of Africa, the Arabs had conquered a vast amount of territory there and converted the people from their indigenous belief systems to Islam. Later, Christian missionaries from Europe reached the continent and converted some people to Christianity, as a precursor of colonization. Therefore, before they were brought to the Americas, some of the Africans who became enslaved had already been converted to Islam and Christianity.

[2] "Africans in America: Religion and Slavery." http://www.pbs.org/wgbh/aia/part2/2narr2.html

[3] "Africans in America: Religion and Slavery.

[4] Interview with Vickie Oldham, August 2015.

[5] Burns, Susan. "The Boycott." *Sarasota*, June 1999.

[6] "Horizons Unlimited Christian Academy: Mission." http://www.horizonsunlimitedchristianacademy.com/mission.html

[7] "The Giving Partner: Partner's roles in Grade Level Reading." http://www.cfsarasota.org/Portals/0/Uploads/Documents/Connect/CGLR%20Partners.pdf

[8] The Westcoast School for Human Development. http://digifxlive.com/wcs/

[9] The History of Bethlehem Baptist Church. Church Archives. Author Unknown.

[10] The History of Bethlehem Baptist Church.

[11] LaHurd, Jeff. "Early African American Settlers." *Herald-Tribune*. 16 April 2014.

[12] Shank, Ann A. "Bee Ridge Turpentine Camp." http://www.sarasotahistoryalive.com/history/articles/bee-ridge-turpentine-camp

[13] McElroy, Annie M. *But Your World and My World: The Struggle for Survival, A Partial History of Blacks in Sarasota County 1884-1986.* Sarasota, FL.: Black South Press, 1986, 88-89.

[14] *But Your World and My World*, 90.

[15] *But Your World and My World*, 6.

[16] Interview with Vickie Oldham. November 20, 2015.

[17] Interview with Vickie Oldham. 31 August 2015.

[18] Interview with Flannery French (New College). November 5, 2015.

[19] Interview with Vickie Oldham. August 24, 2015.

[20] Interview with Vickie Oldham. August 10, 2015.

[21] Interview with Vickie Oldham. August 18, 2015.

[22] Interview with Vickie Oldham. August 2015.

[23] Interview with Vickie Oldham. August 18, 2015. The "protest" was the 1969 School Boycott.

[24] Interview with Vickie Oldham. September 4, 2015

[25] Interview with Vickie Oldham. August 18, 2015.

[26] Interview with Hope Black. September 22, 2015.

[27] Interview with Vickie Oldham. October 19, 2015.

— -

# CHAPTER 10: MEDICAL CARE

Professional medical care for African Americans in Sarasota started out in a dismal state and remained that way for almost one-third of the community's 100-year history. Sarasota's early African American settlers in Overtown and Newtown, and African American migrant workers relied on self-care with homemade treatments or patent medicines, and the care of midwives. Midwives Lula Jones, Georgia Ann Haygood, and Elnora "Madam" Brooks helped pregnant women to give birth. **Helen Dixon** stated in her interview with Vickie Oldham that:

> I was born August 8th, 1936 here in Sarasota. My grandmother, who was a midwife at that time, Lula Jones, she brought me into existence because at that time they wouldn't allow us to be at the Sarasota Memorial Hospital (SMH). So midwives would bring different babies into the world and she brought me into the world.[1]

**Jetson Grimes** was also familiar with midwives:

> My godmother was a midwife. ... My mother contracted tuberculosis when I was one years old, and during that period they didn't have a cure for it. So she had to go off to a sanitarium isolated from the public sphere. And the midwife that delivered me was Madam Brooks. ... I was in her care until I was eleven years old ... and then I moved in with my aunt.[2]

## FOLK MEDICINE

Turpentine became a cure-all internal and external remedy for many people. It was abundantly available because they lived close to the turpentine camps in the area. Turpentine is becoming popular again as a natural treatment for many ailments:

> Turpentine and petroleum distillates similar to kerosene have been used medicinally since ancient times and are still being used as folk remedies up to the present. They were used in ancient Babylon to treat stomach problems, inflammations and ulcers.[3]

Folk remedies, for example using cobwebs for cuts, were what most African American people in central and southwest Florida resorted to out of necessity because segregation prevented them from seeking professional medical care. Robert L. Taylor recalls when cobwebs saved the day for his toe and when turpentine was used as a cure-all:

> There was no medical care. Not only here. I remember up in Zellwood, you had no doctor. I remember when I was out in the yard playing and I ran into a shovel and my big toe was almost cut off. And they took it...with cobwebs and all this stuff, and wrapped it up, and it healed. And never saw a doctor...there was no doctor that would treat black people. ... So you learned to do your own treatments. Bandages was a standard thing or tapes and cotton balls and all that kind. ... I remember playing football, the coach, the only [thing] he had ... was some tape and some turpentine. Everything was treated with turpentine. And so that was a big joke, get the turpentine [Laughter].[4]

Good dental care was difficult to obtain as well. Taylor recalls a bad experience:

> Well the instruments they had ... you had to go at night after they close the office. ... I must have been fifteen or sixteen or something like that. I went there and ... these utensils. This was disgusting. You know they wasn't sanitary. The silver tarnished and that kind of stuff. And so, I didn't go back to the dentist until I was twenty-five.[5]

Sarasota's first African American dentist, Dr. William McAllister, was located on Osprey Avenue. African American dentists Drs. Stafford and Fabio had offices on 34th Street. A few white dentists treated black patients, but only after regular office hours.

When Mary Alice Simmons got sick, she remembers that her mother or her grandmother took care of her. There was no trip to the doctor. They would cure whatever ailed her with:

> Old remedies. Well, of course, castor oil, everybody knows castor oil. I remember something called salapatica. I don't know if they still make it. We were always given a laxative once a month. I don't remember having a headache as a kid. The colds: Father John. Everything was done at home. I don't remember seeing a doctor until, my goodness, I was grown.[6]

In the early days, if African Americans received any treatment at Sarasota Memorial Hospital (SMH), it took place in a separate structure, a former military barracks, installed at the rear of the hospital. Years later, a separate floor inside SMH was dedicated to the care of only African American patients: 1-North. As told by Mary Alice Simmons:

> The hospital had an old building for black people. I used to have epileptic seizure. … So my mom said my dad would just pick me, they had no transportation, and he'd run to the hospital … [with me] in his arms. … On foot. That's what I hear. … There was a section there they had for blacks. … As we grew up, when it came to dental work, they had newer dentists that would see us after five o'clock.[7]

There were few white doctors who would treat African Americans. Most of the NCHD project's interviewees who saw doctors at all only remembered being treated by Dr. Chenault, an African American physician. Dr. Chenault, a board certified orthopedic surgeon, was the first African American physician to receive practicing privileges at Sarasota Memorial Hospital. He also treated the elderly, children impacted by polio and private patients.

Several interviewees mentioned a white doctor who treated African Americans. Alberta Brown remembers being examined by Dr. Specht:

> I had to have surgery for one thing and I was bleeding...to death almost. I didn't have a doctor. … I finally found Dr. Specht. … He waited on me, he took care of me. And then when I had to have surgery, he just said I had to have surgery. And they did it.
> Most black people went to Dr. Specht's. … He was a nice person. He treated everybody the same way. That's what I like about him. His wife's mom, she was one of the people that was in that office … and she was not always nice. She'll have you wait longer than you should be waiting and she put someone else in there if she felt like it. And you got wait on when you could. But all that ended too.[8]

Annie M. McElroy's book, *But Your World and My World*, lists the following African American physicians: Drs. Simpson, Hughes and Rivers. Newtown residents also received treatment from white physicians Dr. Joe Halton and his African American assistant Leroy Blue, Dr. Harry O. Specht, Dr. Patterson, and naturopath Weil King.

Two organizations that made valiant efforts to improve health care for African Americans in Newtown were: the Lily White Security Benefit Association #59 in the 1940s, and the Colored Women's Civic Club in the 1950s.

## LILY WHITE SECURITY BENEFIT ASSOCIATION #59

A saving grace for African Americans who needed health care in the Jim Crow days of Sarasota was the Lily White Security Benefit Association, a benevolent society organization run by black residents in Tampa. The Lily White group provided medical care to poor black people throughout Southwest Florida. Sarasota joined the Lily White Security Benefit Association (LWSBA) in the 1940s under the leadership of Deacon Jack Harris. If they required medical treatment, African American members of the LWSBA in Sarasota could be transported by a Lily White ambulance to the air-conditioned 33-bed Lily White Hospital in Tampa, where they could receive medical care. The LWSBA also had an air-conditioned, 20-bed full service nursing home for those who required long term care due to injury or age.

## THE COLORED WOMEN'S CIVIC CLUB

The Colored Women's Civic Club was on the forefront of the battle for equal treatment and civil rights. Formed by women in Newtown, it achieved some major changes for the Newtown community. Mary Emma Jones, grandmother of Dr. Ed James II, was a Newtown community leader. Dr. James II stated that his:

> Grandmother was a member of the Colored Women's Service Club. That club of ladies sought permission to get some barracks moved to the site of Sarasota Memorial Hospital because blacks could not go to the hospital or stay in the hospital because of the stupidity of segregation. So initially when blacks were allowed to go to Sarasota Memorial Hospital they stayed in a separate wing, which was the military barracks.[9]

Through the efforts of the Colored Women's Service Club, African American patients finally would be admitted – indoors – to Sarasota Memorial Hospital. Many of the Club's members were involved with the Red Cross volunteer programs in the battle against tuberculosis, a disease that was killing many people in Newtown as well as other parts of Florida. According to Annie M. McElroy:

> In the 1930s tuberculosis was a dreaded disease in the State of Florida. We were losing our friends, loved ones and acquaintances to this powerful invader of the human body. The state needed many kinds of resources to conquer this dreadful enemy. … In the fall of 1939, a group of women and one man met with Mrs. Mary

Emma Jones, a volunteer health worker, at Jones Barbecue to discuss the issue. As a result of this night of sharing ideas, the T.B. Health unit was organized. The group elected Mrs. Mary Emma Jones as their first president. They purchased a mobile x-ray unit.[10]

## SARASOTA SICKLE CELL FOUNDATION

The Sarasota Sickle Cell Foundation was established in 1980 with Mrs. Clara Williams as President. The Foundation offered financial & medical assistance along with counseling and education. Sickle cell refers to a group of inherited red blood cell disorders that are primarily found among people of African ancestry.

## NURSING

African American nurses who were primarily trained at first as Licensed Practical Nurses (LPNs), not registered Nurses (RNs), began working at Sarasota Memorial Hospital when it finally integrated its staff. Georgia Thomas started working there in 1945 and was congratulated in 1970 for her 25 years of service.[11] Community volunteers provided additional medical assistance. According to McElroy:

> Lay persons in the black community expressed their concern in various ways: volunteer services to local health organizations, enrollment in workshops, completion of first aid and survival courses are examples.[12]

Others took courses in school, like Shelia Atkins who was in "the first class that had nurses aid training at VoTech, which is now Suncoast Technical College. So I worked in the hospital, in the nursing homes."[13] Gwendolyn Atkins graduated from Florida A&M University (FAMU) nursing school in 1964 and got a job that year at Sarasota Memorial Hospital (SMH). She was told that most of the African Americans in the hospital were on 1-North, but she never worked on 1-North. She left SMH after two years and chose to work in Public Health Nursing for the Sarasota County Health Department (SCHD).

In addition to the hospital, healthcare was delivered to Newtown residents by visiting nurses from SCHD. Henrietta Gayles Cunningham was the first African American public health nurse in Newtown, and she

Henrietta Gayles Cunningham
(left) and Gwendolyn Atkins.
Courtesy: Gwendolyn Atkins Collection.

also treated people in the migrant camps. Gwendolyn Atkins became a public health nurse in the Newtown projects and spent most of her nursing career as a Public Health nurse.

During each visit, she said, she would set up a card table and put a white tablecloth on it in the parking lot at the projects, and "the kids would come running." She treated children for ringworm, colds, abrasions, impetigo, and gave many immunizations, such as DPT, tetanus, polio, and smallpox. She was there to help the people in any way that she could. Even in retirement, Gwendolyn Atkins is known as a health educator and advocate in the community.

## "SARASOTA'S NEWTOWN HEALTHCARE ICONOCLASM"

The term "iconoclasm" is defined as 'rejecting established beliefs and institutions.' This word is totally appropriate for the topic of the 2009 White Paper[14] written by James E. McCloud, President/CEO of Genesis Health Services, Inc., about the Newtown healthcare situation at that time. The lengthy title of the paper is: "A White Paper 2009, Sarasota's Newtown Healthcare Iconoclasm© An Under-served and Ill-served African American Community Building Capacity To Meet their Basic Healthcare and Wellness Needs And A Challenge To Sarasota County Health Department's, "Communities Putting Prevention To Work."[15]

This publication was a scathing indictment of the healthcare system in Sarasota because of its inhumane neglect of Newtown's residents' healthcare. It outlined in great detail the institutionalized racism that pervades the history of healthcare services in Sarasota, Florida. According to McCloud's documentation, not a lot had changed in the system since the days of Jim Crow. Only the methods used to withhold care and ignore the health crises in the African American community of Newtown had changed. These methods were hidden in the fine print of grant 'deals' made between health care funders such as the Centers for Disease Control (CDC), the "middle man"— the Florida Department of Health, and the local healthcare provider — the Sarasota County Health Department, according to McCloud. Many of the details in this publication were mirrored in the stories told by Newtown residents to the NCHD Project's interviewers.

## THE MULTICULTURAL HEALTH INSTITUTE (MHI)

MHI was founded in 1995 by Dr. Lisa Merritt, as a way to:

> Level the healthcare playing field by promoting, educating, and ensuring equal healthcare access and treatment for underserved communities and individuals who are traditionally uninsured and receive a poor quality of care." [16]

MHI supports programs that educate, identify, and test for diseases that often affect underserved communities, such as cancer, diabetes, obesity, stroke, cardiovascular disease, infant mortality, and HIV/AIDS. Dr. Merritt has a holistic approach to healing and combines Western medicine with alternative therapies such as healing circles, acupuncture, herbal and nutrition medicine, detoxification protocols, craniosacral therapy, and mesotherapy. Her approach to medicine and healing focuses on health disparities, their effect on our nation's multicultural citizenry, and the economic impact of sickness prevention strategies. [17]

## A NEW CLINIC IN NEWTOWN

The City of Sarasota and Sarasota Memorial Hospital finally took long overdue action with regard toward improving healthcare for its citizens who happen to live in their most underserved neighborhood – Newtown. The Newtown community hopes that this new clinic, scheduled to open in 2017, will help to close Sarasota's chasm of inequity in healthcare. According to a *Herald-Tribune* article:

> The $2.2 million project is part of Sarasota Memorial Hospital's new internal residency program, which it announced in April, through a partnership with Florida State University College of Medicine. The first 10 residents are expected to arrive in the summer of 2017, and the clinic will serve as their *training ground*. [emphasis added] [18]

It is hoped that Newtown patients using this clinic will not suffer from being the residents' "training ground." Many people, African Americans, especially, are keenly aware of the tragic history of how African Americans were abused for medical research and "training" in the infamous Tuskegee Syphilis Experiment. Therefore, their use of the phrase "training ground" is culturally insensitive. Dr. Merritt's responses in a recent interview are on point:

> As hospital leaders work to make the clinic a reality over the next year-and-a-half, they should also pay attention to delivering care that takes into account the life experiences of the patients they're serving. … I hope the medical residents working there will have a good learning experience, while the population they're learning from also gets proper clinical care," Merritt said.[19]

Many people interviewed for this NCHD Project recalled numerous negative experiences at Sarasota Memorial Hospital. The hospital needs to gain the trust of this predominantly African American community that it has neglected for many years.

---

**ENDNOTES**

[1] Interview with Vickie Oldham. October 19, 2015.
[2] Interview with Vickie Oldham. September 4, 2015.
[3] Last, Walter, "Kerosene and Turpentine – Universal Healer." http://augmentinforce.50webs.com/TURPENTINE--HEALER%20COMPLETE.htm; Turpentine Oil." http://www.webmd.com/vitamins-supplements/ingredientmono-508turpentine%20oil.aspx?activeingredientid=508&activeingredientname=turpentine%20oiland; Healing With 100% Pure Turpentine. Dr Jennifer Daniels MD http://www.health-recovery
[4] Interview with Vickie Oldham. August 18, 2015.
[5] Interview with Vickie Oldham. November 20, 2015.
[6] Interview with Vickie Oldham. August 31, 2015.
[7] Interview with Vickie Oldham. August 31, 2015.
[8] Interview with Vickie Oldham. August 10, 2015.
[9] Interview with Haley Jordan (New College student). October 2015.
[10] McElroy, Annie M. *But Your World and My World: The Struggle for Survival, A Partial History of Blacks in Sarasota County 1884-1986.* Sarasota, FL: Black South Press, 1986, 100, 112.
[11] *But Your World and My World.* 1986, 109.
[12] *But Your World and My World.* 1986, 109.
[13] Interview with Kaylie Stokes (New College student). October 20, 2015.
[14] "What is a White Paper? Originally, the term white paper was used as shorthand to refer to an official government report, indicating that the document is authoritative and informative in nature. Writers typically use this genre when they argue a specific position or propose a solution to a problem, addressing the

audience outside of their organization. Typically, the purpose of a white paper is to advocate that a certain position is the best way to go or that a certain solution is best for a particular problem."
Source: "White Paper: Purpose and Audience." Purdue (University) OWL (Online Writing Lab). https://owl.english.purdue.edu/owl/

[15] A complete copy of the White Paper is available in the Appendix of the Newtown Alive? Report that is accessible online or in Sarasota County libraries.

[16] Multicultural Health Institute http://www.the-mhi.org/#!the-history/a5k7e

[17] Multicultural Health Institute.

[18] "Sarasota Memorial to open clinic in Newtown." December, 7, 2015. http://www.heraldtribune.com/article/LK/20151207/News/605206335/SH/

[19] Clark, Maggie and Billy Cox. "New clinic will target adults." *Herald-Tribune.* December 8, 2015. http://www.heraldtribune.com/article/20151208/ARTICLE/151209650

# CHAPTER 11: NEWTOWN AND OVERTOWN ORGANIZATIONS

## BENEVOLENT SOCIETIES

Newtown, like many other African American communities across the US, developed self-help organizations — benevolent societies and mutual aid societies — to meet various needs of their communities' members. After the Civil War, some African Americans became free people of color.[1] While they had their freedom they had no safety nets. Segregationist policies prevented them from accessing the necessary medical and other facilities that were available solely to white citizens. Forming self-help organizations became a critical matter of self-preservation:

> African American benevolent societies were first and foremost a product of exclusion from white organizations, hospitals, and schools. While the earliest African American benevolent society dates back to 1780, most were founded after the Civil War to meet the challenges of freedom during a time when the ability of African Americans to survive on their own was seriously debated.
> The benevolent societies that Free People of Color created provided a sense of security, especially financially, to people in an uncertain position. ... The benevolent societies they created allowed for community bonding and financial security in the event of death or sickness. Free People of Color did not enjoy the civil liberties granted to white citizens[2]

Though benevolent societies undoubtedly improved the quality of life for African Americans, it is important to recognize that many of them were not all-inclusive. The societies usually imposed age restrictions for new members, often between 21 and 50 years old. Members also had to prove that they were in good health and provide references from others in the community testifying to their good social standing.[3] A number of these organizations had discriminatory policies based on skin color:

> Some societies only granted membership to light or fair-skinned African Americans as a result of the often prevalent misconception that mixed-race African Americans were more intelligent,

attractive, and civilized than their darker-skinned counterparts — a claim that was bolstered by white Americans as well. Exclusivity based on complexion allowed these associations to protect their status as more privileged members of a racially hierarchical society.[4]

In Newtown, there may have been some degree of organizational exclusivity. According to the available information, most of Newtown's benevolent organizations were led by the upper income, educated members of the community such as business owners, educators and religious leaders and their wives. This does not necessarily mean that "ordinary" or non-elite community members were excluded from participating, nor from benefitting from their programs.

In the South, especially, establishing these organizations could attract negative attention from people who wanted to prevent African Americans from bettering their lives. Some whites, particularly, poor whites, held grudges against African Americans who appeared to being doing better financially than they were. Despite their actual life circumstances, most whites still considered themselves to be superior to any African American.

W.E.B. DuBois, African American scholar and graduate of Harvard University (1895 Ph.D.), called attention to this when he stated that the actual life circumstances of poor whites – lower wages, lower social and lower economic status in the white community – were supplemented by the "public and psychological wage" associated with being white.[5] So no matter their circumstances, they considered themselves to be superior. Therefore, when African Americans formed organizations that outwardly gave the appearance of grandeur, such as the social events held by the Free and Accepted Masons, the Eastern Star and the Elks Club, some whites could be resentful and sometimes dangerous. The people of Newtown, however, did not allow that possibility to deter them from pursuing all non-violent means necessary to improve the lives of their community members. Whether or not all community members were actually members of an organization, they could benefit from the works of that organization.

In Sarasota, African Americans established various types of mutual aid or benevolent societies that had civic as well as social functions. These organizations included, but are not limited to: The Free and Accepted Masons (since 1916; pictured below); Household of Ruth, Eastern Star, Sarasota Lodge #3538T (pictured below); Knights of Pythias, Pride of Sarasota Lodge #104 (since 1916); Knights of Pythias St. Mary's Calanthe Court #73 (since 1916); Elks Club (1940s); Organization of Seth; Northside Progressive Men's Club (1980s); North County Civic League

(1980s); Old Folks Aid Home; Church Union; Organization of Seth; Choirs Union; Bingo Club; Old Folk Aid Club; Bingo Club; International Order of Odd Fellows; Lily White Security Benefit Association; Sarasota Sickle Cell Foundation; and the Colored Women's Service Club.

Members of the Free and Accepted Masons.
Courtesy: Lymus Dixon Collection.

Members of Household of Ruth Lodge.
Courtesy: Michael Dixon Collection.

The women of Overtown and Newtown took the lead in bringing aid to their community before the era of the Civil Rights Movement. One of the most prominent was the Colored Women's Service Club. Its remarkable history of political leadership and civic accomplishments in

Newtown was revealed in an article from the *Herald-Tribune* and in an interview with **Dr. Edward E. James II:**

> Years before the more-famous triumphs of the civil rights era in the 1960s, the women of this club won some early victories in Sarasota. The group began during World War II, successfully lobbying for a serviceman's club for black soldiers who weren't allowed to mix with other enlisted men. The club later became a recreation center, to be rebuilt as the Robert L. Taylor Community Complex. Many of the women also led Red Cross volunteer programs and efforts to stop tuberculosis, a feared killer in Newtown in those times.[6]

Through this club's efforts, African American patients eventually would be admitted to the hospital — indoors, not a separate facility such as the barracks adjacent to it. The group also pushed state officials to open up Myakka River State Park to African American residents, started voter registration drives and made possible the Booker High School band.

## SOCIAL AND COMMUNITY-ORIENTED CLUBS

Other clubs had social and civic functions.

## THE ELKS

Dr. Fannie McDugle remembered the Elks as:

> [An] organization for the blacks. ... We travel from town or city to city ... get together and have 'turn outs.' You would have meetings and you would have banquets. Just different things you would have.[7]

## THE CHARMETTES

Another social club that also made civic contributions was the Charmettes. Newtown businesswoman Allease Suarez was a member of this organization. The Charmettes' stated mission was: "To work for the betterment of the community." The major objective of the group of ladies was to promote better and higher education.

Dr. Mary McLeod Bethune, president of Bethune Cookman
College/University, with members of the Charmettes.
Courtesy: Michael Suarez Collection.

## AMARYLLIS PARK

Mrs. Viola Sanders, a resident of Amaryllis Park, organized the community in 1964. She was very concerned about her neighbors who were grieving after the death of a loved one and sent them cards, flowers and resolutions and asked for donations.

Today, the neighborhood association's mission has changed. Members have the ability to collectively confront neighborhood challenges, such as: speeding cars; drug dealers; prostitution, noise and air pollution; disputes among neighbors; upkeep of public roads and sidewalks; and assisting with the Newtown Redevelopment Plan. On June 6, 2000, the neighborhood association was reorganized as the Amaryllis Park Neighborhood Association and elected Mr. Calvin Bryant as president. Barbara Langston serves as president in 2017.

## THE NEWTOWN FRONT PORCH NEIGHBORHOOD REVITALIZATION COUNCIL, INC.

The Newtown Front Porch Neighborhood Revitalization Council, Inc. was a group of concerned citizens committed to the revitalization of the Newtown community. Newtown was designated by the State of Florida as a 'Governor's Front Porch Neighborhood' from 2002 to 2012.

## ENDNOTES

[1] "Since Lincoln issued the Emancipation Proclamation as a military measure, it didn't apply to border slave states like Delaware, Maryland, Kentucky and Missouri, all of which had remained loyal to the Union. Lincoln also exempted selected areas of the Confederacy that had already come under Union control in hopes of gaining the loyalty of whites in those states. … The only places it applied were places where the federal government had no control — the Southern states currently fighting against the Union." http://www.history.com/news/5-things-you-may-not-know-about-lincoln-slavery-and-emancipation

[2] Martin, Kimberly Martin. *Community and Place: A Study of Four African American Benevolent Societies and their Cemeteries*. Master's thesis. Clemson University and College of Charleston, 1-2.

[3] A Brief Historical Account of Early Benevolent Societies." http://www.100menhall.org/about-us/history-of-benevolent-associations

[4] "A Brief Historical Account of Early Benevolent Societies."

[5] "The psychological wage of whiteness meant that: The white group of laborers, while they received a low wage, was compensated in part by a sort of public and psychological wage. They were given public deference and titles of courtesy because they were white. They were admitted freely with all classes of white people to public functions, public parks, and the best schools. The police were drawn from their ranks and the courts, dependent on their votes, treated them with leniency as to encourage lawlessness. Their vote selected public officials, and while this had small effect upon the economic situation, it had great effect upon their personal treatment and the deference shown them" (DuBois, W.E.B. [1935] 1969, 700-701). Accessed on website: http://what-when-how.com/social-sciences/whites-social-science/

[6] Cummings, Ian. "Leading the way before civil rights era." *Herald-Tribune*, February 1, 2015. http://newtown100.heraldtribune.com/2015/02/01/leading-way-civil-rights-era/

[7] Interview with Vickie Oldham, August 10, 2015.

# CHAPTER 12: MILITARY SERVICE

*"Black Sarasotans have been answering the call to serve their country since the early 1900s."*
*- Annie M. McElroy*

## AFRICAN AMERICANS SERVING IN THE UNITED STATES MILITARY

The United States joined the battle against Germany in April 1917 during World War I. Military Recruiting Officer Charles Ayler was stationed in Bradenton; his territory included Sarasota, where he visited on October 26, 1917. According to the *Sarasota Times,* Ayler was recruiting "both white and colored men from ages 18 to 40. White men able to handle colored men are much in demand for the army and will be made non-commissioned officers."[1] African American men across the US saw joining the fighting ranks as:

> An opportunity to win the respect of their white neighbors. America was a segregated society and African Americans were considered, at best, second-class citizens. Yet despite that, there were many African American men willing to serve in the nation's military. ... They viewed the conflict as an opportunity to prove their loyalty, patriotism, and worthiness for equal treatment in the United States.
>
> When World War I broke out, there were four all-black regiments: the 9th and 10th cavalries and the 24th and 25th infantries. The men in these units were considered heroes in their communities. Within one week of [President] Wilson's declaration of war, the War Department had to stop accepting black volunteers because the quotas for African Americans were filled. While still discriminatory, the Army was far more progressive in race relations than the other branches of the military. Blacks could not serve in the Marines, and could only serve limited and menial positions in the Navy and the Coast Guard.[2]

On May 18, 1917, Congress passed the Selective Service Act that required all men from 21 to 31 years of age to register for the draft. Because of the large population of African Americans living in the South at that time, the majority of African American men who were 'selected' for military service came from the South. African American men from Bradenton and Sarasota joined the military and were eager to demonstrate their bravery. McElroy lists over 100 "Colored Selects" who were sent by train to Camp Devens, Massachusetts on August 4, 1918. Another group (unspecified number) was supposed to have embarked for Fort Dix, New Jersey in February, however, "at the urgent recommendation of the Surgeon General of the Army, this was not done because it was considered dangerous to transfer southern Negroes to a northern camp during the winter months."[3]

Much to their dismay, after serving their country in the armed forces, African American men returned to an even more racist society in the US than they had left, one that did not reward their contribution to the war effort. France, however, did provide them with the recognition that they never received from their own country. Several all-African American regiments, including the 369th Infantry nicknamed the "Harlem Hellfighters," received France's award for heroism in combat with the enemy, the *Croix de Guerre*. According to an article about their treatment:

> Expecting to come home heroes, black soldiers received a rude awakening upon their return. Back home, many whites feared that African Americans would return demanding equality and would try to attain it by employing their military training. As the troops returned, there was an increase of racial tension. During the summer and fall of 1919, anti-black race riots erupted in twenty-six cities across America. The lynching of blacks also increased from 58 in 1918 to 77 in 1919. At least ten of those victims were war veterans, and some were lynched while in uniform.
>
> Despite this treatment, African American men continued to enlist in the military, including veterans of World War I who had come home to such violence and ingratitude. They served their county in the brief period of peace after WWI, and many went on to fight in WWII. It was not until 1948, after the war had ended, that President Harry S. Truman issued an executive order to desegregate the military, although it took the Korean War to fully integrate the Army.[4]

Several of the persons interviewed for the NCHD report discussed their time in the military. **Eddie Rainey** was a paratrooper for two years. He trained at the United States Army Infantry School in Fort Benning, Georgia. Anthony "Tony" Major never served in the military, but his father, **"Suit" Major**, and his mother's two brothers served in the Army and returned home to Newtown.[5] **Johnny Hunter Sr.** served in the Air Force. He enlisted, "When I was eighteen years old. And I stayed there for four years."[6]

**Robert L. Taylor**'s military service interrupted his education at Morehouse College:

> I went to service in March of 1943. I was in the Army. ... I began over at Fort Sill in the radio department ... down in Fort Clark, Texas. ...I learned your Morse Code. ... We were there for about a year before we went overseas.

**Willie Charles Shaw's** military experience began, "Right after Gibbs [Junior College]. I joined the Air Force on August the 24th 1967. ... My dad was a veteran, family members had been veterans, served the country, and I, too, wanted to serve. ... I was a security policeman. My rank was Staff Sergeant. I was 19. It was a life changing experience.

**John "Buck" O'Neil**, the famous Negro League Baseball player from Newtown, interrupted his baseball career to serve from 1943-1945 in the US Navy.

**Lymus Dixon** (below) served in the US Army during WWII.

Courtesy: Michael Dixon Collection.

**Oscar Manigo** served in the US Navy during WWII. His son, **Eugene Manigo**, served in the US Army and was a casualty of the Vietnam War.

**Robert "Baldy" White** served in Vietnam.

 Numerous men from Newtown earned the Purple Heart medal, which is awarded to members of the US armed forces who are wounded by an instrument of war in the hands of the enemy and, posthumously, to the next of kin in the name of those who are killed in action or die of wounds received in action. It is specifically a combat decoration.

Courtesy:
Sheffield Family
Collection.

**Horras Sheffield** was awarded the Purple Heart medal in 1968 at age 23. While serving with the US Marines, Sheffield recalls that: "When I was in Vietnam, my whole company, Foxtrot 2nd Battalion, 1st Marine was annihilated in 1967. We were to check on a village that had underground tunnels. When we made an approach, enemy fire mowed the guys down, everybody. Only two of us survived. I was wounded that day and played dead. I kept my M-14 rifle underneath my belly, up to my throat. We slept in the rice patty dikes on our guns.

The Vietnamese fighters picked up the rifles from the wounded. It took two days to be rescued. I was shot twice in my left leg and left side. After the rescue, I was treated and recuperated for four months aboard the USS Sanctuary, a hospital ship; then was transferred to Walter Reed National Military Medical Center in Bethesda, Maryland."[7]

Gabrielle Russon published a moving tribute to **Michael Campbell** in the *Herald-Tribune* titled "Remembering a Fallen Soldier" – 49 years after his death. She wrote that:

He joined the military a week after graduating from high school in 1964, following in the footsteps of his father, a World War II veteran. A headstone was placed on Campbell's grave in Galilee Cemetery in 2014, thanks to the efforts of "Debora Livingston, a Newtown historian who visited the cemetery one day, about two years ago, and stumbled on the site. [Livingston said to Russon,] "There was a bed of grass over him. He was overlooked. That's when I went to work."[8]

Pfc. Michael "Kaydo" Campbell.        Courtesy: Becky Zremski
Courtesy: Dorothye Smith.

## TWO HIGHLY RANKED NEWTOWN VETERANS

According to Mayor Shaw, "**Lieutenant Colonel Doxey Byrd Jr**. was responsible for logistics in Vietnam, the movement of equipment."[9] Annie M. McElroy wrote about Lt. Col. Doxey Byrd Jr., a 1953 graduate of Booker High School. He was:

> The first black from Sarasota to attain Field Grade Rank in the US Army. In September 1953 he enrolled at Florida A&M University. During his four years there he was part of the ... ROTC programs. Based on his achievements in both academics and military skills he earned the status of Distinguished Student and this provided the basis for his being awarded a Regular Army Commission. ... Doxey Byrd's military career was both varied and distinguished. Some of his duty tours include Europe, the Far East the Middle East and Southeast Asia. ... He has received three awards of the Army Commendation Medal, two awards of the Meritorious Service Medal and the Bronze Star for distinguished combat performance in Vietnam.[10]

Lt. Col. Byrd Jr.'s daughter Kathy writes proudly about her father:

> Lt. Col. Byrd was a Battalion Commander in Okinawa, Japan where he commanded more than 1,200 men and women, a fleet of ships and other equipment. After his two duty tours in Vietnam he was sent to Command General Staff College in Ft. Leavenworth, Kansas, where he graduated in the top five of his class. After that, he was stationed in Washington D.C. where he worked at the Pentagon and was a professor at Howard University teaching Military Science. Lt. Col. Byrd retired after serving 21 years in the Army and returned to Sarasota with his wife Ethel Byrd, whom he had married in 1958. They had one daughter Kathy Byrd-Pobee. After returning, he was active in his church, New Bethel Missionary Baptist. He also decided to go back to school to obtain another degree. He went to University of South Florida and obtained a BA in Criminal Justice. He owned and operated his own trucking business until his health required him to retire completely. Lt. Col. Byrd passed away on August 7, 1996 at the age of 61.[11]

McElroy also wrote about another distinguished African American military officer – **Captain Cornell McKenzie**. He was "the son of

McDonald McKenzie and Mary Mays ... the third generation of the Willie McKenzie family and the fourth generation of the John Mays family" — two of the earliest settler families in Sarasota.[12] Cornell McKenzie was "the first black man from Sarasota to attend West Point Military Academy. He graduated from West Point in 1976 with a commission of Second Lieutenant and a B.S. degree. ... McKenzie was commissioned Captain in 1980."[13]

## WOMEN IN THE MILITARY

V.F.W. Auxiliary #4412 North Sarasota.
Courtesy: of *The Bulletin*.

Lt. Col. Doxey Byrd Jr. Conducts Swearing In Ceremony.
Courtesy: Kathy Byrd-Pobee Collection.

Leon Byrd served in the US Army during the Gulf Wars — Desert Storm and Desert Shield.
Courtesy: Leon Byrd Collection.

There are many other men and women from Newtown, not mentioned here, who served in the military to protect their country.

## THE USO IN NEWTOWN

During WWII, what is now the Sarasota-Bradenton International Airport was a US military air base. Mayor Shaw states that, "There were barracks there and quite a few black [soldiers] were stationed at that air base from all around the country." Because of segregation laws, African American soldiers could not use the USO on the military base. A USO building for the African American soldiers was constructed in Newtown in 1940. "The 'Black USO,' Shaw continued, "That's where I learned how to do the hully gully. We rocked in the old USO."[14] When the war ended, the building was no longer needed for that purpose. It first became a hospital building, relocated behind Sarasota Memorial Hospital where African Americans received medical care, and later became the "The Rec" center for the Newtown community that was run by Robert L. Taylor. [15]

---

## ENDNOTES

[1] *Sarasota Times.* November 1, 1917. In McElroy, Annie M. *But Your World and My World: The Struggle for Survival, A Partial History of Blacks in Sarasota County 1884-1986.* Sarasota, FL.: Black South Press, 1986.
[2] Bryan, Jami. "Fighting for Respect: African-American Soldiers in WWI."

Managing Editor, *On Point*. An <u>Army Historical Foundation</u> publication.
http://www.militaryhistoryonline.com/wwi/articles/fightingforrespect.aspx
[3] *But Your World and My World*, 1986, 73.
[4] "Fighting for Respect: African-American Soldiers in WWI."
[5] Interview with Dr. Rosalyn Howard. December 20, 2015.
[6] Interview with Vickie Oldham. October 19, 2015.
[7] Interview with Vickie Oldham. March 22, 2016.
[8] Russon, Gabriel. "Remembering a Fallen Soldier." *Herald-Tribune*. Monday, October 13, 2014.
[9] Interview with Vickie Oldham. March 16, 2016.
[10] *But Your World and My World*, 1986, 73-74.
[11] Biographical notes submitted to Vickie Oldham on March 20, 2016.
[12] *But Your World and My World*, 1986, 2, 74. John Mays was among the first African American settlers of Sarasota in the late 1800s and was a founding member of Bethlehem Baptist Church.
[13] *But Your World and My World*, 74.
[14] Interview with Vickie Oldham, March 16, 2016.
[15] *But Your World and My World*, 1986, 69. The "Rec" was replaced with the Robert L. Taylor Community Complex.

# CHAPTER 13: SPORTS

Newtown residents have had a noteworthy history in amateur, semi-professional, and professional sports. The three major sports have been baseball, basketball, and football. Golf was also popular among some African Americans.

## NEGRO LEAGUES BASEBALL

In the late 1800s, there were some integrated baseball teams, but after 1900 the pressure of the Jim Crow laws, enforcing racial segregation, prevented African Americans from playing on any teams with white players. "The term "Negro Leagues," as it is used by the [Negro Leagues] museum, refers to the highest level of play for black baseball during segregation."[1]

The Negro Leagues Baseball Museum, located in Kansas City, Missouri, was created to preserve an important part of African American history and culture. The Negro Leagues Baseball Museum in the 18th and Vine District owes its existence to John "Buck" O'Neil, chosen president of the infant organization in 1990. From that time on he gave hundreds of talks, working without a salary, to raise money for the facility. It opened in 1997.[2]

John "Buck" O'Neil.
Courtesy: Jetson Grimes Collection.

The Negro Leagues were organized in 1920 in response to the lack of opportunity for talented African American athletes to play ball.

Unofficial groups of players began:

> 'Barnstorming' around the country to play anyone who would challenge them. ... An organized league structure was formed under the guidance of Andrew "Rube" Foster — a former player, manager, and owner for the Chicago American Giants. In a meeting held at the Paseo YMCA in Kansas City, Missouri, Foster and a few other Midwestern team owners joined to form the Negro National League. Soon, rival leagues formed in Eastern and Southern states, bringing the thrills and innovative play of black baseball to major urban centers and rural countrysides in the U.S., Canada, and Latin America. The Leagues maintained a high level of professional skill and became centerpieces for economic development in many black communities.
>
> In 1945, Major League Baseball's Brooklyn Dodgers recruited Jackie Robinson from the Kansas City Monarchs. Robinson now becomes the first African-American in the modern era to play on a Major League roster. While this historic event was a key moment in baseball and civil rights history, it prompted the decline of the Negro Leagues. The best black players were now recruited for the Major Leagues, and black fans followed. The last Negro Leagues teams folded in the early 1960s, but their legacy lives on through the surviving players and the Negro Leagues Baseball Museum.[3]

The Jacksonville Red Caps are the only team recognized in Florida as a member of the Negro Leagues. However, there is a proud tradition of African Americans playing baseball in Sarasota and Bradenton. Although the Bradenton Nine Devils were considered a semi-pro team,[4] and were not part of the nationally recognized Negro Leagues, they occasionally played against Negro Leagues' teams.

## SEMI-PRO BASEBALL

### The Sarasota-Bradenton Nine Devils

> [The Nine Devils baseball team] was [Bradenton's] black baseball club, comprised of players from Sarasota and Manatee County, who enjoyed prolonged success during the segregation era in the independent Florida State Negro League from 1937 to 1956. Originally the Aces, they were renamed Nine Devils after winning their first nine games one season.

The players were owners of dry cleaning shops, field workers, golf course groundskeepers and sanitation workers who excelled on the baseball diamond. "When we knocked off work, we'd go behind the projects and practice," said Copeland, a McKechnie Field caretaker. "Sundays we'd play ball."

The Nine Devils played 70 to 75 games a year against ball clubs from Daytona, Miami, Orlando, St. Petersburg and West Palm Beach. They also played Negro Leagues ball clubs like the Cleveland Buckeyes, Homestead Grays and Indianapolis Clowns. Home games at McKechnie and long gone Roush Field were festive affairs, usually drawing big crowds. "Women wearing their Sunday hats, people laughing," said Morris Paskell, a second baseman. "Everybody knew each other. It was beautiful." The Nine Devils were a great source of local entertainment and civic pride to the African American communities in Bradenton and Sarasota.[5]

In 1983, Harry Robinson, manager of the Sarasota-Bradenton Nine Devils baseball team said:

The original Nine Devils team was organized 40 years ago and it was pretty much an all-black team playing against all-black opposition. The general idea of the organization was, and still is, a place for kids of any color who don't have the chance to go to college or sign with the pros. It's a chance for them to show their stuff in front of the scouts ... For some of the kids, it's their last chance or only chance.[6]

(above) The Nine Devils team.
Source: The Robert "Bud" Thomas Collection.

## The Sarasota Tigers

The second local African American semi-pro baseball team was the Sarasota Tigers, whose most famous team member was Buck O'Neil. One of O'Neil's teammates was Carlos Suarez.[7] The Sarasota Tigers:

> Served as a jumping-off point for John "Buck" O'Neil, a Sarasotan [from Newtown] whose fame as a player for the Kansas City Monarchs, a Negro American League team, gained renewed recognition in 1994 when he helped narrate Ken Burns' PBS documentary, "Baseball."[8]

Les Porter writes that:

> Buck O'Neil lived in Newtown as a youth and worked alongside his father in the celery fields. His father also owned O'Neil's pool hall and recreational center that became the "hang out" place for baseball players. His parents, Lou Ella and John Jordan O'Neil Sr. encouraged him to pursue his passion, and that was playing baseball. Several major-league baseball clubs held Spring Training in Florida, including the New York Yankees who trained in Sarasota, and the New York Giants who trained in Tampa ... Buck and his friends would gather outside the local stadium and retrieve balls for sale to tourists. He also got to see Negro league players from teams such as the Chicago American Giants and the Indianapolis ABCs. During the winter, these players worked in the posh Palm Beach hotels as waiters, cooks, bellhops and chauffeurs, and played some of the best baseball in the country on their days off. They included Andrew Rube Walker who established the Negro National League in 1920.[9]
>
> As a teenager, in the spring [O'Neil] watched from a tree beyond the outfield fence while major league teams trained at Payne Park. Occasionally his teacher, Emma E. Booker, would let him leave class to play for the Sarasota Tigers. She saw to it, however, that he advanced in his studies as much as he could in her classes so that, when he entered Edward Waters College in Jacksonville on a baseball scholarship, he tested out for the 11th grade in the school's high school program.[10]

# BUCK O'NEIL

## Professional Career

John "Buck" O'Neil began his professional baseball career with a semi-pro league, but was soon chosen to play in the professional Negro Baseball Leagues:

> O'Neil signed to play baseball with the Miami Giants, a Negro barnstorming team, and in 1937 he was signed by the Memphis Red Sox of the Negro Baseball League, and the following year with the Kansas City Monarchs. Buck's career with the Monarchs as a smooth building first baseman and savvy manager (1948 to 1955) spanned 1937 to 1955. The Monarchs won consecutive Negro American League pennants from 1938 to 1942. His Negro League baseball career was interrupted by service in the U.S. Navy from 1943 to 1945. As a manager, O'Neil led the Monarchs to two Negro Baseball League championships and one title. He compiled a lifetime batting average of .288, and led the league in hitting with a .345 batting average in 1940, and .350 in 1945, his best season. He was manager of the Western team at the annual All-Star game from 1951 to 1954.
>
> In 1955 Buck signed with the Chicago Cubs thus becoming the first African-American scout in the major leagues, and subsequently became the first African American coach in the major leagues as well. However, due to the enduring racism of the times, this accomplished baseball veteran never got the opportunity to coach on the field during a major league game. However, O'Neil was credited with signing Hall of Fame shortstop Ernie Banks, and outfielder Lou Brock and many other successful black major league ball players. He became a scout with the Kansas City Royals in 1988 and earned the Midwest Scout of the Year in 1998. His association with the Royals would continue throughout his life.[11]

## Buck O'Neil's Awards

Buck O'Neil received numerous awards and recognition of his outstanding performance on the field and promotion off of the field including:

- Presidential Medal of Freedom.
- Buck O'Neil Lifetime Achievement Award – National Baseball Hall of Fame.

- Civil Rights game "Beacon of Light" award — Major League Baseball.
- Honorary doctorate degrees from the University of Missouri, Kansas City, and Duquesne University.
- Florida State Hall of Fame.
- Statue of O'Neil in the Negro Leagues Baseball Museum.
- Bust of O'Neil in the Hall of Famous Missourians.
- The Baltimore Orioles' spring training complex was named after O'Neil.
- Honored in 1995 with a special graduation ceremony at Sarasota High School from which he had been denied admission 65 years earlier, due to segregation.[12]

Buck O'Neil died in 2006 at the age of 94. The fact that he was never inducted into the Baseball Hall of Fame is a controversial issue, especially among his supporters. However, the Baseball Hall of Fame erected a statue of him at Cooperstown, New York, its headquarters, and created a Lifetime Achievement Award in his honor.[13]

## ADAIR JAMES FORD

Ford's baseball career began by playing as a younger man:

> With the first all-Negro teams — Huntsville Rockets and the All Star Team. Later, he signed with one of the St. Louis Cardinals' minor league team[s] and played with the Winnipeg Goldeyes, Mattoon Phillies and Gainesville G-Men. During 1954-1955, he traveled to several cities in the United States and Canada. His love for the sport encouraged him to teach young males to attain their baseball aspirations. Some of them pursued college and a professional sport. ... For over 35 years he worked at the Sarasota Parks & Recreation (part-time) in the Newtown community. The newly constructed gym was named in his honor by the City of Sarasota.[14]

## WILLIE "CURLY" WILLIAMS

> Williams began playing with Negro teams in Charleston, Lakeland and Jacksonville in the 40s. He'd win a spot on one of the "major" Negro League teams in 1948. Williams, then a shortstop, was a member of the Newark Eagles (and its successors) from 1948 to 1951 and was selected to play in the 1950 East-West All-Star

game. He also played winter ball in the Dominican Republic and Puerto Rico. In late 1949 in Puerto Rico, Williams, on a homer spree, attracted the attention of the Caribbean scout for the New York Giants. ... Then after the 1950 All-Star game the Chicago White Sox came calling. He took his game to the Triple-A level in the White Sox organization, which, however, already had a young Chico Carrasquel at shortstop with Luis Aparicio soon to replace him. Noting the limited opportunities in pro ball, especially as he reached his late 20s, William headed north and joined the Carman, Manitoba, Cardinals and [a] host of other former Negro League players in the ManDak [Manitoba-Dakota] League. He had a strong season, .286, 12 homers and 40 runs batted in over just 199 at bats.

He was lured back to the Negro Leagues in 1954 when he was one of the stalwarts of the Birmingham Black Barons. The following season, he'd begin a nine-year hitch with Lloydminster of the Western Canada and Northern Saskatchewan Baseball leagues. Not only was he one of the most popular players, Williams continued to perform at a high level and also took up managerial duties for the final few seasons of his career. He retired from baseball after the 1963 season. Williams put in twenty-seven years with the Sarasota Coroners office before he retired in 1990. ... In 1997, the Sarasota, Florida Council declared "Curly Williams Day" in honor of his efforts to raise funds (through the Curly Williams Foundation) to provide college scholarships for needy students. Williams died in Sarasota in August 2011 at age 86.[15]

## MAJOR LEAGUE BASEBALL

Four African Americans from Sarasota played Major League Baseball:
- **HUGH YANCEY JR.,** Chicago White Sox, 1968 and the Cleveland Indians; Manager of Chicago Cubs rookie team in the Gulf Coast League, 1985;
- **EDWARD "DUKE" WHEELER** – St. Louis Cardinals, 1970;
- **ROBERT "POOKIE" WILLIAMS** – Texas Rangers, 1971;
- **JOHNNY JENKINS** – Texas Rangers, 1972.

# YOUTH BASEBALL IN NEWTOWN

Baseball has traditionally been very popular in Newtown. In 1954 the American Legion Post #295:

Fielded a baseball team for Newtown's youth that was to eventually develop into a four-team league. These teams went on to win two district and divisional titles. In 1958, the Post's teams won the 8th Division Title and in 1963, the 11th District Championship.[16]

Perhaps due to the strife created in Newtown and Sarasota by desegregation and civil rights issues, the organized youth baseball teams ceased to play. McElroy wrote in 1986 that:

The rebirth of youth baseball in the Newtown area came about as the result of hard work by two dedicated parents ... [who] had boys in the 9-13 year old range. ... Ervin Crummer and Robert White are the two of many who began the drive to have our black youngsters play organized baseball. ... They went around and begged for donations, for uniforms, travel expenses and refreshments. While doing this, they interested Fredd Atkins in their quest to have a league. Fredd was the sports writer for the *Bulletin*, which is our black newspaper. While the coaches were doing their best ... the columnist continued to bombard the sports section with pleas for help.

George Parson, regional director for Little League Baseball, read about their desire to become a league. ... After several meetings ... Newtown Little League was embraced into Little League International.[17]

According to Fredd Atkins, "the Newtown Little League incorporated in 1982 and he was the founder and president. Ricky Thomas was the vice president and Ervin Crummer was head of officials."[18]

# GOLF

Leonard Reid, one the early leaders in Sarasota's African American community, was "the right-hand man and confidant of Colonel John Hamilton Gillespie, first mayor of the township of Sarasota."[19]

Reid assisted Col. Gillespie in mapping the first golf course in Sarasota:

> That covered 110 acres in the eastern end of downtown. The first hole was where the Terrace Building, on North Washington and Ringling boulevards, stands ... When Gillespie was designing the [nine-hole] golf course in 1901, the pair walked through the palmetto covered land ... After the design was completed, Reid and a crew of 50 men went to work pulling out the palmettos to create the fairways and the greens. The Gillespie Golf Course opened in 1905 and closed in 1925.[20]

African Americans were unable to enjoy the beautiful Bobby Jones Golf Course. That is until Robert "Bud" Thomas took a stand on the matter. His good friend, Jetson Grimes recalls that:

> [Bud] was the one that forced the integration of the Bobby Jones Golf Course. ... I can remember ... when it started out with the golf course ... they had the Caddie Club. ... At four o'clock the caddies could go out and play. And if they had friends, they could bring their friends to play. And Bud, he never was a caddie, but loved to play golf. So he would play ... in the afternoon, after work. ... And after a while he said, "Well hey. If I can go out there at four o'clock, we can go out there at eight o'clock or nine o'clock, in the daytime." So he formed a group and they went out and got on the tee and teed off. And the City Manager at that time ... they had a big commotion. ... They had these black people out there on the golf course. And in fact, as I was told, he didn't get any kind of repercussion [from the white players on the course]. ... They was just like, "Okay we just got some black people out there." But the city was up in arms ... [not] ready for integration ... They finished eighteen holes and they called them in [off the course] but Bud said, "We gonna go back out here the next day." "We gonna continue to play." So I think Sarasota didn't want any kind of controversy because it was a tourist town. You know, they didn't need that kind of publicity. So that's how the golf course was integrated.[21]

The Robert "Bud" Thomas Golf Tournament is organized by Grimes and held at Bobby Jones Golf Course during the Dr. Martin Luther King Jr. Celebration in honor of Thomas.

# BASKETBALL

**Howard Porter** was arguably the greatest basketball player from any high school in the state of Florida, and some go further to say he was the best in the country. Porter was born on August 31, 1948 in Stuart, Florida, and later moved with his family to Newtown. As fate would have it, the family moved next door to Booker High School basketball coach Al Baker. Baker had received communication from a coaching colleague about the talented high school basketball player's move to Sarasota. Porter would not disappoint. Together with teammates Hugh Yancey and Arthur Johnson, the powerful 6'8" center/power forward led the Tornadoes to an undefeated 35-0 season. The team averaged 102 points and won the Florida Interscholastic Athletic Association Championship for all-black teams. Coach Al Baker said his team could have scored 200 points. Indeed, on January 21, 1967 the Tornadoes defeated Marshall 166-66, at the time the highest total by a team in Florida, and this was before adoption of the three-point shot.[22]

Excitement about the team went far beyond the Newtown community. Howard averaged 35 points as a senior, and in one game he scored 37 points, pulled down 28 rebounds and blocked six shots. In another memorable game, he shattered the backboard on a dunk. Coach Baker said Porter was not just a superbly talented athlete, but also the hardest worker on the team. First in the gym and the last to leave; an ideal team leader.[23]

There was much excitement not only in Newtown, but also throughout the Sarasota community about the exploits of the exciting Booker team. It seemed as though the entire city supported the team and, increasingly, white Sarasota residents started coming to the games. The all-black team was a "uniting" force in an otherwise racially divided Sarasota community.[24] "Until that particular time, there was a fear of coming into our community," longtime Newtown barber Jetson Grimes says. "I thought it had a lot of meaning for the relationship between whites and blacks."[25]

Buried in the excitement of winning, though, was a foreboding sense of loss. Integration took place after 1966 to 67 school year, and Booker High was shut down for the next three years. The team was the last great thing residents of Newtown had to hold onto for a while. "It was a sense of pride," Frazier says. "You had something you could focus on, rather than knowing you were going to get shut down the next season. So many things happened after that and it wasn't nice. Booker had a lot of pride and it was destroyed, and Booker has never been the same since."[26]

Several universities heavily recruited Porter, but none in Florida, a state steeped in the Jim Crow racism of the segregated South. Colleges across the country wanted Porter. But [Coach] Baker was also intercepting a lot of hate mail from towns like Gainesville [Florida] and Tallahassee [Florida], where people were not too keen on having a black player at the local university. Lou Watson, then head coach of basketball powerhouse Indiana University, came to see Porter play – the first time he had flown to see anyone. Porter didn't score in the first seven minutes. Then he exploded with 54 points over the next 25. Watson was quoted in the *Herald-Tribune* as saying, "I gave Howard a 98 percent rating out of 100 percent the first time I scouted him, and my first comment on the scouting report was 'Superstar.'"[27]

Villanova was among the first northern schools to recruit blacks in the South, and it dispatched assistant coach George Raveling to scout Porter. "By halftime I knew there couldn't be five guys in the universe his age better than him," Raveling told the *Orlando Sentinel*.[28]

Porter decided to play at Villanova University in Philadelphia. A three time All-American selection, he compiled a career average of 22.8 points a game and 14.8 rebounds per game. He holds the Villanova career record for rebounds and led his team to the 1971 NCAA Championship game. Porter scored 25 points, grabbed eight rebounds and was named the tournament's Most Valuable Player, despite his team losing the final game to UCLA, 68 to 62.[29]

Unfortunately, following the bad advice of his agents, Porter signed a contract on Dec. 16, 1970 with the American Basketball Association (ABA) Pittsburgh Condors while still playing for Villanova. This was a violation of the NCAA's rules. That mistake resulted in three major negative events: "The NCAA made Villanova forfeit every game of the 1970-71 season dating back to Dec. 16, 1970. That included the two Final Four games, played in March 1971. The school also had to return close to $72,000, its cut from the tournament."[30] Porter's MVP award was also withdrawn. An *Orlando Sentinel* reporter who interviewed him said the professional contract issue crushed Porter and denied him the chance to become an NBA star. As Porter told the reporter, "My understanding was it wasn't binding. It was just a document and not a contract. I think the whole Villanova thing carried over and affected my confidence. I had always been the nice, easygoing, good guy, but back then I was viewed as a crook." [31]

Porter played professional basketball in the NBA for seven years with the Chicago Bulls, the New York Knicks and the Detroit Pistons. In 1997, the Villanova University Wildcats retired Porter's #54 basketball jersey … and it hangs from the rafters in the Pavilion. Returning to his alma mater in 2001 for a Wildcats Legends Gala, he was greeted warmly by teammates, administrators and students. "He is a beloved figure here," said Villanova coach Jay Wright. Following his NBA career, Porter struggled for a time with alcoholism and drug abuse. He had seemingly turned his life around, however, and was working as a respected probation officer in Minneapolis, Minnesota, when he was tragically murdered. [32] Howard Porter died on May 26, 2007. He was 58 years old. [33]

## PROFESSIONAL FOOTBALL

Sam Shields Jr. was a star athlete in football, track and field, and baseball at Booker High School. He was an excellent wide receiver in high school and, in 2014, he signed a $36 million contract that included a $12.5 million signing bonus with the NFL's Green Bay Packers.

Two other Newtown athletes who beat the odds and made it into the NFL were Tony Green and Wendell "Pat" Carter. Green played for the Washington Redskins and the Seattle Seahawks. Carter played for the Detroit Lions, the Los Angeles Rams, the Houston Oilers and the Arizona Cardinals. [34] Green and Carter were inducted into the Riverview High School Hall of Fame in September 2015.

## THE ATHLETIC LEGACY OF BOOKER HIGH SCHOOL

All of the stories about Newtown athletes, except one, have a common thread – Booker High School (BHS). Buck O'Neil did not attend Booker High. At the time he was ready to attend high school, BHS did not exist. African American students could only advance to the eighth grade; white high schools would not accept them.

Desegregation forced the community to spread out its talented African American athletes to various Sarasota schools. Prior to desegregation, BHS had been called "The School of Champions." It was a powerhouse in local and state sports, winning numerous awards and trophies. Both boys and girls from BHS represented some of the best athletes in the State of Florida.

---

**ENDNOTES**

[1] Negro Leagues Baseball Museum. "Leagues and Teams." https://www.nlbm.com/s/team.htm

[2] Montgomery, Rick. "Buck O'Neil: Played key role in establishing the Negro Leagues Baseball Museum." January 15, 2016. http://www.kansascity.com/news/local/article54962555.html "Life hasn't been so good for the Negro Leagues Baseball Museum since Buck's passing five years ago. The facility in the 18th and Vine Jazz District has gone through financial and leadership struggles. This spring, the museum's board picked Bob Kendrick to take over the museum in hopes of drawing in new fans and turning a profit." "A Century to Remember: Bob Kendrick, NLBM and Buck O'Neil." KCPT, Kansas City PBS. 2013. http://kcpt.org/news/a-century-to-remember-bob-kendrick-nlbm-and-buck-oneil/

[3] Negro Leagues Baseball Museum. "Leagues and Teams."; "Buck O'Neil: Played key role."

[4] Mannix, Vin. "Bradenton's first baseball heroes: Nine Devils to be Honored." *Bradenton Herald*. October 16, 2011. http://www.bradenton.com/news/local/news-columns-blogs/article34528767.html

[5] Beardsley, Howie. "Sarasota-Bradenton Nine Devils Special to Manager Robinson." *Herald-Tribune*, June 22, 1983. https://news.google.com/newspapers?nid=1755&dat=19830622&id=O9geAAAAI BAJ&sjid=dWgEAAAAIBAJ&pg=4440,1172267&hl=en

[6] "Sarasota-Bradenton Nine Devils Special to Manager Robinson."

[7] Shank, Ann. "Leagues of Their Own." Sarasotahistoryalive.com http://www.sarasotahistoryalive.com/history/articles/leagues-of-their-own/

[8] "Leagues of Their Own."

[9] Porter, Les. "Newtown Sports Personalities." Unpublished paper, 2016.

[10] "Leagues of Their Own."

[11] "Newtown Sports Personalities."

[12] Sullivan, Paul. "A Lesson in Diplomacy." *Chicago Tribune*. March 12, 1995.

[13] O'Neil, "Negro Leagues player, dies at 94." MLB.com. October 7, 2006.

[14] Quoted from the Obituary of Adair James Ford. He died on March 19, 2016.

[15] *Western Canada Baseball* "Willie 'Curly' Williams." http://www.attheplate.com/wcbl/profile_williams_curly.html

[16] McElroy, Annie M. *But Your World and My World: The Struggle for Survival, A Partial History of Blacks in Sarasota County 1884-1986.* Sarasota, FL.: Black South Press, 1986, 175.

[17] *But Your World and My World*, 175.

[18] Communication with Vickie Oldham.

[19] Rodriguez, Yolanda. "Home in Path of Progress." *Sarasota Herald-Tribune.* July 18, 1998. Section A1.

[20] "Home in Path of Progress."

[21] Interview with Vickie Oldham. Sept 4, 2015.

[22] "Newtown Sports Personalities."

[23] "Newtown Sports Personalities."

[24] "Newtown Sports Personalities."

[25] Anderson, Chris. "Former Coach Talks about Booker High Basketball." Newtown 100. *Herald-Tribune.* December 14, 2014. http://newtown100.heraldtribune.com/2014/12/14/former-coach-talks-booker-high-basketball/

[26] "Former coach talks about Booker High basketball."

[27] Anderson, Chris. "Finally forgiven: The Howard Porter story." Newtown 100. *Herald-Tribune.* http://newtown100.heraldtribune.com/2014/12/14/finally-forgiven-howard-porter-story/

[28] "Finally forgiven: The Howard Porter story."

[29] "Finally forgiven: The Howard Porter story."

[30] "Finally forgiven: The Howard Porter story."

[31] "Finally forgiven: The Howard Porter story."

[32] "Newtown Sports Personalities."

[33] "Finally forgiven: The Howard Porter story."

[34] "Green and Carter Inducted Into Riverview Hall of Fame." *Tempo News.* September 3-9, 2015, 1.

# CHAPTER 14: REDEVELOPMENT OF NEWTOWN

*"As in many African-American communities, what is necessary for revitalization goes well beyond streetscape and beautification. These physical solutions must be combined with social and economic ones in order for the community to reach its full potential."*
— Newtown Community Redevelopment Area Plan

     The above statement is an excerpt from the Executive Summary of the Newtown Community Redevelopment Area (CRA) Plan. It declares the intention to implement a comprehensive approach – addressing the social as well as the physical and economic infrastructure – in the planning process for revitalizing the Newtown community.

     Since African Americans first settled in Sarasota, access to professional medical care was nonexistent. For many years, Jim Crow laws left residents to care for themselves. Healthcare is a vitally important aspect of social revitalization and its inclusion in the CRA Plan advances the comprehensive approach designed to address the wellbeing of Newtown residents. Heart disease and diabetes are two serious illnesses that are prevalent in the Newtown population. The announcement of Sarasota Memorial Hospital's plan to establish a clinic in Newtown is overdue but welcomed news. "This is a game changer," said Mayor Willie Shaw, a strong advocate of revitalization efforts in Newtown.[1]

     In a newspaper article about the clinic's opening, Dr. Lisa Merritt, founder of the Multicultural Health Institute in Sarasota, commented that hospital leaders should also pay attention to delivering care that considers the cultural aspects of medical treatment. Dr. Merritt is an expert regarding racial health disparities and she asked: "Will the [post-graduate medical] residents speak Spanish? Will they look like the patients they're serving? And will they understand what local resources are available to patients?"[2] These are critical questions that have serious consequences for the quality of care patients receive.

     Planners may also want to consider collaborating with the faculty and graduate students in the University of South Florida Department of Anthropology's program in Biocultural Medical Anthropology (Biocultural Dimensions of Human Health and Illness).[3] The field of Medical Anthropology, a sub-section of Cultural Anthropology, asks the same types of questions as Dr. Merritt. Medical Anthropologists work with physicians, helping them to understand how cultural factors influence health and wellbeing, and how the physicians' awareness of these cultural factors can improve healthcare programs and services. Since treatment in the Newtown clinic will be administered by post-graduate residents, it is hoped that the hospital's planning process for their training includes cultural competency education, and, possibly, consulting Dr. Merritt for her expertise in this area. If adopted, these suggested measures could make the Newtown healthcare clinic a true "state-of-the-art" healthcare facility.

## A "NEW" NEWTOWN

Extensive planning and millions of dollars have been invested by various entities collaboratively to revitalize Newtown. In the City of Sarasota's fiscal year 2000-2001 budget, the Commissioners demonstrated their support for revitalizing Newtown by allocating funding for this purpose. Following is a portion of the report:

> The Newtown Comprehensive Redevelopment Plan, also known as the Newtown Community Redevelopment Area Plan (CRA) was prepared by the citizens of Newtown as a blueprint for the revitalization of their community, which has experienced a decline in its economy, a decline in living conditions as the housing stock deteriorates, and a decline in their quality of life.
>
> Concern over the community's decline prompted several community leaders, represented by the Coalition for African American Leadership, to organize an effort to get the City Commission of Sarasota to verify the severity of these issues, identify the causes and, where appropriate, assist them in turning these trends around. There have been numerous isolated organizational efforts and specific public improvements made in this neighborhood in the past. However, the commissioners agreed that it was time to make a more comprehensive examination of the factors contributing to the area's economic decline and to devise a series of strategies for the redevelopment of the community.
>
> The city's goal is to revitalize the entire community through the stimulation of commercial and housing development and redevelopment within Newtown. This Community Redevelopment Area Plan is the summary of this planning effort and shall act as the blueprint for the Newtown community renaissance. The plan outlines detailed strategies for achieving this goal, and identifies specific projects to be included as part of the city's Ten-Year Capital Improvement Program. The plan also identifies other financial resources and partners to assist with the implementation of plan strategies.

Outside funding is required to bring the revitalization process to reality. However, outsiders cannot "fix" these community problems. A grassroots, bottom up strategy is required. Therefore, the fact that

Newtown citizens prepared the CRA plan is good news. Too often community projects are dictated, top down, by people who may be well meaning but do not know or understand the particular culture of the community nor bother to consult community members about solutions. In this case, it is apparent that residents' input was heard because, for example, changes were made with regard to hiring practices after Janie Poe's Gardens Phase I was completed.

The Sarasota Housing Authority and its developer, Michaels Development, were responsible for the redevelopment of the Janie Poe public housing projects. The housing facility was named in honor of a well-respected Booker High School math teacher.

Janie Poe.
Courtesy: Dorothye Smith.

Over the years, the buildings became severely deteriorated and a haven for illegal activities. The Janie's Garden construction project was designed to renovate or demolish structures, revitalizing that part of Newtown. Phase I began in 2008 with the renovation of a number of low-income housing units into 86 modernized mixed income units. That project, however, revealed disparities in hiring practices that led to the establishment of a community taskforce to address hiring concerns before additional projects were started, specifically the Janie's Garden Phase II and the Robert L. Taylor Community Complex redevelopment projects.

In the effort to increase the number of local people hired for the project, Suncoast Technical College developed an introduction to construction class and training programs to teach job readiness skills. Area residents who graduated from the program were hired by four construction companies.[4] The involvement of local workers provided an income for people in the community that, during the time of the Janie Poe Phase I, had a 17% unemployment rate.[5] One third of the workers who constructed Robert L. Taylor Community Complex lived in the community. They experienced an enormous sense of pride and personal investment while working on the project.

The 2005 documentary film, "Condemned," brought negative attention to the City when it illuminated the great disparity in living conditions between the white and African American residents of Sarasota. It highlighted the Janie Poe housing projects. One summary of the documentary film reads:

> One of the wealthiest cities in the country has a secret. In the shadow of the swankiest downtown hi-rises, children are sleeping with roaches swarming their beds, black mold invading their lungs, and raw sewage bubbling up in the yards where they play. For decades, the 128 poor families who live in the Janie Poe housing project in Sarasota, Florida, were out of sight, out of mind. "Condemned" gives a voice to the families living inside the tenement, and shows how poverty and neglect are interlaced with racism, politics and power.[6]

The renovation of housing and other buildings is key to the success of the Newtown CRA. The deteriorated condition of some areas attracted crime. The second phase of Janie's Garden began in 2011 and was completed in 2012. It added 68 affordable housing units and new retail space. The transformation of the rundown Janie Poe housing projects began with tearing down the Mediterranean Apartments, a haven for undesirable persons who moved into the community over the past few decades.

Eager to bring noticeable change to Newtown, local and federal housing officials pledged to tear down the projects and transform them into modern, colorful mixed-income housing complexes. Eddie L. Rainey Jr., a retired postmaster lived near the Mediterranean Apartments and was glad to see their destruction. Rainey attended the ceremonial demolition held on a December day in 2011 and told a reporter, "This was the nest" … "By taking the nest down, those birds got to fly somewhere else."[7] The King Stone Townhomes Complex replaced the demolished Mediterranean Apartment complex, which had 68 small apartments. The new complex consists of 28 spacious units of mixed-income housing. Displaced residents received relocation assistance, according to William Russell, President and CEO of the Sarasota Housing Authority.[8] "Fourteen townhomes are restricted to very low income families earning less than

50% of the area's median income. The other 14 townhomes are restricted to families earning up to 80% of the area's median income."[9]

Currently, investors, not community residents, own approximately 60% of Newtown real estate. The trend began when the economy took a nosedive in 2008. Homes went into foreclosure, which opened opportunities for outside investors to purchase distressed properties.

The Newtown-North Sarasota Redevelopment Office (NRO) is on the front line of redevelopment efforts in Newtown. The NRO, a division of the City of Sarasota's Neighborhood and Development Services Department, works with the community, developers and other stakeholders to implement the Sarasota City Commission's priorities and goals related to the CRA plan. The NRO lists these major projects (completed from 2008-2013) in its April 2014 report: the North Sarasota Workforce Initiative (NSWI); North Sarasota Entrepreneur Collaborative (NSEC); StoreFront Grant Program; Youth Empowerment; Alice Faye Jones, a volunteer at the Robert L. Taylor Community Complex, offers the program "Brothers and Sisters Doing the Right Thing;" Booker High School Rebuild — also a part of the CRA; The Neighborhood Stabilization Project (NSP); and a Walmart Neighborhood Market.

The redevelopment plans appear to be proceeding in a very positive direction for Newtown. The data presented in the NCHD Project's Final Report will provide the NRO and others additional insight into the community, its people and their visions for the future by:

- Providing the Newtown community with a deeper knowledge of its history, intermingled with the personal stories of community residents' experiences;
- Presenting historic preservation analysis, an inventory of the community's structures and information about those that hold special historical and cultural significance to community members;
- Contributing to the cultural knowledge base of the community's residents and leaders as well as the governmental agencies working to redevelop Newtown-North Sarasota.

In 2009, the Sarasota City Commission made Newtown's uplift a priority. It was the catalyst needed to complete many of the initiatives. A major factor in the progress now occurring in the Newtown area has been the commitment and longstanding support of City Commissioners and their desire to garner strong community consensus. There were challenges in navigating people, place and politics, but having CRA/TIFF funds assisted greatly in accomplishing their goals.

It is gratifying to learn about cooperative ventures between the Newtown community and outside entities that seek to work together to rebuild and revitalize, rather than gentrify, a historic African American community. These CRA projects benefit the city's economy and demonstrate that Sarasota is striving to become an inclusive city that acknowledges and respects the diversity of its citizenry.

---

## ENDNOTES

[1] LeCoz, Emily. "Sarasota Memorial to open clinic in Newtown." http://g52-shweb.newscyclecloud.com/article/2015151209678

[2] Clark, Maggie and Billy Cox. "New Clinic will target adults." *Herald-Tribune.* December 8, 2015. http://g52-shweb.newscyclecloud.com/article/2015151209650

[3] "Biocultural Dimensions of Human Health and Illness." http://anthropology.usf.edu/research/themes/

[4] "Local area residents were defined as: a person who resides within the Newtown boundaries, which are from the North: Myrtle Street, from the East: Tuttle, from the South 17th Street, from the West: Orange Avenue, then back South: 10th Street to the West: U.S. Highway 41 (Tamiami Trail)." Source: Newtown-North Sarasota Redevelopment Project Report.

[5] 2010 census data reported in the Demographic Survey prepared by the Newtown-North Sarasota Redevelopment Office. April 2014.

[6] "Condemned." http://www.imdb.com/title/tt1500158/

[7] "New day for Newtown housing." http://www.heraldtribune.com/news/20111202/new-day-for-newtown-housing

[8] Personal correspondence with Vickie Oldham. January 30, 2017.

[9] Newtown-North Sarasota Redevelopment Project Report.

# CHAPTER 15: VISIONS FOR THE FUTURE

*"We know that neither institutions nor friends can make a race stand unless it has strength in its own foundation. In order to succeed, it must practice the virtues of self-reliance, self-respect, industry, perseverance and economy."*
— Paul Robeson

Human rights advocate Paul Robeson aptly described the fortitude of the founding fathers and mothers of Newtown. Through determination, enterprise, self-reliance and self-respect, they accomplished great feats. Their silent mantra, "I shall either find a way or make one," is a recurring theme that emerges throughout their history.

Even though the conditions under which residents lived were unacceptable, undesirable and in many cases deplorable, the pioneers continued working and building the communities of Overtown and Newtown with available resources for future generations. Residents found a way to pool their assets to ensure that neighbors and neighbors' children had food to eat, access to electricity, and were educated. Those who could afford to purchase consumer goods such as cars and televisions shared them. Teachers worked overtime to prepare students for college and life. African American-owned businesses thrived because Newtown residents had to patronize them for their survival.

Today, many residents of the Newtown community are observing ongoing construction projects near where they once lived in the downtown corridor, and the expansion of Ringling College of Art and Design along Dr. Martin Luther King Jr. Way. Gentrification is the term that describes what many residents suspect is happening in Newtown. Don't mention the "g" word, though, among some developers and new residents who moved into Overtown — now rebranded as the Rosemary District — where Sarasota's African American community had its beginning. The word has too many negative connotations.

There was only one historic marker to remind visitors and residents that African American residents built a beloved district tin Overtown. In early 2016, a contractor, constructing a multimillion dollar condominium and office complex, took the marker down. Overtown and Newtown residents flooded City Hall with calls. Mayor Willie Charles Shaw called for city workers to locate the marker. They did find it, but, ultimately, it was not reinstalled at the construction site. It was placed in storage and a temporary sign was posted on the construction gate amid a sea of other construction signs, making it hard to distinguish.

Municipalities throughout the country are grappling with how to find the right balance between improving blighted communities and avoiding the displacement of the original residents who wish to remain in their neighborhoods. Mixed-income housing, quality schools, childcare and job training services are a few amenities that are changing neglected neighborhoods in Atlanta, Austin, Boston and beyond. It is our hope that Sarasota planners will meet with community leaders from other cities that have similar redevelopment issues as Newtown to discover mutually beneficial solutions for stimulating revitalization.

## PERSONAL VISIONS

Newtown residents were asked about their visions for the neighborhood's future. Some older residents long for days of old, but others are embracing inevitable changes in the community. Below are a few of their remarks:

**Anthony "Tony" Major,** interview with Dr. Rosalyn Howard.
*(Dr. Howard): What do you see as the future or what would you hope for the future of Newtown?*
*(A. T. Major):* Well … I think the history needs to be told and needs to be preserved. … what it went through to get to where it is. Then … the people who live in the neighborhood will have a sense of pride and get rid of all the drugs and … and have a sense of caring about the community. Right now, it's like every other black community; it's the old folks who are carrying it on. The youth could care less. But I think if we can instill that in the youth, probably get some more black teachers at Booker. So it's a mixture … I think then the future would be bright.

**Carolyn Mason**, interview with Hope Black.
*(H. Black): How can we, the community at large, influence teenagers who might be going astray, to come back and make a life for themselves?*
*(C. Mason):* I think programs like Community Youth Development, and then the city has a youth group. I think as much as we can, we need to try and touch not only those groups, but any … organized groups of youngsters like at community centers and Boys' and Girls' Clubs and Girls, Inc. and the YMCA. As much as we can, start to talk to those groups of children or … wherever they are. We ought to be taking our messages there, and then inviting them to our places of business and volunteer. Give them

the opportunity to learn what we have learned. And I think that can help build our community going forward.

**Dorothye Smith**, interview with Vickie Oldham.

*(V. Oldham): What would you have to say to this Newtown community about moving forward in the coming years and decades and centuries? What can they learn, this new generation, from the early years?*

*(D. Smith):* They can learn there's close relationship. It should be always between the school, the home, and the community. And also that children learn by sharing and people in general learn by sharing, not just in the community, but remember there are people over – we call it "other side of the track"– and their bodies work the same way yours work. And if you show love and respect, they'll show love and respect. Because sometimes we can be kinda hostile. … Forget about things that happened in the past and remember the good things that's happening now and the good things we expect to happen in the future. That's one of the best things that they can do.

**Dr. Edward James II**, interview with Haley L. Jordan (New College student).

I'm glad that you all are doing something that you believe is good for posterity, for everybody, because I always believed that folk would do better if they knew better. But they don't understand.

**Eddie Rainey**, interview with Vickie Oldham.

*(V. Oldham): In Newtown's going forward, what is going to need to happen for its future?*

*(E. Rainey):* For the future of Newtown? Well that's a good one. I would say we've gotta find a way to gainfully employ our young people and to educate them. To let them know the benefits of an education and have them get out and earn. And I hate to bring this to the topic, this drug situation. We've got to find something that is going to deter this situation out of the community. You know it's a hard thing to hear a child say, "Well he's driving a Mercedes, he's driving a Cadillac and he does not work." And they understand, "Wow," they say, "Well I want to be that way." But I think that if we could educate them, provide them with jobs and give them better guidance from the churches, from the schools, from the neighbor down the street, talk to them and let them know, "Hey, there's a better life if you just apply yourself. "

**Dr. Harriet Moore,** interview with Vickie Oldham.

*(V. Oldham): Yes, our leaders are aging and we need a new crop of leaders to take this community to the next level. What is it gonna take?*

*(Dr. Moore):* We absolutely do. One of the things that I try to do through my church, Trinity Christian Fellowship Center, we have a mentoring program, The Youth United for Success Mentoring Outreach Program. ... So we work with young people to help them and develop them, kinda like we were nurtured coming up. And all of us that are here that know and understand should all be working with young people to mentor them and to train them and to instill in them the wisdom, the knowledge, the understanding and the values of our parents and grandparents and great-grandparents. And helping them to understand the history of our people.

**Dr. Fannie McDugle**, interview with Vickie Oldham.

*(V. Oldham): What's your vision for Newtown's future? If you could envision a future for Newtown, what would it look like?*

*(F. McDugle):* Well, if I could do it, it would look like downtown. [Laughter] ... It would take a lot of money to do it. So, I'm not dreaming about it right now, but maybe you and the other generation coming on might step up and can do it.

**Fredd Atkins**, interview with Vickie Oldham.

*(V. Oldham): Okay, answer that question about where we're going as a community.*

*(F. Atkins):* Where we are going as a community has been a very serious struggle for myself and people of conscience and awareness, because we are trying so hard to save this community for our own...posterity. And with that, we want to make sure that Newtown don't get gentrified out of Sarasota and be scattered like they did down there in Lee County or they did in Overtown in Miami in some sections or they did in Palm Beach and Riviera Beach in West Palm Beach. This system has a way of dispersing us — just like they did Overtown and Sarasota—and replacing you with a different kind of energy and culture. And so our biggest struggle now is to figure out how we maintain our history and our ownership of this community as we grow and develop economic prowess. ... If we don't create a way to maintain our community and our ownership, which is rapidly leaving, we will not have a Newtown. ... That's so important to me.

**Helen Dixon**, interview with Vickie Oldham.

*(V. Oldham): What do you think are important issues to improve Newtown?*

*(H. Dixon):* Well I'm a retired social worker and I have been here for years, and years, and years. I came back in 1982 to put back in my own neighborhood that had been so good to me. So I've counseled kids for all those years. And I see that education is the key here for our kids because they're not getting the education that they should get. ... We've got to go back ... and give some things that our parents gave to us for them to change. Because when I counsel kids, they don't have any 'get up' about them at all. ... What my father pushed in me the parents [are] not pushing that in the kids to let them know, they're free, they can do the things they want to. Put your mind to it. Get good grades, stay in school. ... I love Sarasota, I love Newtown, I love what we're doing, but we just have to do more. And it takes us, the older ones, to come back to say, "I can do all things through Christ who strengthens me." And help the others.

**Rev. Jerome Dupree**, interview with Jessica Wopinski.

*(J. Wopinski): What do you feel are the most pressing issues that we still need to work on?*

*(Rev. Dupree):* Most pressing issue that we need to work on today is to start as early as we can to work with our young people. We need people who are available for our young people as mentors. I mean start in the grade school, and work with those young people, and kind of guide them. .... fathers have walked away from the homes, the mothers are raising children by themselves. Sometimes it's the grandmothers. ... I'd like to see us come together, and be ready to assist anybody in the community when they have children and they're having a hard time. ... to be ready to assist them in as many ways as we possibly can. Because the young people that we raise now, I just want them to look at our lives and find them worthy to emulate.

**Jesse Johnson**, interview with Vickie Oldham.

*(J. Johnson):* We got to just keep on going and do better.

*(V. Oldham): Keep on going. Learning from our ancestors, learning from you all.*

*(J. Johnson):* We can learn and we can go on up the mountain 'cause this a hill we climbing and if we ain't ready to climb it, let us just give up and walk away. ... People *want* us to walk away.

'Cause someone else can come in line. And I say, "No sir. I know about these people, these my people I'm talking about." That's what I tell people.

**Jetson Grimes**, interview with Vickie Oldham.
*(V. Oldham): What can it be as we move into the future?*
*(J. Grimes):* Well I think mentally from a city perspective and a community perspective, it can't continue to be a black enclave off to itself. ... We're unique ... [but] ... We need to be inclusive with the rest of Sarasota. ... You'd have to break down that polarization of this community. ... Because it's just like being contained in a environment when you not getting any air. If we don't have the ability to open this environment up where we can get the resources and get the air that the rest of Sarasota gets, we gonna continue to slowly ... fade away. ... And mentally we have to start changing ourselves. We got to say, "Okay if we gonna participate in this city, we got to be able to participate throughout the city." And people that's living outside the community ... they can have ability to come in this community and spend money. Because if the money not circulating in the community, whether it's through the jobs, whether it's through businesses, the community is going to die. ... We need to bring ... talent back in the community and if not to stay in here, but to be able to work in here, to be able to utilize their talent to enhance the community and I think once we can do that, we gonna see our thing change.

**Johnny Hunter Sr.**, interview with Vickie Oldham.
*(V. Oldham): What do you envision for Newtown's future?*
*(J. Hunter Sr.):* Well let me tell you this, one of the main problems is, we are not organized. Politics controls everything that we do in this world. From the air we breathe to this interview we doing, there's some regulation that governs that. You have to be politically active in this society. If you cannot vote, you don't even count.

**Rev. Kelvin Lumpkin,** interview with Vickie Oldham.
*(V. Oldham): The same reason that people came, young people, professionals, leave because there is not adequate employment and they don't come back except for holidays and weekends.*
*(Rev. Lumpkin):* I think that part of the problem is that some our kids are being brought up without an obligation to serve. I feel an obligation to serve this community. Some people want to live their lives for their pleasure and so they want to live in a city where

entertainment is readily available. I'm not saying there's anything wrong with that, but I believe with the problems in the African American community, any African American who's made it, I think has a responsibility, just like Harriet Tubman, to go back and help those who are less fortunate. And so I hope that we can instill … in them, a heart to serve and a burden to serve. I think if we can instill in our kids a greater sense to serve, then maybe some will come back. And I see some coming back, but maybe more will come back because this community needs the talents of individuals who've been fortunate enough get a degree to be exposed to greater things. This community really needs that.

**Dr. Louis Robison**, interview with Vickie Oldham.
*(V. Oldham): You've seen its ups and its downs and what do you think? Where are we going? What should we stop doing, what should we start doing?*
*(Dr. Robison):* That's a good question. I think any community, in order to recognize its greatness or its benefits it has to begin with what you're doing, this. I think this is so important. You have to recognize the history. There's so many people that are gonna listen to this and hear this, they aren't gonna know anything about this community, and when a culture denies or does not understand its past, then it's doomed to failure. As a historian we know that. We look [at] any culture in the history of the world that decays, the decay is always based on morals or lack thereof, decadence and the kinds of things we find to be important that take us away from our beliefs in God and takes us away from our belief in church and our fellow man. When those things begin to get in the way, then we begin to see an erosion of society.

We could talk about education, we could talk about politics we could talk about who the next governor is gonna be, but it all has to start in the home and what we're teaching our children to be. Because we were poor. I'll tell you. We did not have a lot growing up and my mother lost that restaurant, probably in less than a year. So I can say to you that there were some very, very tough times, but the foundation was always there, church, education, reading books, making sure that health was as best it could be at the time. Those kinds of basic needs. We talk about that in the hierarchy of needs. Those things are important.

**Mary Alice Simmons**, interview with Vickie Oldham.
*(V. Oldham): What do you envision Newtown's future to be in looking beyond today?*

*(M. Simmons):* You know what, I've always thought about it. I was working for a lady, I asked, "How did Longboat Key become Longboat Key? How did these cities become?" That's what I envision for Newtown. I understand we don't have the tax base right now, but I think Newtown should be a town within Sarasota. I think Newtown should have its own mayor, its own police department. If the tax base ever gets there where that can be supported.

**Nathaniel Harvey**, interview with Vickie Oldham.
*(V. Oldham): What kind of advice do you have for our town leaders or community as far as what it's gonna take for us to improve even more and progress?*
*(N. Harvey):* I think we got to stick together. We got [to] work a little harder. We got to keep on working 'til we get it to work. So it's not quite where it should be, but it's getting there. So all we got to do is keep doing what we doing and maybe get a little aggressive and things will turn out for us fine.

**Robert L. Taylor**, interview with Vickie Oldham.
*(V. Oldham): What is it going to take to change this community as we move into the next century? What you think needs to happen?*
*(R. Taylor):* I think teaching kids gonna have to change. We are bringing up kids to be victims because it's everybody's fault that you are like you are. But we not doing anything on the other end of the spectrum to make these people be responsible for themselves. And if you don't respect yourself, how can you expect others to respect you? Our leaders are making people victims. You don't have to be a victim. You can get out of that rut if you want to, but you got to want to do it. And you got to have the family to encourage you to do it.

Nobody make you stop, drop out of school in the eighth grade. Nobody make you wear your pants down around your behind. And nobody make you do these things you know will be harmful. ... You have no parents now that's willing to make them do it. Right now the kids are in charge of the family. They say, "I'm gonna do this." If I got ready to go somewhere, I didn't tell my mother I'm going here, "May I go there?" You didn't have permission, you didn't go. But now kids roam the street. I wasn't allowed to roam the street, I didn't allow mine to roam the streets.

**Wade Harvin**, interview with Vickie Oldham.
*(V. Oldham): What does this community need to do to reinvent itself? To be self-sustaining?*

*(W. Harvin):* Go back and get some of the things that we dropped. There are some folk in Galilee Cemetery would say, "But why did they drop this?" About thirty years ago, if I needed a stepladder at ten o'clock on Saturday night, I could go to Chapman hardware and get a stepladder. If I needed to touch up some paint ... they were open. We gave up things that were really good for us. ... We had three, four cleaners, dry cleaners. Now] I have to drive to Main Street to put my clothes in the cleaners, my suits.

*(V. Oldham): So there's a need for more entrepreneurship?*

*(W. Harvin):* Yes, and I can understand the reason why is because we haven't told the children the story well enough.

**Wendell Pat Carter**, interview with Vickie Oldham.

*(V. Oldham): When you come back driving through the neighborhood what do you think?*

*(W. P. Carter):* Well, obviously it's changed. It's not the same any longer. When I was growing up, there were families. We don't really have the same type of families. You don't see that anymore. You see a lot of younger mothers. ... It's a lot of younger parents than my generation.

*(V. Oldham): What does Newtown have to do? What does Sarasota have to do to attract them?*

*(W. P. Carter):* Jobs. I mean obviously the bigger the city, the better the opportunity is to have a nice decent paying job and I'm sure there are some here in Sarasota, but it's limited and obviously you have a few more people competing for the same amount of jobs. And that would be the first thing that comes to my mind because upon graduating from college with a degree you want to go, obviously, where it's easiest to find a job.

**City of Sarasota Mayor**, **Willie Charles Shaw**, interview with Vickie Oldham.

*(V. Oldham): What kind of vision for the future do you have for Newtown, having seen it from its very beginnings?*

*(W. Shaw):* Well one of the things that has driven me more than anything is the identity of Newtown. ... I'm very, very big on changing the landscape, restoring the landscape and bringing about a greater vitality to North Sarasota as a whole. ... Right now ... the median income for the city of Sarasota is $49,000 a year. In our area it's about $24 [thousand]. We're 46% living under poverty.

*(V. Oldham): Why so far behind? Why the gap you think?*

*(W. Shaw):* I think that quite frequently we become distracted. There are ... other voices. And our priorities are very difficult to set

because we have yet as a community learned how to work together.
... One of my visions is to work ... with others to bring about a
greater understanding. ... I want to see the landscape change.

*(V. Oldham): What about grooming new and young leaders?*

*(W. Shaw):* Oh very much so. In talking to some of our youth,
younger people ... in a recent meeting, that was my conversation.
How do we create succession? Who comes behind me? Who do we
want to represent? And if you're not at the table ... if you're not on
our advisory boards, if you're not becoming [a] participant in your
neighborhood association, if you're not seeking these things, then
those challenges remain the same.

**James Brown and Yvonne Brown**, interview with Vickie Oldham.

*(V. Oldham): What does this community do to go into the future?*

*(J. Brown):* I think we go right back to our roots. I see us not feeling
the struggle as much, so there is no urgency. That is troublesome. I
started work at age thirteen. I would get home from school and the
next day, if it wasn't Sunday, I was up on the corner trying to catch
what you call "a hustle." Whoever comes by wanting to hire
somebody for the day, I'm gone, working my way through college.
See this is what I'm talking about. ...The struggle is no longer there.
.... The struggle builds character.

*(Y. Brown):* I also feel that we have to try harder in the educational
arena. We have to make sure that we get our children prepared for
their first day of pre-school as parents, grandparents, relatives.
We've got to make sure we get our children in an educational
system of some sort at a very early age. We had a Head Start
[program] for a long time and in most of our communities we still
have something that is akin to Head Start. So those of use that love
working with children and families, we've got to reach out a little
more and make sure that we're establishing that pride in being
whoever they are. ... It's not enough for us to get it. We got to try to
help the others get it.

And I think when we look at ourselves as a race, we've
always had that pride, we've always had that love for community,
love for each other. ... Try not to be too afraid of all the things that
we see on TV and the looks that you might get when you want to
help someone. Try to look beyond that and just quietly go and see if
there's something you can do because there's a lot of people that
need a lot of help and we see them everyday.

*(J. Brown):* Knowing what my generation came through, knowing
the opportunities that my parents missed, I feel obligated, moved,
driven to walk through every door that they could not, but I'm

prepared to walk through that door. I'm not asking for anything, I'm paying my way and I've earned the right to be there.

## Vickie Oldham's Vision for the Future

Residents, especially those who have made Newtown their home for generations, want to maintain the integrity of this historic community; enjoy its streetscapes, upgraded parks and community center; and lure talented graduates home. There is concern, however, about the displacement of residents, the loss of cultural assets and traditions as major construction projects are completed along Dr. Martin Luther King Jr. Way.

It is my hope that young leaders will emerge and devise strategies to alleviate residents' fears about gentrification and any other community issues that arise. I think there are valuable lessons to learn from our trailblazers.

For me, one of the most interesting themes that emerged from our research of Newtown's history was the youthful age of Newtown's leaders who upended Jim Crow laws that blocked equal access to Sarasota banks, restaurants, downtown shops, the hospital, libraries, and schools. The creative, bold actions and persistence of residents such as Neil Humphrey, Jack and Mary Emma Jones, John Rivers, Dr. Fannie McDugle, Dr. Edward James II, William Jackson, James Logan, Robert "Bud" Thomas, Fredd Atkins, Walter Gilbert, Betty Johnson, Sheila Sanders, John "Buck" O'Neil, Howard Porter and many others were extraordinary. These leaders are now considered community heroes and she-roes, but it was as young people that they began shaping Newtown's future, and inspiring others to move the needle of community progress.

Retired educator Dorothye Smith recalls Edward James II asking many questions in second grade. "He always asked 'why' about everything," she said. So as a Florida A&M University college freshman home on Christmas break in 1957, the first question he asked was "why?" when a librarian denied him and three classmates the right to check out books. Undeterred, James kept asking until a meeting was arranged on the spot with Sarasota City Manager Ken Thompson.

I hope a new generation of Newtown residents will continue asking "why" or "why not" and agitate as Dr. James has. The college student's tenacity opened library services to Newtown residents and students. As a 26-year-old on staff at the library, Betty Johnson advanced James' efforts by working behind the scenes, persuading her bosses at the main library to open a reading room in Newtown. Her idea morphed into a library outreach program that eventually led to the construction of the North Sarasota Public library.

As a 12-year-old, Walter Gilbert attended NAACP meetings with his mother and was inspired by local NAACP president Neil Humphrey. "I thought he was a meek man. But his persona changed in my face. I wanted to be a leader like him," said Gilbert, who at 25 became an NAACP member. Gilbert was mentored by NAACP president John Rivers and board member Dr. Edward James II, then later became the NAACP's president from 1981 to 1985.

In third grade, Sheila Sanders and her classmates saved pennies, nickels and dimes to learn about money management. They deposited the coins in passbook savings accounts at Sarasota Federal Bank. When that bank would not allow African American students to tour the facility and vault like other district students could, Sanders persuaded her 8- and 9-year-old classmates to close their accounts and open up new ones at the Palmer Bank.

As a teen, she routinely studied the agenda of the Sarasota County School Board and rode a city bus to attend the meetings. Years later, Sanders became Gilbert's campaign manager during his first bid for city commissioner. The team of James, Jackson, Sanders, Gilbert and Atkins made sure that Newtown in District One would have representation on the City Commission through a federal lawsuit that they filed and won.

Growing up in Newtown, I knew about the community leaders' work, but realized during this project the youthful age in which they changed community history.

Education, exposure, civic engagement and mentoring prepared the young adults for leadership. My vision is that the same components can transform, inspire and energize today's millennials to lead Newtown's renaissance.

# CHAPTER 16: CONCLUSION

Overtown and Newtown were the first and second African American communities formed within Sarasota, Florida. Until now, a comprehensive history of these communities has not been easily available to the general public. The details of the lives of African Americans in Sarasota were widely dispersed in public and private collections of artifacts, news stories, personal photographs and letters that had been stored away. Many memories were sealed in the unrecorded oral tradition of the residents.

The City of Sarasota provided the funding that Newtown residents had sought for over a decade, which made it possible to form a team of scholars, professionals and community consultants who would finally combine all of these fractured details. The team conducted in-depth research about these historic African American communities with an emphasis on Newtown, which celebrated its centennial in 2014. The research included: oral history interviews, an inventory of Newtown's historic buildings, how the community developed through an examination of original plat maps, and an extensive review of written sources. The important legacies of courage, dignity and determination among the people of the Newtown community mirror those legacies in other African American communities across the United States. Providing this space for the ancestors, elders and descendants to tell their stories expands our vision of the mosaic of American history, adding pieces to it that have been missing for too long.

Preservation and interpretation of the Newtown community's history will now be shared with the public on a heritage interpretive trail, a website, an app, and a brochure. All of these products will spark pride in the past, confidence about the future and respect for the contributions of Sarasota's African American trailblazers.

A byproduct of promoting Newtown's historic resources will be a transformation of the community. When Sarasota's Laurel and Gillespie Park neighbors promoted their assets through the creation of a map and walking tour, a change occurred. Residents began improving their properties block by block. A movement started and the value of real estate increased. Properties are now in demand. Other examples of success can be found in several other Florida communities. The City of St. Petersburg's 22nd Street Corridor was once considered blighted and undesirable. Today, a heritage trail that highlights the African American community's history has attracted new businesses. According to Derek Kilborn, a City of St. Petersburg urban planner, "the historic markers and heritage trails are revitalizing the African American community's business district and neighborhoods, changing its landscape, attracting visitors, and triggering economic development." The City of Fort Pierce developed a heritage trail that highlights its Highwaymen artists. The Cortez Historic Fishing Village and the Venice Train Depot have experienced dramatic increases in visitor traffic and increased revenues at its restaurants, galleries and gift shops.

Communities that are similar to Newtown in character are discovering the benefits of showcasing and leveraging local history. Often misunderstood and unfairly maligned, Newtown's assets have been underutilized. A key element in economic stimulation and revitalization will be recasting its image through the lens of history, which will shatter myths and misconceptions. The time is right for Newtown to promote its abundance of historic treasures through heritage tourism.

Public and private partnerships to fund multiple additional phases are envisioned. Newtown's residents are getting ready to share with diverse audiences their stories of courage, dignity and determination. Newtown is Alive!

# ABOUT THE AUTHORS

**Rosalyn Howard, Ph.D.** is a cultural anthropologist, ethnohistorian and retired associate professor from the University of Central Florida (Orlando), Department of Anthropology. Dr. Howard taught courses in cultural, general and linguistic anthropology and conducted in-residence ethnographic (community) research studies in Jamaica, the Bahamas, and Bermuda. She has conducted additional research and teaching projects in Florida, in the Caribbean region, and in Africa. Dr. Howard has written several books and numerous articles focused on her research about African and Native American peoples in the African Diaspora, particularly the Black Seminoles of Florida and The Bahamas. She has collaborated on several films about her research. Dr. Howard has been a member of the "Looking for Angola" research team since its formation in 2004.

**Vickie Oldham, M.F.A**, a consultant and community scholar, is well known as a former broadcast journalist and 'daughter' of Newtown. She has worked in higher education marketing and communications for nine years. Her responsibilities included branding and marketing three Historically Black Colleges and Universities. Oldham completed a documentary short about Newtown's history in 1992, "Triumphant Struggle," and was one of the producers of the documentary "Reflections: A History of Sarasota County" in 2003. She founded the interdisciplinary "Looking for Angola" (LFA) project in 2004 to identify archaeological and historical evidence of the early 1800s Black Seminole settlement, Angola, located in the Tampa Bay area. Traces of cultural artifacts have been unearthed. Before the LFA project began, this history was not well known. Through multi-platform marketing and communications, the story is now available to worldwide audiences.

# APPENDIX

## A PARTIAL LIST OF BUSINESSES IN OVERTOWN AND NEWTOWN

**Locations:  (O) = Overtown    (N) = Newtown**

### Rooming/Guest Houses and Motels

- Colson Hotel (later named Palms Hotel) (O)
- Edith Olave Major (O) then moved to (N)
- Elmo Newton (O) then moved to (N)
- Chicago Flats – 256 W. 6th St. (run by Sarah Robinson)
- Mary Emma Jones (Barbeque, Cab Stand, Guest House)   (N)
- Annie Carmichael (O) then moved to Church Street (N)

### Barber Shops, Beauty Salons (also located in homes and on porches)

- Budd's Barber Shop  (N)
- Timmon's Barber Shop   (N)
- Jetson's Creative Trend (Barber Shop and Salon) (N)
- Jones Beauty Parlor  (N)
- Josephine Green Beauty Parlor  (N)
- Dorothy and Florence Thomas  (O)

### Builders, Contractors, Plumbers, Electricians

- Charlie Jones, Sr.        (N)
- J.E. Rainey             (N)
- James W. King          (N)
- John H. Floyd          (N)
- Tom DeLaughter         (N)
- Calvin Bryant          (N)

### Farming Contractors

- Elmo Newton (first to contract celery in the county) (N)
- Johnny Newton        (N)
- Eddie Williams        (N)
- Nathan Coons         (N)

- Abe Jones        (N)
- Mack James        (N)
- Edward "Grand Pa" Gordon    (N)
- Wade Thomas    (N)

## Corner food stands; Grocery stores

- Neil Humphrey's Sundries (N)
- Moore's  (N)
- Cann's  (John Major's) (N)
- Orange Avenue  (N)
- Carner's (at the corner of MLK and Pershing Avenue)  (N)
- Eurkhart's  (N)
- Britt's  (N)
- Mays Family (O)
- Henry and Birdie Solomon's  (N)
- Ella Garrett's  (N)
- Brockston's  (N)
- Eddie's Fruit Stand (N)
- Josie's  (N)
- Wright Bush merchandise and grocery  (O)
- Fish sold from home of Katie Frazier  (N)

## Child Care
- Helen Payne Day Nursery (formerly Newtown Day Nursery) - renamed for white benefactor Helen Payne (N)
- Lenora "Madame" Brooks, day care and midwife (delivery room set up in her home)  (N)

## Pressing Clubs and Dry Cleaners

- James Major – Osprey Avenue   (N)
- Walter Pearcy, Sr. – Osprey Avenue  (N)
- Joe Jackson & Plezzie Davis     (N)
- Frank Davis and Ed Payne – 33$^{rd}$ Street  (N)
- Royal Palm 12$^{th}$ Street  (O)
- Red Light Pressing Club  (O)

## Restaurants, Entertainment

- Luella O'Neil Restaurant (N)
- Mary Emma Jones Barbecue Stand (N)
- J&L Bar-B-Que (N)
- Manhattan restaurant and bar/lounge on Central Avenue – Johnny "Buddy" Abnar (Father of Booker High School Principal Dr. Rachel Shelley, among first African American lifeguards at "the Rec") (O)
- Town Hall Restaurant (owned by Louis Robison's mother) (N)
- John "Buck" O'Neil – poolroom and recreational activities – baseball team 'hang-out' (N)
- Clyburn's Bar    (O)
- Miss Susie's Social Club (N)
- Savoy bar and hotel – Central Avenue, Early 1950s (N)
- Twelfth Street Pool Room (O)
- Bamboo Club    (N)
- Danceland (N)
- Capricorn Lounge II (O)
- Savoy Lounge    (O)
- Airdome Theater – 1376 5$^{th}$ St. (O)
- Ace Theater (O) (many old time residents remember this place as a movie house where one could see movies for 10 cents.) 1419 Fifth Street (O) (see photo below)

Ace Theater.
Courtesy: Jetson Grimes Collection.

## Taxicab Companies (1908-1985)[1]

- Seniors Cabs: Herbert Seniors and Jimmie Howard  (N)
- Elam Cabs: Arthur and Richard Elam   (O)
- Texas Cabs: Luther Aldridge     (O)
- Brantley Cabs: Arthur Brantley (N)
- Cooper Cabs: Isaac Cooper (N)
- Jones Cabs: Jack and Mary Emma Jones  (N)
- Huffman Cabs: John, Willie "Bo" and Nathaniel Huffman  (N)
- Black Hawk Cabs: Frank Woodard(N)
- Thomas Cabs: Wade Thomas, Sr.  (N)
- Brown Cabs: Jack Brown  (N)
- Johnson Cabs: James Johnson  (N)

## Newspapers

- Bulletin  (N)
- Tempo News    (N)

## Gas Stations

- Jenkins' "Union 76 Service Station"  (N)
- Johnny's Auto Repair   (N)
- Suarez's Gas Station and Post Office (N)
  Allease and Carlos Suarez  (right)

Courtesy: Jetson Grimes and Michael Suarez Collections.

- Baker's Gas Station (below)  (N)

Courtesy: Photographer Jenny Acheson.

## Funeral Homes

- Stevens Funeral Home  (N)
- Holton's Funeral Home  (O)
- Jones Funeral Home  (N)

## Additional Businesses

- Hudson Essex Showroom Auto dealership
- Cleaning businesses (Various office buildings, Van Sky building, Terrace Hotel, Ritz Theater, private homes) (O)
- New West Florida Ice Company Ice House – Central Avenue. (O)
- Sewage Removal: Mr. Ledbetter (N)
- Garbage Disposal: Jack "Deacon" Harris  (N)
- Mr. Joe's Bike Shop (N)
- Bill Bryant – Hatter – Osprey Avenue
- Sam "Major" Brook's Cigar Factory  (N)
- Malcolm's Seamstress Shop (Dr. Fannie McDugle's mother)

---

[1] McElroy, Annie M. *But Your World and My World: The Struggle for Survival, A Partial History of Blacks in Sarasota County 1884-1986.* Sarasota, FL.: Black South Press. 1986, 32.

# BIBLIOGRAPHY

"A Brief Historical Account of Early Benevolent Societies."
http://www.100menhall.org/about-us/history-of-benevolent-associations

"A Century to Remember: Bob Kendrick, NLBM and Buck O'Neil."
KCPT, Kansas City PBS. 2013. http://kcpt.org/news/a-century-to-
remember-bob-kendrick-nlbm-and-buck-oneil/

"Africans in America: Religion and Slavery."
http://www.pbs.org/wgbh/aia/part2/2narr2.html

Anderson, Chris. "Finally forgiven: The Howard Porter story." Newtown
100. *Herald-Tribune*.
http://newtown100.heraldtribune.com/2014/12/14/finally-forgiven-
howard-porter-story/

Andrus, Patrick W. *National Register Bulletin* 15: "How to Apply the
National Register Criteria for Evaluation." Washington D.C., U.S.
Department of the Interior, National Park Service, 1990, Revised, 1991,
1995, 1997, 2001 and 2002.

Baram, Uzi. "Learning Service and Civic Engagement." In Michael S.
Nassaney and Mary Ann Levine. *Archaeology and Community Service
Learning.* Gainesville: University Press of Florida. 2009.

Beardsley, Howie. "Sarasota-Bradenton Nine Devils Special to Manager
Robinson." *Herald-Tribune*, June 22, 1983.
https://news.google.com/newspapers?nid=1755&dat=19830622&id=O9ge
AAAAIBAJ&sjid=dWgEAAAAIBAJ&pg=4440,1172267&hl=en

"Bee Ridge Turpentine Camp."
http://www.sarasotahistoryalive.com/history/articles/bee-ridge-turpentine-
camp/?back=history

"Biocultural Dimensions of Human Health and Illness."
http://anthropology.usf.edu/research/themes/

Black, Hope. "Zora Neale Hurston: Studies in Anthropology."
Unpublished paper. March 9, 2005.

Black, Hope. *Mounted on a Pedestal: Bertha Honore Palmer*. MA thesis. University of South Florida, 2007.

"Booker High School."
http://www.digplanet.com/wiki/Booker_High_School_ (Sarasota, Florida)

"Booker School."
http://www.sarasotagov.com/LivingInSarasota/Contents/PublicWorks/Publ
icWorksHistoricBookSchool.html

"Briefs from Barwin." May 27, 2016.

Brown, Canter Jr. "The Sarrazota or Runaway Negro Plantations;" Tampa Bay's First Black Community 1812-1821. *Tampa Bay History*, Vol 12 No. 2, 1990, 5-29.

Bryan, Jami. "Fighting for Respect: African-American Soldiers in WWI." Managing Editor, *On Point*. An Army Historical Foundation publication. http://www.militaryhistoryonline.com/wwi/articles/fightingforrespect.aspx

Burns, Susan. "The Boycott." *Sarasota*, June 1999.

Byrd, William Allan Jr. *A Survey And Analysis of School Problems Associated with the Desegregation of Florida High Schools—1962-1966*. Diss. College of Education. University of Miami: 1969.

Caldez, Jose Maria and Joaquin Caldez. Land grant applications, Spanish Land Grants (Unconfirmed Grants, 1828), film file 2.1. (Microfilm available at John German Public Library Special Collections Department, (Tampa), Florida A & M University, Tallahassee and Tampa Public Library).

"Caples Convinced Ringlings to Come to Sarasota."
https://www.sarasotamagazine.com/articles/2014/11/17/caples-ringlings-
sarasota

Carr, Madeline Hirsiger. *Denying hegemony: The function and place of Florida's jook joints during the twentieth century's first fifty years*. Dissertation. Florida State University, 2002.

Cave, Damien. "In a Town Apart, the Pride and Trials of Black Life." *The New York Times*. September 28, 2008.

"Celebrating 50 years of integration at the University of Florida."
University of Florida. September 15, 2008.
http://news.ufl.edu/archive/2008/09/celebrating-50-years-of-integration-at-the-university-Of-florida.html

"The Celery Fields: Past, Present and Future."
https://www.scgov.net/Sustainability/Sarasota%20Sustainability%20Partnership%20Meeting%20Presen/2014_02%20Celery%20Fields-%20Dubi.pdf. (Sarasota Audubon Society)

Celery Fields History Panel: Cultural Resource Center (CRC) NSPL

"Celery Production in Florida."
http://ufdc.ufl.edu/UF00027543/00001/2j?search=workers
http://www.sarasotaaudubon.org/capital-campaign/the-celery-fields/

"Celery Fields." https://www.scgov.net/parks/Pages/CeleryFields.aspx
Sarasota Audubon Society: Economic Impact.
http://www.sarasotaaudubon.org/capital-campaign/economic-impact/

"The Celery Fields." http://mustseesarasota.com/listing/the-celery-fields/

City of Sarasota, Florida, Code of Ordinances, Division 8 – Section IV-806, Designation Standards for Review, 2002, Revised 2008.

"Civil Rights 101: Voting Rights."
http://www.civilrights.org/resources/civilrights101/voting.html

"Civil rights pioneer led era of change in Sarasota."
http://www.heraldtribune.com/article/20141205/ARTICLE/141209813

Clark, Maggie and Billy Cox. "New Clinic will target adults." *Herald-Tribune*. December 8, 2015.
http://g52-shweb.newscyclecloud.com/article/2015151209650

Cleary, Joe. "Sarasota History of Turpentine and Pine Woods." Search For Sarasota Homes Blog.

"Condemned." http://www.imdb.com/title/tt1500158/

Constitutional Rights Foundation. "Race and Voting in the Segregated South."
http://www.crf-usa.org/brown-v-board-50th-anniversary/race-and-voting.html

Cummings, Ian. "Looking back, and ahead." *Herald-Tribune*. April 17, 2014. http://newtown100.heraldtribune.com/looking-back-ahead/
Cummings, Ian. "Caravans to Lido broke beach barrier." *Herald-Tribune*. July 13, 2014.

Cummings, Ian. "Leading the way before civil rights era." *Herald-Tribune*, February 1, 2015.
http://newtown100.heraldtribune.com/2015/02/01/leading-way-civil-rights-era/

Daniel, Pete. *The Shadow of Slavery: Peonage in the South 1901-1969*. Urbana: University of Illinois Press, 1972.

DeGruy, Joy. *Post Traumatic Slave Syndrome*. Joy DeGruy Publications. 2005.

DuBois, W.E.B. [1935] 1969. Accessed on website: http://what-when-how.com/social-sciences/whites-social-science/

Eckhart, Robert. "Remembering a Newtown that taught character." *Herald-Tribune*, February 21, 2011.

"Economic Impacts of Historic Preservation in Florida – Executive Summary." Tallahassee, Florida, State of Florida, Department of State, Division of Historical Resources, 2003.

Elder, Amy A. *Sarasota: 1940-2005 Images of America*. Charleston: Arcadia Publishing, 2005.

"First Black Community."
https://www.scgov.net/History/Pages/FirstBlackCommunity.aspx)

"Forgotten Chapter of History."
https://www.pinterest.com/dropdeaddiva56/forgotten-chapter-of-black-historyturpentine-camps/

"For Sarasota fraternity, an anniversary and an evolution."
http://www.heraldtribune.com/article/20150409/ARTICLE/150409682

Gardner, Andrew. "Agency." In R. Alexander Bentley, Herbert D.G.
Maschner, and Christopher Chippindale eds. *Handbook of Archaeological
Theories*. Lanham, MD: Altamira Press, 2009.


"The Giving Partner: Partner's roles in Grade Level Reading."
http://www.cfsarasota.org/Portals/0/Uploads/Documents/Connect/CGLR%
20Partners.pdf

Gorman, Juliet. 2001. "What is a jook joint and what is its history."
http://www.oberlin.edu/library/papers/honorshistory/2001-
Gorman/jookjoints/allaboutjooks/whatisjook.html

"Grand Lodge Knights of Pythias."
http://knightsofpythiasfl.com/history/

"Green and Carter Inducted Into Riverview Hall of Fame." *Tempo News*.
September 3-9, 2015, 1.

Grismer, Karl H. *The Story of Sarasota- The History of the City and
County of Sarasota, Florida*. Sarasota, FL: M.E. Russell, 1st Ed., 1946.

Handelman, Jay. "A More Colorful Sarasota Theater Scene."
http://newtown100.heraldtribune.com/2014/11/14/colorful-sarasota-
theater-scene/

"The History of Bethlehem Baptist Church 1876-1997." Church Archives.

"History of the Newtown Community."
http://www.sarasotagov.com/Newtown/history.html

"Horizons Unlimited Christian Academy: Mission."
http://www.horizonsunlimitedchristianacademy.com/mission.html

Howard, Rosalyn. "Looking For Angola": Public Anthropology and the
Archaeological and Ethnohistorical Search for a Nineteenth Century
Florida Maroon Community and its Circum-Caribbean Connections.
*Florida Historical Quarterly*, 2013.

Howard, Rosalyn. "Black Towns of the Seminole Indians." In Poynor, R. ed. *Africa in Florida: Detangling Diasporas in World Culture*. Gainesville: University Press of Florida, 2012.

Hughes, Dan. "A Look Back. "The History of Florida Turpentine Camps." *Herald-Tribune*. Monday, March 1, 2004.

Hurston, Zora Neale. "Characteristics of Negro Expression." 1934. https://genius.com/Zora-neale-hurston-characteristics-of-negro-expression-annotated

Ifill, Sherrilyn. *On the Courthouse Lawn: Confronting the Legacy of Lynching in the Twenty-First Century*. Boston: Beacon Press, 2007.

James v. City of Sarasota, Fla., 611 F. Supp. 25 (M.D. Fla. 1985). http://law.justia.com/cases/federal/district-courts/FSupp/611/25/2003811/

"Jim Crow and the Great Migration." (https://www.gilderlehrman.org/history-by-era/progressive-era-new-era-1900-1929/jim-crow-and-great-migration).

"John Hamilton Gillespie." https://www.scgov.net/History/Pages/JohnHamiltonGillespie.aspx

Johnson, B.J. "The Village as I Knew It: 1950 —." Unpublished Essay. 2013.

"Knights of Pythias." http://www.pythias.org/index.php?option=com_content&view=article&id=57:pythian-principles&catid=41:about-the-order&Itemid=27

LaHurd, Jeff. "Early African American Settlers." *Herald-Tribune*. April 16, 2014.

LaHurd, Jeff. *Sarasota: A History*. Arcadia Publishing, 2006.

LaHurd, Jeff. "1920s was time of racial strife in Sarasota." *Herald-Tribune*, July 28, 2014. http://newtown100.heraldtribune.com/2014/07/28/1920s-time-racial-strife/

Last, Walter, "Kerosene and Turpentine – Universal Healer."

http://augmentinforce.50webs.com/TURPENTINE--
HEALER%20COMPLETE.htm;

LeCoz, Emily. "Sarasota Memorial to open clinic in Newtown."
file:///Users/rosalyn/Desktop/Sarasota%20Clinic%20in%20Newtown.web
archive

"Leonard Reid Family House."
http://www.sarasotahistoryalive.com/history/buildings/leonard-reid-
family-house/

Levey-Baker, Cooper. "Rosemary Rising." *941CEO, Real Estate*.
September 4, 2015.

Little, Barbara J. and Paul A. Shackel. *Archaeology and Community
Service Learning.* Walnut Creek, CA: Left Coast Press. 2014.

"Looking Back and Ahead."
http://newtown100.heraldtribune.com/looking-back-ahead/

Lopez, Yadira. "Saving and celebrating Newtown's stories." *Herald-
Tribune*. Friday, September 25, 2015.

Mannix, Vin. "Bradenton's first baseball heroes: Nine Devils to be
Honored." *Bradenton Herald*. October 16, 2011.
http://www.bradenton.com/news/local/news-columns-
blogs/article34528767.html

Martin, Kimberly. *Community and Place: A Study of Four African
American Benevolent Societies and their Cemeteries*. Master's Thesis.
Clemson University and College of Charleston.

Matthews, Dylan. "Voting Rights Act ruling: Here's what you need to
know."
https://www.washingtonpost.com/news/wonk/wp/2013/06/25/voting-
rights-act-ruling-heres-what-you-need-to-know

Matthews, Janet Snyder. "Booker Earned Degree While Teaching Others."
*Black Educator*. Centennial Profile. 1985.

McElroy, Annie M. *But Your World and My World: The Struggle for Survival, A Partial History of Blacks in Sarasota County 1884-1986.* Sarasota, FL: Black South Press, 1986.

Miller, Ernest H. *Bradenton Florida City Directory.* Ashville, Florida-Piedmont Directory Co., 1916.

Miller, Ernest H. <u>*Sarasota Florida City Directory*</u>. Ashville, Florida-Piedmont Directory Co., 1918.

Miller, Ernest H. <u>*Sarasota Florida City Directory*</u>. Ashville, Florida-Piedmont Directory Co., 1921.

Miller, Ernest H. <u>*Sarasota Florida City Directory*</u>. Ashville, The Miller Press, 1923.

"Mob Lynch Negro Last Monday Night." *Manatee River Journal.* 7 July 1912, 3.

Montgomery, Rick. "Buck O'Neil: Played key role in establishing the Negro Leagues Baseball Museum." January 15, 2016. http://www.kansascity.com/news/local/article54962555.html

Multicultural Health Institute. http://www.the-mhi.org/#!the-history/a5k7e

Murdock, Zach. "City to seek help redeveloping Marian Anderson Place." *Herald-Tribune.* January 1, 2017.

Negro Leagues Baseball Museum. "Leagues and Teams." https://www.nlbm.com/s/team.htm

"New day for Newtown housing." http://www.gainesville.com/article/SH/20111202/ARTICLE/111209898/0/ david.mcswane@heraldtribune.com?p=2&tc=pg

Newspaper article, 10/26/1916. Newspaper title unknown. Sarasota County Historical Resources.

Newspaper article, 11/21/1916. Newspaper title unknown. Sarasota County Historical Resources.

Newton, Michael. *The Invisible Empire: The Ku Klux Klan in Florida.*

Gainesville: University Press of Florida, 2001.

*Newtown-North Sarasota Redevelopment Project Report*. April 2014.

Oldham, Vickie. "Emotional Welcome Home for BHS Class of 1968." *Tempo News*. Vol. 28, No. 42 Oct 15-21, 2015.

"Overtown Historic District." United States Department of the Interior, National Park Service, National Register of Historic Places, 2002.

Porter, Les. "Newtown Sports Personalities." Unpublished paper. NCHD volunteer researcher, 2016

Praught, Hailey Erin. *A Bare Bones History: Lynching in Manatee County*. University Honors Program. University of South Florida, St. Petersburg. August 5, 2009.

Rainone, Donald F. *The Role of the Sarasota Visual Performing Arts (VPA) Magnet in Desegregation and Resegregation of Booker Neighborhood Schools*. Diss. University of South Florida. Tampa, FL. 2003.

"Remembering a Newtown that taught character." February 21, 2011. http://www.heraldtribune.com/article/20110221/ARTICLE/102211040/0/search?p=1&tc=pg

"A Religious Portrait of African-Americans." http://www.pewforum.org/2009/01/30/a-religious-portrait-of-african-americans

Rodriguez, Yolanda. "Home in Path of Progress." *Sarasota Herald-Tribune*. July 18, 1998. Section A1

Russon, Gabrielle. "At modern new Booker campus, a room for history." June 29, 2013. http://www.heraldtribune.com/article/20130629/article/130629585?p=2&tc=pg

Russon, Gabrielle. "Seeing Newtown in a new light." *Herald-Tribune*. http://newtown100.heraldtribune.com/2014/08/15/seeing-newtown-new-light/

Russon, Gabriel. "Remembering a Fallen Soldier." *Herald-Tribune*. Monday, October 13, 2014.

Rylee, J. Whitcomb, "History of Overtown, Sarasota, Florida." 1997.

"Sarasota Audubon Society: Economic Impact." http://www.sarasotaaudubon.org/capital-campaign/economic-impact/

"Sarasota County, Florida Soil Survey." Map; (United States Department of Agriculture, Soil Conservation Service, series 1954 No. 6, issued 1959). "Sarasota, Florida: Paradise on the Gulf Coast." *The Western & Central Florida Cooperator*. April 2014.

"Sarasota County NAACP." http://sarasotacounty.naacp-fl.org "60 years ago, blacks desegregated Florida beach" http://www.washingtontimes.com/news/2014/jul/19/ 60-years-ago-blacks-desegregated-fla-beach/? page=all

"Sarasota County Parks, Recreation and Nature Centers." www.scgov.net

"Sarasota, Florida: Paradise on the Gulf Coast." *The Western & Central Florida Cooperator*. April 2014.

"Sarasota Memorial to open clinic in Newtown." December, 7, 2015. http://www.heraldtribune.com/article/LK/20151207/News/605206335/SH/

"Sarasotan students' school boycott stops neighborhood schools from closing, Florida, United States, 1969." http://nvdatabase.swarthmore.edu/content/sarasotan-students-school-boycott-stops-neighborhood-schools-closing-florida-united-states-1

Shank, Ann A. "Bee Ridge Turpentine Camp." http://www.sarasotahistoryalive.com/history/articles/bee-ridge-turpentine-camp

Shank, Ann. "Leagues of Their Own." Sarasotahistoryalive.com http://www.sarasotahistoryalive.com/history/articles/leagues-of-their-own/

Shea, Jennifer. "Pastor touts power of prayer." August 30, 2012. www.heraldtribune.com/article/20120830/ARTICLE/120839982

"60 years ago, blacks desegregated Florida beach."
http://www.washingtontimes.com/news/2014/jul/19/

Smith, Mark D. "The Payne Chapel AME Assembly Church".
http://www.sarasotahistoryalive.com/history/articles/the-payne-chapel-
ame-assembly-church/

Soaries, Rev. DeForest Jr. "Black churches and the role of empowerment."
*CNN Opinion, Black in America*, August 1, 2010 10:56 a.m. EDT
(http://www.cnn.com/2010/OPINION/08/01/soaries.black.church/)

Stevens, Albert C. *Cyclopedia of Fraternities*. New York: E. B. Treat and
Company, 1908.

Sullivan, Paul. "A Lesson in Diplomacy." *Chicago Tribune*. March 12,
1995.

Sulzer, Elmer G. *Ghost Railroads of Sarasota County, The Turpentine
Track: Manatee to Arcadia*. Sarasota County Historical Commission,
Sarasota County Historical Society, 1971.

"The Colored Methodist Church of Sarasota." Sarasota Times. April 21,
1910. Subjectfiles, Sarasota County Historical Resources.

"The Rosenwald Schools: An Impressive Legacy of Black-Jewish
Collaboration for Negro Education." http://abhmuseum.org/2012/07/the-
rosenwald-schools-an-impressive-legacy-of-black-jewish-collaboration-
for-negro-education/

"The Westcoast School for Human Development."
http://digifxlive.com/wcs/

"Things You May Not Know." http://www.history.com/news/5-things-
you-may-not-know-about-lincoln-slavery-and-emancipation

Turner, Linda. Collection. Courtesy of the Sarasota County History
Center.

"Turpentine Oil." http://www.webmd.com/vitamins-
supplements/ingredientmono-

508turpentine%20oil.aspx?activeingredientid=508&activeingredientname
=turpentine%20oiland; Healing With 100% Pure Turpentine.

United States Supreme Court; N. A. A. C. P. v. ALABAMA, (1958)
No. 91 Argued:Decided: June 30, 1958.

Western Canada Baseball: "Willie "Curly" Williams."
http://www.attheplate.com/wcbl/profile_williams_curly.html

"What is a Brownfield?"
http://brownfieldaction.org/brownfieldaction/brownfield_basics

White, Norval. *The Architecture Book*. New York: Alfred A. Knopf, 1976.

Whittle, Patrick. "Memories of Laurel: Black Community Celebrates its
History This Week." *Herald-Tribune*. February 20, 2007.

Wilkerson, Isabel. *The Warmth of Other Suns: The Epic Story of
America's Great Migration.* New York: Vintage Press, 2011.

Williams, John Lee. *The Territory of Florida: 1775-1856 or, Sketches of
the topography, civil and natural history, of the country, the climate, and
the Indian tribes, from the first discovery to the present time, with a map,
views, &c.* New York, A.T. Goodrich, 1837.

Woodson, Carter G. *A Century of Negro Migration*. Washington, D.C.:
Association for the Study of Negro Life and History, 1918.

WPA Guide to Florida #27. Federal Writer's Project. (Sarasota section),
1939.

Ziel, Deborah L. *Which Way to the Jook Joint?: Historical Archaeology of
a Polk County, Florida Turpentine Camp,* MA thesis. Department of
Anthropology. University of Central Florida, Orlando, 2013.

# INDEX
## for
# Newtown Alive: Courage, Dignity, Determination

### compiled by
### David Harralson, Ph.D.


**(ohi):** Oral History Interview
*passim*: "here and there," (throughout (the book)
**123ff:** The ff means "subject continued through the pages following" 123
**c.:** *circa*, meaning "about"
**#:** indicates footnote number on that page

Washington, Thomas "Mott", 14
Watson, Lou (Indiana basketball), 196
Wenzel, Christopher, NCHD Team (Architectural Preservationist) v, 4
Westcoast Black Theater Troupe, 141
Westcoast Center for Human Development Church (1980, K-12), 153-154, 158
Wheeler, Edward "Duke" (ML baseball), 192
White Paper, what is? 170 #14
White, Robert "Baldy," 180, 193
Wiggins, Lucinda, 108
Williams, Clara (President of Sickle Cell Foundation), 167
Williams, Frank T. & Madeline, 14
Williams, Glenda, 125
Williams, John Lee (historian), 6
Williams, Robert "Pookie" (ML baseball) 192
Williams, Ruby (teacher), 111
Williams Turpentine Camp (Venice), 71
William's Stationery, 89
Williams, Willie "Curly," 191-192
Williams, Yvette, 74
Woolworth, 137
Wopinski, Jessica (New College interviewer), 82, 95, 96, 112, 210
World War II, end of tolerance of racism, 137
WPA Guide to Florida, 62-63
Wright Bush House, 18

Wright, Jay (Villanova basketball), 197

**Y**
Yancey, Hugh (basketball), 195
Yancey Jr., Hugh (ML Baseball), 192
Youth Baseball in Newtown, 193
Youth Empowerment, 204
Youth United for Success Mentoring Outreach Program, 209
Young, Mamie Baker, 114

**Z**
Ziel, Deborah (archaeologist), 73

**Photos**

## Photos in alphabetical order by person, place, or subject

Made in the USA
Columbia, SC
19 August 2020

16825428R00146